# THE BILLIONAIRE'S FOLLY

# THE BILLIONAIRE'S FOLLY

## THE UNTOLD STORY OF ETHEREUM AND THE UNICORN THAT WASN'T

Faisal Khan

Waterside Productions

First Printing, 2022

ISBN-13: 978-1-958848-15-9 print edition
ISBN-13: 978-1-958848-16-6 e-book edition

**Waterside Productions**
2055 Oxford Ave
Cardiff, CA 92007
www.waterside.com

*The events depicted here occurred mostly between March 2017 and March 2020. In service of the narrative, I have condensed or combined certain persons or conversations. But rest assured, I saw all this stuff happen at some point.*

*Out of respect for my fallen colleagues, I have altered most names. But for anyone offended by their depiction, you probably deserve it.*

*For my parents, for teaching me to dream big.*
*And how to read.*

# TABLE OF CONTENTS

# PROLOGUE

*New York, August 2019. ETH:* $224.

"I should sue the shit out of them, too," Omar said angrily as he crossed one leg over the other. We had been colleagues and were still friends, at least for now. We were sitting in Washington Square Park on a warm summer evening, the kind when all of New York goes for a stroll and thinks, *Maybe it is worth living here* as the breeze spirits away the stench of hot trash and dogshit more typical of the city sidewalk.

Omar and I had only sat down by the central fountain when we took in the headline that Harrison Hines, a once rising star at ConsenSys – the world's biggest company focused on blockchain, where Omar had once worked and I still did – had ended his lawsuit after suing the firm for a cool $13 million. Harrison claimed he had been promised equity and profit-sharing but then unceremoniously fired before receiving any. I'd heard that, supposedly out for revenge, he had hired Mark Zuckerberg's lawyer to come after us. I imagined it was the one who had saved Zuck from the Winklevoss twins in *The Social Network*. "I heard" is in this case literal, because in our headquarters our legal team sat in the middle of the room, and everyone was talking about it.

I could taste the bitterness in Omar's words. He too had been a star at ConsenSys, tossed out due to conflicts with Joe, the CEO. ConsenSys was less a single company and more an incubator for dozens of startups, and Omar had led one of the most promising teams. He too had been promised the world—equity, investments, the opportunity to build a team and use blockchain technology to completely upend the real estate industry. But when the market turned against us, leadership backtracked, and the promises turned to smoke.

"Vanessa emailed me again asking about real estate," I said, trying to change the subject. She worked on our business development team and perpetually confused me for Ritesh or Vinay or a half dozen other brown guys, this time for Omar. "I told her I'd start calling her Victoria if she didn't start getting our names straight."

He smiled for a moment. "I could throw her in the lawsuit too," he said, pausing before looking angry again. I might have felt that anger. For two years we had worked on the hottest tech of the decade and the money monsoon had rained all around us. We had tasted the addictive rush of entrepreneurial success and our turn felt inevitable. But while I admired his drive to get what we deserved, I myself was on the verge of taking a deal with ConsenSys that might save me from being laid off in the wake of the collapse in Bitcoin in late 2018. I knew I had to take the offer, too afraid of ending up in Omar's shoes. In fact I had insisted we meet miles away from the Brooklyn office so no one would see us together. Two brown guys slinking around making secret plans for revenge? That's what the FBI calls a sleeper cell, and I wanted to stay out of trouble. I considered explaining my thought process but realized I would only feel ashamed. Years later, when Omar had built a war chest large enough to take on even Joe's billions, I would recall our discussion on the park bench and how many times I had slinked away from conflict. But at that time I was beyond the point of caring who was right and who was wrong. I simply wanted to survive.

This is a story about idealism. ConsenSys aimed as a company to do nothing less than to completely rewire the Internet itself, which we saw as irredeemably broken, dominated by Big Tech companies. We would succeed by using the blockchain, more specifically Ethereum, the software *cum* cryptocurrency *cum* "world computer" that our CEO and founder Joseph Lubin helped to create in 2014.

The mental image you likely have of cryptocurrencies like Bitcoin is a bunch of nerds playing with Monopoly money, trying to convince everyone of its importance. Fair. But Ethereum is an upgrade from Bitcoin – a currency combined with computer programs called 'smart contracts,' which can automate anything related to the movement of money – from regular salary payments to instant lending to creating digital bank accounts for everyone in the Third World at no cost. To open a bank account, governments and Big Banks required an address and a form of ID, leaving billions without either out in the cold. Ethereum would have no such requirement to transact on the blockchain. And through Ethereum, we saw a window to redefine financial services and even how money itself functioned.

Like Bitcoin, Ethereum is decentralized – no person owns it. It is a computer program run simultaneously by tens of thousands of people, rather than by an individual or a profit-motivated company. We could use that collective resource, we reasoned, to replace Facebook and Apple and the other overlords of the Internet. Once we re-built all of these profit-seeking apps on Ethereum's smart contracts, we would have a new, *decentralized* Internet: what we called web 3.0. Smart contracts could provide free and secure services to everyone, rather than turning our own data against us as these corporate behemoths did.

Ben Franklin wrote that time is money, and money is time. We buy things for two reasons: either to save time, or to make our time more valuable. We value time so dearly because none of us knows how much we have. Franklin came up short. Money is not time; money is life itself. And so for us, disrupting currency was too low a target. By reprogramming money, we could reprogram society for the better.

That idealism drew me in like a magnet. After spending my twenties floating aimlessly in corporate America, I wanted a job with positive impact. In my childhood my Asian immigrant parents had given me two lifelong assignments: to make the world a better place, and to be rich. When I turned thirteen I complained these might be difficult to do at once, and my father helpfully pointed out that Bill Gates had done it. And he didn't even have a college degree, my father added. I nodded along dutifully.

I spent my college years traipsing from NGOs in Africa to the halls of Congress to studying in the Middle East, another liberal arts student full of ideas and no direction, hunting for that magical combination. When I noticed that the NGO's chief economist mostly spent his time booking first class tickets to conferences, I started to have doubts about my parents' first assignment. They thought that I might be making a dent in the world when an invite came by mail to a luncheon for Muslim interns hosted Vice President Joe Biden at the White House. But the pride was fleeting, as the *Obama is a Muslim* rumors led to some second thoughts in the West Wing and worries about feeding the conspiracy mill, and they soon reorganized the event to be a joint Muslim-Jewish lunch hosted by an Indian flunky who was neither Muslim nor Jewish. (President Biden, you still owe me.) Without that cachet, and noting that my manager in Congress lived off whiskey and ramen given her long hours and pitiful salary, I soon decided my parents' second assignment was more realizable. I would deal with the world's problems later.

Now a decade later I had come across blockchain and Ethereum. I had, I thought, finally struck (moral) gold. We could use blockchain to build an Internet that was decentralized and fair rather than exploitative and foul. We could build a financial system with access for everyone. ConsenSys saw a society dominated by corporations and a path to create the tools that would inevitably lead to a better world. All I had to do was help build the movement.

This is a story about greed. "Never before have so many unskilled twenty-four-year-olds made so much money in so little time as we did this decade in New York and London," Michael Lewis wrote in his classic memoir *Liar's Poker* about the investment banking floors of Solomon Brothers. A modern gold rush, he claimed.

Well, eat your heart out, Michael, because Ethereum was not only a means for saving the world, but also happened to be one of the most profitable trades in history, returning nearly 5000x, going from thirty cents to $1400 in three years. Even more so, Ethereum was the launchpad for other cryptocurrencies, which grew ten, twenty, even one hundred times during the pandemonium of 2017. Many of our friends and enemies in the blockchain universe spent their time not writing code to save the world but trading obsessively in these "coins," trying to make another ten or twenty times return on the 1000x profits they had already made on Ethereum. Those who bought at the right time had investing returns that made Warren Buffet look like a nobody. And those who bought at the wrong time saw fortunes vanish.

How did blockchain, an interesting if complex technology, fuel the largest bubble of this century, peaking at nearly a trillion dollars? The idea that anyone could own Ethereum, the blockchain that could be the basis for *the next Internet*, was what truly drove everyone into a mania. Imagine buying a piece of the Internet in 1990. That potential profit was what drove everyone crazy, from your Uber driver to your grandmother, to buy Bitcoin.

I was not immune. Since college, I'd lived the high life working in corporate, the $5000 a month apartment in Midtown and all expenses paid meals. Now I was the one booking first class. When I left to join ConsenSys, I knew the potential return in Ethereum meant my equity might someday be worth millions – and in the meantime I could trade in these obscure cryptocurrencies, doubling and tripling my money along the way. All I had to do was help spread the word.

This narrative began with idealist techies like us who hoped to make money, but we were not the only guilty party. The consultants of McKinsey and Accenture and others wanted fees, and so put out white papers encouraging companies to invest in blockchain. Venture capitalists also saw the profits from Ethereum and were dying for the chance to earn high returns without having to wait ten years for an IPO. The press and publishers saw the chance to cover a potential societal shift. Authors had a chance to write bestsellers. *Blockchain Revolution. Blockchain: The Next Everything.* Perhaps this memoir even sits next to one of these tomes.

And no one thought to question this tale of an amazing future, because everyone was going to make lots of money off of it.

This is a story about people. As it turns out, ConsenSys was no ordinary company. It was, in some ways, perhaps the grandest social and business experiment of our times. Joe, our CEO, chose not to give us orders or instructions on how to lead this revolution. He simply gave us funding and asked us to use blockchain to make the world a better place. He had placed a billion dollar bet on humanity, as was explained to us in our onboarding video by a cartoon unicorn.

Most of us worked hard out of gratitude to him. He could have screwed off at any point with his Bitcoin wealth and lived out his days on an island. Which, in fact, many ConsenSys employees did—a large number moved to Puerto Rico, where they could avoid paying federal income taxes. But Joe stayed the course, even through the hard times. In turn, we built the software and spread word of the revolution in order to further his experiment.

But who was scientist and who was subject?

Indeed, we were also experimenting on you. We helped write the headlines covering blockchain and cryptocurrency, and we smiled for the photos that ran above the fold on blockchain's promise to remake finance, the government, and everything else. We fed the journalists, who we knew could not differentiate private key cryptography from hieroglyphics, and they graciously turned our words into clickbait. I myself learned some of these tricks, on how to drop just the right hints or spin up a controversy for a headline. We spun a beautiful narrative that the 'thought leaders' in consulting and tech and venture capital repeated like the colorful parrots they are. Groupthink based on hearsay fed the fire. Blockchain is not unique in this – in much of tech and finance, a similar polluted river runs, flowing from the builders to consultants to 'thought leaders' to journalists, whether the subject is "artificial intelligence" or automated drones or the 'Internet of Things.' Finally it flows to you, the dumping ground of empty buzzwords.

I do not want to imply we led a massive conspiracy to dupe the masses. No, we believed in blockchain's ability to reshape finance and technology, and what that could do for the world, and so many followed us because they wanted to believe, or because they thought they could make a quick profit. Blockchain was the Rorschach test of our tech-obsessed era, the bubble within the bubble, and a moral fable of the perpetual conflict in the heart of every tech entrepreneur between greed and idealism: a battle for the soul of tech. Unfortunately, greed won.

But just your luck – your guide today is one of the very few non-coders who spent his days helping to build the blood and guts of the blockchain itself. There is yet time to pull back the curtain. And as our opening crawl comes to an end, our story, like another well known futuristic epic, begins in a space age desert far, far away...

# PART I

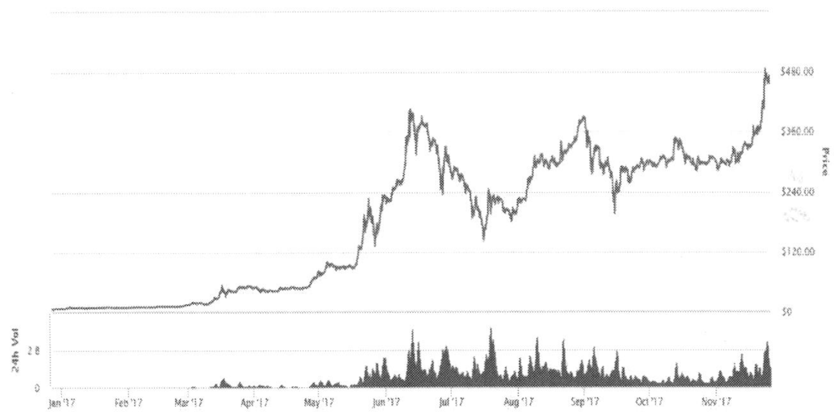


# THE DESERT UNICORN

# ROCKET SHIP

*Dubai, August 2017. ETH:* $296.

We read the questions aloud, one by one. Most of our team had not yet met Joe, and their eyes and mouths opened wide at the idea of being in the same room as a billionaire, a revolutionary, someone who had invented something that the entire world was talking about. *COO of the Ethereum Project, co-founder of Ethereum, founder of ConsenSys.* Joe had more titles than a character on *Game of Thrones.* I was a few months into the job at ConsenSys and had met Joe one on one last month, so I felt less nervous than the rest of the team. But I was still impressed that he had flown from New York to help us handle what we were jokingly calling "growing pains." It spoke volumes about the value of our fledgling office, halfway across the world, and the importance of our work to his grander vision.

The government of Dubai had recently announced it was dedicating massive funding to becoming a global leader in blockchain, which they (and we) saw as the next revolution in tech. The experts kept saying blockchain was soon going to be a change agent 'on the scale of the Internet.' ConsenSys had been one of the first companies to fully dedicate itself to building blockchain software since 2014. Finally, blockchain's moment in the sun had arrived, and Joe wanted the Dubai office to be the vanguard of ConsenSys's growth worldwide. The hype train was about to leave the station, and it was speeding towards Dubai. But right now, we needed Joe's help, and badly.

We were sitting in the conference room at a five-star hotel in the heart of downtown. It would have been an understatement to describe the weather outside as *sweltering*, but the building AC was cranked to the max as panes of gold-tinted glass kept the room from getting too bright as the sun bore down outside. Whenever Joe visited ConsenSys' offices around the world we typically held town halls like this. Clem, our new receptionist, wiped her brow a bit. She was friendly but always nervous, and when Joe had plopped down in the adjacent seat her eyes bugged out a little behind her glasses. She tried to put her tea cup down without too much of a *clink* as Bilal, our local operations lead, read out questions the team had submitted beforehand in his best podcast voice.

"What are our plans for growth in the next year?"

Joe had come from our NYC headquarters to meet with senior officials in the government here, who were now our flagship clients globally. Everyday they paid a publicist to announce in the press that these blockchain investments would unlock the door for Dubai to become the "Silicon Valley of the desert." CNN, CNBC, and other international news were serving up cheesy headlines on Dubai and blockchain daily with dramatic shots of men in headdresses looking out over the desert from a helicopter. The entire room strained to hear Joe's low, even voice. Someone had just asked Joe if he saw himself as the 'Elon Musk' of blockchain, which made him chuckle. The collective awe in the room seemed to float in the air. Years later, I look back and wonder if Joe had let the feeling sink in and enjoyed the moment. Our future town halls would not show the same deference.

"Blockchain is going through a hypergrowth phase," Joe answered. "We are now firmly in the geopolitical orbit, with our clientele spanning major banks in Europe and governments in Asia. We cannot estimate this kind of exponential change, but I assure you it will be a great and wild ride. The work of this team will be critical and we will continue to prioritize it." Everyone on the team smiled in triumph. Our techno-messiah had spoken. The Dubai team had narrowly avoided catastrophe, as we ran into walls trying to close deals in a country where no one took startups seriously. We preached a technological revolution to government agencies that saw virtue in moving slowly. No one seemed to believe us when we said a cryptographic database would change their lives forever by re-engineering the financial industry from the ground up and automating bureaucratic processes like issuing land titles. Our projects were understaffed, leading to tedious infighting from overwork.

The infighting led to accusations of a lack of leadership. We felt the NYC and other offices had done little to help, abandoning us to our lonely crossings of the desert.

Have patience, Joe was telling us, because the best is yet to come. The company would continue to grow, and help would soon be on the way. Why else was Joe here except to tell us of the coming rapture?

I felt similar relief at Joe's words. There was a power vacuum in Dubai, and I saw an opening for myself, a washed up management consultant, to redeem my career by taking the reins and leading us into battle against IBM, our chief competitor. I had just been tapped to try and beat them in what could be our biggest deal yet. Just before this meeting Joe and I had met with the CEO of one of Dubai's largest companies who I thought could help us win the contract.

"But didn't they just hire you?" my soon-to-be fiancee Saira had asked me over FaceTime before Joe's visit, wondering how the biggest deal could be handed to a new hire. She lived in New York still and was bewildered by everything I did, given she worked in medicine where experience and training were what counted. Not here. Blockchain had made some sense to her when I explained it, but mostly she said it "sounded like the future" and trusted that I was right.

"Everyone's new in this industry," I explained. "Did it matter if you joined Apple in 1985 instead of 1984?" I was counting my chickens' grandchildren already. But I knew I was not the only one doing so in the industry.

Bilal moved on to read the next question. "Would you ever sell the company?" he asked. The room stirred at this one. Bilal and a few others had been hired early enough to have equity shares in ConsenSys, and an acquisition would make them rich. I myself had yet to find out how many shares I had, but I half-assumed half-hoped that if I closed the multi-million dollar deal I was working on it would inevitably be a large number. I had been doing the math in my head recently on how many billions we would have to be worth for me to retire.

Joe was unmoved by the question about selling the company. "Who would buy us?" he posed to the group. The idea of an acquisition was not as exciting to him. Selling the company would mean passing up on his vision, which was not to just replace all traditional money with digital currency – a mind bogglingly audacious goal in itself – but to use money as a base for redefining the economy, using smart contracts on Ethereum to automate government services like real estate deeds or even getting a passport. Society could be *trustless*, he liked to say.

I believed we could achieve some of that at least, and we could start by digitizing the ministries here in Dubai. So far, we had only found bloated bureaucracies, but we knew that here shaking the right hands might lead to eye watering sums being thrown at the seemingly impossible. In that I had another advantage on my side, another reason I had come to Dubai: "brown privilege," my term for my ability to seamlessly code switch from a greeting in Urdu to the Pakistani CTO to presenting to a group of clients in my American accent. I had never appreciated until moving here the authority that accent carried, the association with Hollywood and Coca-Cola and all things capitalism, although these days the rest of the world was more addicted to Netflix and Facebook than the caffeinated offerings of Brand America™. I knew how to play my part.

Joe had another reason for his disinterest in the question about an acquisition: he was already astronomically wealthy. It was well known that he had been the biggest investor in Ethereum, purchasing a significant sum when the cryptocurrency was only worth a few pennies on its first day. The price of Ether was in the hundreds of dollars now, and so he could easily be worth $5 billion – or more. No one, in the company or out, knew the exact number. We constantly speculated, as did the media, about how much he was actually worth. What we did know was that our project in Dubai was helping Ethereum to be taken more seriously by big corporations than a few years ago, when cryptocurrency was considered a scam and pastime for drug dealers. More positive news was good for the price. Joe repeated his question. "Would someone buy us?"

"IBM!" Amir exclaimed, waving one hand in the air above his head. "Their blockchain team needs us badly, and we have the best technology!" Amir was a technical manager who had joined a month prior and his enthusiasm for Ethereum was still infectious. *Genius*, he would proclaim every time we reviewed an architecture diagram on the whiteboard. Still, even though Amir was right about IBM's shortcomings, Joe would never sell to them. They represented the opposite of his vision: big corporates maintaining control over the status quo.

Joe grinned in response, with the assuredness of a talking head on your favorite talking head network. "They won't be buying us," he noted.

"No?" Amir asked, slightly surprised.

"We will buy IBM before IBM buys us," Joe said, with a slight smile.

The room broke out in spontaneous applause.

# IN THE BEGINNING

*"This planet [Earth] has – or rather had – a problem, which was this: most of the people living on it were unhappy for pretty much of the time. Many solutions were suggested for this problem, but most of these were largely concerned with the movement of small green pieces of paper, which was odd because on the whole it wasn't the small green pieces of paper that were unhappy."* – Douglas Adams, *The Hitchhiker's Guide to the Galaxy*

In the beginning, there was the Code.

And the Code was with Satoshi, and the code was Bitcoin.

And Bitcoin was full of bugs. Satoshi fixed these bugs, whomever he was. We will probably never know who, since Satoshi was just a pseudonym used on an Internet. He (or she) has never existed anywhere else.

But we know a few things about his motives. In September 2008, as the world economy was in flames, Satoshi posted the code for Bitcoin online, as well as a paper entitled, "Bitcoin: A Peer-to-Peer Electronic Cash System." For decades, hackers had been trying to build something similar: a secure, digital currency. They had been perpetually blocked by the "double spend" problem, which meant that, because anything digital can be simply copied and pasted, there was no truly secure way to ensure that any "e-money" could not be counterfeited. Digital bills could be easily counterfeited, which meant software-based money would be worthless. But now Satoshi believed he had a solution.

This might seem to the reader like a hobby for Internet oddballs living in basements, but it had the potential to redefine something we all care about: money. (Try not to clutch your pearls too tightly.) "Fiat" is worthless by itself: it only has value because we believe it does. Humans have used different things – paper, rare seashells, gold – but each was held up by the same belief. It can be shocking if you really process it: that people slave everyday for things that come out of printers, or out of mud, or washed up on the beach.

The year is 2009. The price of Bitcoin (BTC) is $0.

Money represents something else: control. The US government regulates money, which means it controls the banks, and therefore has an iron grip on much of the economy across the globe. Developing countries from China to the Caribbean, desperate for a stable, secure currency, use the dollar for their economies. Without an alternative, the world is stuck with an American superpower. We can send an email to China in a thousandth of a second, but sending $100 to your neighbor takes three days. All thanks to US laws.

The famed economist Milton Friedman had once said, years before the Internet existed, that reliable e-money was what would make computers truly revolutionary and reduce the power of governments. But with the dollar under a stranglehold, that revolution was stalled.

Satoshi created software to solve that problem. He called it Bitcoin. And then he disappeared.

This goal is so bold as to invite ridicule. Was Bitcoin really meant to be taken seriously as a currency? Or was it meant to be a joke? Was the fact that Satoshi gave himself the first million Bitcoins proof that he was serious or that he was playing a prank on us all?

The year is 2010. The price of BTC is one third of a penny.

At first, Bitcoin was just a toy for a few bored cryptographers to play with in the sandbox. But in 2010, Bitcoin arrived in the public consciousness through the website Silk Road. Silk Road was a marketplace for drugs, sex, syringes, *anything* illegal you could imagine and often worse. Ross Ulbricht, its founder, declared his Satoshi-like ideals on LinkedIn: he built Silk Road "to use economic theory as a means to abolish the use of coercion and aggression amongst mankind."

The year is 2011. BTC is worth $1.

Silk Road soon became the first reliable and safe way to buy weed without meeting a shady dealer. Word got out, and the demand for Bitcoin began to grow with the demand for cannabis lollipops, and the price of the cryptocurrency started to increase. Suddenly, one could make a killing simply "investing" in Bitcoin. Only 21 million Bitcoins would ever be created, which gave it more worth than flimsy fiat issued on paper, or even gold. The seashells had become digital.

The year is 2012. BTC is now $12.

Thanks to Silk Road, the first crypto-enthusiasts turned out to be potheads and anarchists. These soapbox libertarians preached the new "Bitcoin standard," and proclaimed that it would be the future of money. Unfortunately, their safe haven quickly turned dark: sinister users turned to selling harder drugs than weed, or worse, child pornography. It was like Amazon crossed with a penitentiary, but with Bitcoin instead of cigarettes as currency.

The year is 2013. Bitcoin reaches nearly $1000.

Ulbricht's ideals ceded to power and paranoia. Enemies proliferated. Ulbricht soon offered Bitcoin to a drug dealer to take care of his 'problems':

> (FriendlyChemist) is causing me problems. Are you still looking for him or now that you've found Xin have you given up? I would like to put a bounty on his head if it's not too much trouble for you. What would be an adequate amount to motivate you to find him? Necessities like this do happen from time to time for a person in my position.

People would live and die over Bitcoin, just as they did over the green pieces of paper. I first heard of Bitcoin around this time, as the mania was attracting its first mainstream media attention. Geoff, one of my nuttier colleagues, put half of his bonus into Litecoin, which I had never even heard of, although I was also pretty sure he had a drug problem and so I felt unsure about his judgment. I had only read bad things about Bitcoin in the headlines, but I was learning to distrust that as well: a project around mortgage lenders I was working on had been in the news two or three times that year, and every story I read seemed to be a caricature of what I knew to be true, as a policeman's sketch says as much about the policeman. There had to be more than met the eye. I stared at the screen, mouse hovering over the buy button, but decided I was better off saving the money for grad school. If only.

The FBI had begun to hunt for Silk Road's mastermind, piecing together Ulbricht's identity from his various screeds on Internet forums. He was arrested a year later and now sits in federal prison. Bitcoin became synonymous with nefarious activity. If the love of money is the root of all evil, Bitcoin was its poisonous flower.

It is late 2013. Bitcoin has crashed to $500.

But not everyone believed that cryptocurrency's potential ended with Bitcoin. Vitalik Buterin, a *wunderkind* at university in Canada, wrote of an even grander vision in 2013 – one where a currency like Bitcoin could be itself made *programmable*. With just a bit more code, crypto could be more than just currency.

Satoshi was Prometheus, having brought Bitcoin to humanity, but Vitalik expanded on the idea with a proposal to create currency 'smart contracts,' to automate everything that involved money. Trade, banking, even salaries could be automated. Ethereum would deduct payment from your account as soon as Amazon delivered a package – no bank or credit card necessary. He named the concept Ethereum, after the *ether* that surrounds all of us. Joe joined Vitalik when the idea was in its infancy, deploying his Bitcoin millions to fund others who wrote the code and created the Ethereum Foundation to market its mission. Ethereum quickly became a rival to Bitcoin, and the fundamentalists hated it, doubling down on their beliefs. But Vitalik, Joe, and the other co-founders had their sights on something bigger: a new trust layer for the Internet, and Ethereum as a computer for the world. An Internet without middlemen.

It is 2014. Ethereum is thirty cents. The time for revolution has come.

# ROCKETMAN

*Dubai, March 2017. ETH:* $41.

Weeks before I ever heard the phrase "world computer," I sat in my apartment in Dubai with the curtains drawn. My cell buzzed. It was Sevag, the partner I worked for, or my boss' boss in other words. My manager had warned me to expect an angry phone call over the weekend. "You know, when I met you," the partner yelled, "you seemed like a 6 out of 10, 7 out of 10 maybe, but now you're more like a 3 out of 10." He had no mercy even on a Saturday afternoon.

I was then working at my job before ConsenSys, at Strategy&, the once legendary consultancy named Booz&Co that was now a distant fourth behind McKinsey, BCG, and Bain. As a high powered consultant, I charged clients thousands of dollars for advice I was not qualified to give, fulfilling the dream of every MBA graduate. By moving to tax-free Dubai, I could see the world and live in the lap of luxury. In the Middle East I would fit in easily as a brown man. Yet my genius plan had now gone horribly awry.

I had returned the day before from Riyadh, where our client was headquartered. On a recent trip, I had been interrogated by a security officer outside the compound where foreigners like us stayed. He asked for my passport and scowled at me when I could not produce it instantly. The automatic rifle slung over his shoulder swung back and forth as I rummaged through my bag and under the seat. I tried not to look at the military jeep behind him, its large gun turret standing ominously. This intense security, I learned, had been put in place after terrorists had attacked a number of expatriate residences, an incident immortalized in a Jamie Foxx film creatively named *The Kingdom*. The guard began to castigate me in Arabic. Where was my passport? I found these guards more menacing than any imaginable terrorist threat. Three phone calls later a colleague located a photocopy of my passport, which was enough for us to pass through. (The passport was later located under a pizza box.) Since that day I had looked over my shoulder constantly.

Now I felt my heart pumping out of anxiety, just as it had then. The fear of everything I associated with this job collided with the fear of being fired. I was not performing great but I did not deserve to be so insulted. It was hard enough to deal with the client, where my days mostly consisted of being yelled at by Saudi men in white headdresses. The evenings then consisted of being yelled at by Lebanese men in black suits. I considered why Sevag had expected so much and now I was rated so lowly. Growing up as a Pakistani-American in Boston, I had always felt the nagging sense of being an *other*, an outsider, but here I was labeled to the contrary: an American. My first day on the job my manager flaunted my credentials to the customer: projects with JP Morgan and the Department of Defense and other names signaling America's corporate supremacy over the world. Both the clients and my team expected a shoot-first cowboy, full of confidence and swag and Big Dick Energy. Instead they felt they had another meek brown man. That was the only explanation I had for why the partners treated me like an Uber driver.

"I think we'll figure things out this week," I said, trying to show the self-assurance I thought he wanted from me. "I've delivered for bigger clients, from JP Morgan to Bloomberg." I hoped the Americana might impress him.

The name dropping did little to buy Sevag's clemency. "Things better improve this week," he growled, "or you're going home." He hung up. The room swayed around me. I fantasized momentarily about taking an Uber straight to the airport, escaping to never return, the way all the other British and American expats had absconded back in 2009 when the Dubai economy went belly up. The local airport had had to tow away all the Ferraris left to gather dust in the parking lots. America, the country which had just elected Mr. Muslim Ban in 2016, beckoned, lifting her lamp by the golden door. So much for feeling more accepted here in the Middle East. I was doubly displaced, and running was no solution.

Consulting usually involves a lot of bullshitting, and some massaging of the numbers and talk of 'best practices' usually works fine in the US. In the Middle East it reaches another level: they do not want to buy advice as much as to be sold a dream. This client wanted to hear our plans for how their backwater IT company could become a world class cybersecurity innovator, and pronto. To win here, I needed to walk on water, and I was in the wrong holy land for that.

I stared at the single ray of sunlight coming through the dark curtains. It was early April and the weather outside was still humanly tolerable, in the high 90s, more so than the 110+ degree climate typical of summer. I needed fresh air. I slid open the balcony door and went to look out over the eighth floor swimming pool in our building, about two storeys below my unit. A few Russian money launderers lounged under a palm tree, trying to peek at the British women tanning their backsides on the chaises a few feet away from their hot tub. About one hundred yards to the right, the Burj Khalifa glinted in the sun, blinding said money launderers and admonishing them into some forced bashfulness. In exchange for the weekly torture I took in Saudi Arabia, I got about a day and half of free time to to enjoy this scene on my own.

My mind came back to the phone call just now. *That asshole,* I thought. One day I would call him from New York and taunt him about who had really won. "You look tired," he scoffed on the first morning we met, as if taunting me, like a sprinter to his rival before the gun, telling me I would be in last place. I had not come this far in my career or so far from home to give up because someone was *mean*. I had to find the fire and pride to prove I could do this.

I ended up in Dubai almost by accident, though some accidents feel inevitable. At Columbia, Ahmad had been my best friend during my MBA, a Lebanese genius who dropped out of his PhD program in artificial intelligence to "make some real money" in consulting. We bonded as I regaled him with stories of my reckless travels in Syria and Lebanon in 2009, before the civil war. Being broke I had bought an old used travel guide before my trip to Beirut. I only realized how outdated its recommendations were – things had changed much after the 2006 conflict between Hezbollah and Israel – when I arrived at my hotel to learn it had long since become a brothel. Be careful of the tensions near the border, the guide helpfully noted. Ahmad slapped the table with laughter.

One day after class he asked me if I would be interested in working in management consulting with him at Strategy&. At first Dubai seemed too far, but I had always been interested in the Middle East. I was twelve years old when 9/11 happened, and the other kids kept calling me Arab long enough that I decided to study the language in college and see what "Muslim" really meant. Now Dubai meant a chance to explore this world in person. Plus, the tax savings would do wonders for my student loans.

I was also running low on options. I had always been terrible at finding jobs, starting with my first full day at a bank during college, when I interviewed at Bear Stearns, the famed investment bank that collapsed in early March 2008 and would become the first domino to fall in the worst global economic crisis since the Great Depression.

My very well timed visit was on February 16, 2008. So you can see my corporate career started with some issues.

Early in college I had decided that I would focus on my parents' second assignment, becoming rich, so I focused completely on becoming an investment banker. I did not know much about it, but banking appeals to those full of ambition and lacking in common sense. What I really wanted to be was the Muslim Jerry Seinfeld, but that seemed like a waste of a degree from a preppy liberal arts college in New England. Working 18 hours a day with a bunch of douchebags in expensive suits seemed more like the kind of thing I was meant to do.

We candidates from Williams were all given a tour of the Bear Stearns trading floor, bright-eyed fools taking in the scene with the frenetic energy of a beehive. Red-faced men pounded red keys on screens that showed red, red, red. The numbers and arrows danced on the TV screens hanging everywhere and all of them pointed down. On this particular day LIBOR, the interest rate for lending between banks, had jumped again, making it difficult for Bear to get the financing to continue its normal business. The stock price for Bear had fallen from $172 at its peak, barely a year earlier, and was down to the $80s and still plummeting. So enamored were we with the Street that these signs of near apocalypse did not even register strongly enough to prevent us from puffing up our plumes of false enthusiasm.

The VP assigned to give us a tour spread out his arms and told us dryly it was not a normal day. "Like it is for the rest of the Street, these are challenging times," he said, pausing. He turned to me with an eyebrow raised. "Are you *seriously* yawning?" he said, as I struggled to quickly cover my mouth. I had taken a 7 am bus from Williamstown to be here, I explained. "Maybe don't work at a nuclear plant," he told me with an expression that was more snarl than smile. I did not get the joke.

I went home without a job but with a large amount of free Bear Stearns swag that is now considered memorabilia. I still keep the pen case on my desk to keep me humble, a reminder of when I had seen genius fail.

Forty interviews later, I had finally learned not to yawn and much better at pretending I was not doing this purely for the money, which, as I have noted, was exactly why I was doing any of it. A respected consulting firm gave me my first job and I arrived on my first day, ready for a life of financial models and filet mignon, only to find I had been assigned to a software team full of Indian uncles who went home at 5pm. The senior partners, old and white, called me by the wrong name while I stewed and silently plotted on how to find other means to scratch my way to the top.

Within a year, I had found another role in consulting but instead with banking clientele. It was not Wall Street per se but it had all the things I had dreamed of: the long hours, endless expense account, and colleagues whose parents had helped them get the job. *Fantastic.* I soon settled happily into my role as the local deity of Microsoft Excel. Being the numbers guy meant I did not have to go to as many meetings as my prep school colleagues, which felt like a victory at the time.

I had just managed to commit to heart the entire menus of the Cheesecake Factory and Morton's The Steakhouse when I nearly lost it all. The firm fired me – only to change its mind and hire me back two days later. One manager, Chris, had protested on my behalf, although he suspected it may have only been because the directors had again mixed me up with someone else. My Excel wizardry was unappreciated because they barely knew who I was. I was perhaps lucky there were other Indians to be mixed up with, since my only Black colleague in my office was fired a week later.

But in those two days I had made a decision. I was not going to resign from this life of privilege and be thrown back with the coders so easily. (Although they would eventually move my desk downstairs next to the IT department, lending credence to Chris' theory. I tried to appreciate the smell of microwaved biryani, remembering the story of Mullah Nasruddin, the star of many fables in the Middle East. One day he slipped walking on a precipice, and was barely hanging on from a plant when he noted a tiger watching below. As he began to pray he noticed a strawberry growing on the vine. "If you should find yourself in a similar position," the Mullah says, "that strawberry will be the sweetest one you ever eat.") As I went home downcast and fearful for my future, the tiny, imaginary Bill Gates on my shoulder spoke a few words of inspiration: *Go get your MBA*.

Two years later I was interviewing with hedge funds and consulting shops, looking for an internship after my first semester at Columbia. Although I had experience in finance, I was disappointed to find out it had been the wrong kind of finance – what the bankers called "back office," meant for the ninnies who went home to their wives in New Jersey or Long Island. Much as I tried to hide it with buzzwords, they somehow always caught on. The stress of these well-coiffed men scoffing at my poor grasp of net interest income broke my brain in many an interview, as if they could sense the back office stink on me – in one case, after a glass of bad milk at breakfast clawed my insides, quite literally.

The MBA did have its positives. I managed to meet my now fiancee, Saira, a medical student who knew my best friend. Powerless without my expense account, and with my finances drained to a level where the numbers had turned red, I tried to impress her by introducing her to the Prince and Princess of Bahrain at our spring gala. Friends from class, you see. It worked, though I never mentioned I had bought the gala tickets for a quarter of the price off a classmate I knew was a CEO's son whose girlfriend had dumped him. We both knew he didn't need the money. I had managed to use my finance education for something, at least.

Now I was job hunting again, with the rejections piling up in my inbox like a barrage of unwanted Christmas email marketing. "You told too many jokes during the interview," the McKinsey partner told me in the call afterward, pretending to have empathy as he stomped on my ambitions. "We do very serious work." I was feeling more desperate by the day.

I had started to realize the universe very much wanted me to be with people who looked like me. The mixed up names and seating maps were losing their subtlety. I would focus on consulting in tech, and in a place far enough where I might just escape the tractor beam of white privilege: Dubai.

Dubai was also desperate, as the region sorely lacked talent. They would gladly overpay for an Ivy credentialed schmuck like me, even as I was five minutes late to the interview. I told the interviewer being perpetually late might help me fit in in the Middle East. He did not acknowledge the horribly lame joke, which I immediately regretted, remembering McKinsey's advice a moment too late. And yet he made me a job offer anyway. I wondered how I had survived the self sabotage. "He did not get the joke," Ahmad explained to me later, "because he couldn't sleep on the flight from Dubai to New York. So he just drank the whole way instead. He was really, *really* hungover." Humorlessness was what had gotten me here to Dubai, getting yelled at on a Saturday. Which, admittedly, was funny.

I accepted the job offer. Now was the time, if any. If it all worked out, I would pay off my loans, weasel my way back into the States, and I'd have Saira to greet me at JFK on my triumphant return. Or Mom, if things went *really* south.

I arrived in the Middle East and was immediately shipped off to work with a client in Saudi Arabia. It was 2016 and the country was rapidly ascending in the world order. A hotshot new Crown Prince announced "Vision 2030," a bold plan to remake the kingdom after oil had collapsed. The Prince believed he was the next Steve Jobs. He went on tours where he posed for photos with Zuckerberg and Trump, who declared Saudi was full of potential. So now here I was in Riyadh, dealing the diktats of the Prince's wishlist which were springing to life like gods from Zeus' thigh. Into this world I was parachuted in, full of confidence that Sevag was looking to chop down with Bunyan-like tenacity.

I sat in the lounge at Riyadh airport four days later, having somehow survived the week. I was flying to New York City – not abandoning Dubai, although that was appealing. I was flying fifteen hours to meet Saira's parents, to show her I was serious. The only thing I knew about her father was that he had come to the US originally as part of the Pakistani Olympic team, and then subsequently turned a few dollars he saved from odd jobs into a carpet store empire. My friend had run into him at a wedding in the hotel gym, where Saira's father challenged him to a push up contest. I could not tell this man my career was in tatters. I had to find a way through. At a minimum, I'd need to start with a very firm handshake.

The flight to JFK was at 2 AM, so I had the entire lounge to myself. I nibbled what was left of my fries, having thrown the rest to the orange tabby who lived in the alley outside my building. I hated the Riyadh airport. I had waited twelve hours here for a flight to my grandfather's funeral in India. I would have to fly back here in barely 48 hours. The call for boarding began and I queued up Elton John's "Rocketman," which like probably many other suitcase warriors is my don't-get-depressed song for long flights. I nodded as he missed the Earth so much, and his wife ...

I was eating a tasteless jam sandwich just before takeoff when I received a whatsapp message. Mohamed was a recent friend, a Sudanese American I had met at some startup-related events. I had been going to a few of these, hunting and hoping for a company less miserable where I could still slake the ambitions that drove me here. Mohamed's startup was on the edge of shutting down, so I offered him my extra bedroom and let him keep things going. I had rented this oversized apartment in part to welcome any friends to stay while passing the city. If I was going to struggle through shitty interviews and corporate jobs my whole life, I could use the karmic diversification of a few good deeds, or at least a few favors.

"Might have a new job for you," he texted. "What do you know about blockchain?"

# INTO THE ETHER

*Dubai, April 2017. ETH:* $48.

Raheem had a laugh that somehow sounded like both a giggle and a guffaw. It was never really clear to me how he managed to make both noises at once, as if he was trying to keep it together and enjoy himself simultaneously. It did seem genuine, at least.

I was nervous. I was behind on my work for the week again and had no desire for another dressing-down. I had to finish another presentation this weekend, more slides on how drones would revolutionize telecom in Saudi Arabia and other fluff. Instead of working, I was across the street having coffee with Raheem. Mohamed had introduced me to him over Whatsapp – he was leading the new Middle East office for ConsenSys. My leg twitched under the table as I tried not to convey my internal panic. There was only one door now – *get the job or get fired*, I kept thinking, although Raheem's laughter put me at ease.

"So, like, we've made a lot of relationships with the government here in Dubai," he told me. "You know, we need someone who gets the culture. We can't just import some guy from New York, you know?" He hinted at having deep connections in the region, and expressed some frustration that other people at ConsenSys did not get how doing business here could be unique or 'sensitive.' One teammate from New York had suggested we use blockchain for voting, which had been met with a mix of consternation and laughter from the ministers. *They don't vote here*, someone had to whisper.

I knew something of what he meant, having lived in the Middle East before. I spent my semester abroad in Syria, before that country became a synonym for limitless misery and conflict. Dictatorship was not new to me.

Recently I had had to convince Saira to call me on some unheard-of video calling app, because as I explained to her FaceTime and Skype were illegal. The government essentially owned all the cell companies, and wanted us to pony up for long distance. This was the logic of a benevolent authoritarianism: we could live in our ultramodern skyscrapers, but for any new business or technology the powers that came along they needed not one cut but many: at each stage of any deal there was a labyrinth of companies that all owned each other, each inevitably leading back to the Royals.

"What if you get caught?" she had asked, her voice signaling concern. To her, the lack of freedom was something to fear. A British citizen had been recently deported for raising money for charity on Facebook – another punishable offense, as only the government's charities were allowed. But to me, the constant surveillance meant safety: I walked around unbothered late at night, alone, both here and in Syria, traveling wherever I wished, knowing an ever-present eye was on me. As long as I never discussed politics, I could continue in these small transgressions, knowing if I ever crossed a line – a thin, invisible line that you only developed from talking to the other expats – each little sin would be used to throw the book at me. I had once tried to discuss politics in Damascus, asking a local friend about the "Lion King," the codename expats told me to use when talking about Bashar al-Assad. I saw the immediate look of fear in my friend's eyes and knew now to press the topic any further.

For all the oddities, it was clear to anyone living there the rulers knew what they were doing. The Emirates had created a rival to London and New York out of literally nothing: in the 1980s it had simply been a highway in the desert, leading to nowhere. They had combined their biggest advantages, oil and empty land, to create massive airport runways as the foundation for the biggest airline outside America. They had made capitalism work for them – just as early Americans had when they arrived on someone else's land. It was a place in transition, but unlike many other dictatorships they were excited by the future, as long as they could shape anything that came along to their liking.

Still, even I had to learn a few things. Sometimes the stereotypes were wrong. The vast majority of Saudis I met drove beat up old Japanese cars they filled with free gasoline. Sometimes the stereotypes were true. A co-worker did not come to meetings in Saudi because the client had no women's bathrooms. They did not see the need.

"I do have a lot of experience with difficult clients," I told him, blandly summarizing these lessons.

His eyes lit up. "Yes! You know how it is then." He related to me how things had started here: ConsenSys had been selected from dozens of startups to join the Dubai Future Accelerators, or DFA, an incubator meant to foster partnerships between exciting startups and the government bureaucracy.

Most startups failed to sign any contracts, but thanks to Raheem, ConsenSys had been able to use DFA as a springboard to get an audience with the Sheikh, the Crown Prince, and their inner circle. Blockchain would be the next hot technology, we explained, and now was the perfect time for Dubai to get ahead of everyone else. Even Silicon Valley had barely begun to understand blockchain's implications. Like Saudi Arabia, Dubai wanted badly to shrink its dependence on the ever-shrinking riches of the oil industry; the Crown Prince Hamdan saw an opportunity to make his mark on the country's history by jumpstarting the tech scene. ConsenSys had flown in its experts from around the world to run workshops on the merits of blockchain. We described how Ethereum improved on Bitcoin and could revolutionize both business and government.

Dubai in particular needed to improve its government services in identity and land registries, and here we proposed a transformation based on Ethereum smart contracts. Dubai could be the first, redefining the concept of government itself. The local leadership was convinced. In late 2016 the "Dubai 2020 Blockchain Strategy" was born: a proclamation to the world that Dubai would use smart contracts to digitize all government services and create a completely paperless administration by 2020.

There was one problem: no one in the government—or really anywhere in the world—knew much about blockchain. They would need an advisor on this journey. Who better to help them than us?

On March 14, 2017, the Dubai government made a head-scratching announcement: it named ConsenSys and IBM as advisors on the blockchain strategy, putting competing visions of blockchain in play. IBM had created its version of a blockchain, one controlled by a central party. They championed a blockchain they had built for Wal-Mart as an example of how corporations could profit from the technology, and they distanced themselves from any mention of Bitcoin or Ethereum or decentralization. Our view of blockchain centered on digital currencies, and theirs was completely antagonistic to them. A rivalry was created that would define my time in Dubai.

Ethereum was already on an uptrend when the announcement hit the press. On February 28, ConsenSys, along with Microsoft and JPMorgan, had announced the Enterprise Ethereum Alliance, a trade group meant to build an Ethereum upgrade to handle smart contracts for big business. The price had doubled from $15 that day to $28 by the Dubai announcement. Within 10 days of the latter, it had grown to $50. Anyone who believed in Ethereum's potential had tripled their money in just a few weeks.

"A few more bucks on Ethereum's price, and Joe will basically be a billionaire. Then we can just hire shit-tons more people here and be a huge unicorn," Raheem explained. He giggled. This was the first time I realized a critical link between ConsenSys and the Ether price. Joe was funding the company with his crypto. Our war chest grew with every success. Raheem hinted that he too had bought a lot of Ether – and might be profiting millions already.

"But more than that, we could do a lot of good here," Raheem noted. "The government runs everything in Dubai, and we could really help them improve people's lives." Dubai could even be the gateway to reforming the whole Middle East with tech, a blockchain revolution to supplant the region's many failed states. "It's a win-win," he guffawed.

How often in life did you find something that could help people and make you rich at once? I was impressed and felt hopeful after a long time. But I also still needed to get back to the office.

"You should meet Joe, actually," he concluded, finally wrapping up our chat. "He likes to interview everybody."

I was taken aback. "He's coming to Dubai?"

"In a couple weeks," he said. "Let's hope he likes you."

It was 2 am and we were still getting yelled at.

"These projections are crap," Sevag had told my team in the conference room. "We need to finish this by Thursday morning. I don't care when you do it, just be ready by then." I felt a deep embarrassment, the red-faced kind from the schoolyard when every humiliation feels life-threatening.

After Sevag stormed out, a younger teammate, maybe twenty-three years old but already burned out, glanced at me wide-eyed. He asked if we would have to stay up all night. I thought about it. I had two days before meeting Joe and I could cut in on precious sleep to learn more about blockchain—or try to salvage what was probably my last chance to save this project. I felt like a prisoner, staring at the watchtower in the yard, calculating how far I could make it before I'd be shot. *Just. Run.* I told the team we would be better off getting some rest. We could start on fixing the projections early in the morning.

I sulked back to my hotel room.

Resting on the bed, I checked the price of Ether. It was up another 15% in the three days since I'd spoken to Raheem. *We can hire a shit-ton of people* ... I thought back to how many interviews it had taken me to get my first job: forty rejections before my first offer. Raheem was Pakistani, like me, so we could connect easily. But now I had to impress a CEO? I had taken some long odds here. I always blamed my interview failures on being brown, which felt accurate since so many of my friends felt like they ran into the same walls. I internalized this kind of thinking, which only made my anxiety around interviews worse. But I had to do so, because I am a millennial, and self-victimization is endemic to our generation, and self-doubt is a major theme of this story.

Joseph Lubin, I googled. This man had made billions off crypto and yet was ready to spend all of it in the cause of advancing blockchain. What made him tick? I found a speech on YouTube from a few weeks prior. "Has anyone heard of blockchain? Or Ethereum?" he asked a lethargic crowd. He looked a little awkward on stage, his right arm clasping his left. "The token is now number 2 behind Bitcoin," he noted, pointing to a chart showing the price going from $0.20 to $4. The crowd warmed up.

Bitcoin, he explained, was so secure because it allowed anyone to have a copy of its database, which is essentially a history of transactions ("distributed ledger"). Anyone could also submit transactions to this ledger, as Alice would try to pay Bob $10. But the transaction would only be *approved* if everyone agreed that the math worked out. If she had the funds, the transaction would be approved and committed to the "block-chain," which was essentially a cryptographically secured ("chained") history of these transactions (stored in groups, called "blocks"). Voila! Secure, digital currency.

Bitcoin was undoubtedly better than the US dollar, Joe explained. It was faster than a traditional bank, was more secure, and did away with the exorbitant fees. The audience began to sit up and listen. "With Ethereum, you can develop any program you can dream up," he said, mentioning burgeoning applications in supply chains, banking and loans, and even music. "Identity is really messed up," he continued. "The poor often have no passport, no license, especially in the Third World. We are building something called uPort, which will enable self-sovereign identity, and will enable you to control your own personal data." The *ums* and pauses in his speech stopped altogether. Now he had the crowd enchanted. "We are also building next generation financial infrastructure," he noted, which would help bring banking to the unbanked left out from the economy and provide credit to those most in need of it, creating a free account on Ethereum for anyone who wanted one. Joe's favorite topic was decentralized music: every time a song was streamed, the artist never received payment directly – most of the money went to record labels, or Spotify, who paid artists a sad and exploitative pittance at less than a penny per stream. Even then, those pennies were split up with managers, and a dozen other intermediaries that were legacies from a world when CDs needed to be printed and most music was played on the radio. Ethereum would remove these middlemen. ConsenSys was already building Ujo, an app to make sure artists would be paid directly for their work.

ConsenSys seemed to have a decentralized application for everything, I thought, a fully fleshed out vision for how the world could run on blockchain. All I had to do was convince this guy on screen that I understood how it worked.

It was 2:25 am but I felt more awake than I had all day. This was more than a hot tech company or an escape from my abusive boss. This was a chance to improve the lives of millions, *billions*, something my aforementioned millennial self wanted deeply.

I had to find out more about how this miraculous software worked. Sleep could wait. I googled "public key cryptography," and started to take notes.

# CRYPTOGRAPHY

*"Any sufficiently advanced technology is indistinguishable from magic." - Arthur C. Clarke*

Part math, part magic.

Cryptography is the game you play with your friends as a kid— trying to send notes in class with the words spelled backward and numbers replacing half the letters so the teacher wouldn't be able to read about your crush on Billy. (Years later, Billy turned out to be a lout.)

Bitcoin, Ethereum, and other blockchains all rely on a special type of math known as public key cryptography. Everyday you log on to wi-fi, use email, check your bank account, or perhaps send some embarrassing selfies. Your private (perhaps, very private) data is floating all around in the air for anyone to steal. Why can't they?

The answer is a very complex version of your secret notes in class. Imagine a special, expensive, fountain pen that can only write *your* signature – no one else's. Everyone knows it is yours, and you signed your marriage papers with it. Forgery is impossible ... but if you lose it, the guy with your pen (key) did not steal your things. No, he *is* you; he can prove it through the papers for the car and the house. He can produce the signature. So it is his house now. And his wife. Hopefully he isn't Billy. All it took was the pen.

Moreover – with a blockchain, the signatures are visible to everyone. The idea is a *distributed* ledger, where everyone has a copy of all the transactions. As long as everyone has their own pen, it is impossible for there to be fraud. Alice can send money to Bob without a bank. You can write a contract over the Internet and know the money is secure. The "signatures" are not your name but instead a random string of numbers and letters, making this semi-private. In a world where banks didn't keep your money safe so much as steal it and tech companies didn't keep your data safe so much as sell it, blockchain had the potential to get rid of both. Dozens of startups would jump into the space, and ConsenSys was one of the first, starting in 2014, fully dedicated to building for Ethereum, an exciting new upgrade over Bitcoin.

Think of blockchain as a little bit like doing an embarrassing dance in a room full of blind people. You're totally fine, as long as they are all actually blind. (Maybe add a few hackers outside, trying to peep inside.)

Governments also use cryptography extensively to protect secret files, and the NSA invented many of the most common algorithms in cryptography. China and Russia tend to worry that the US government built a "backdoor" in these – a master key that could unlock every message from secret plans about their missile programs to Putin's web browsing habits. The NSA is the blind guy who brought a hidden camera. Don't trust that guy.

# SASHIMI AND A KAHUNA

*Dubai, April 2017. ETH:* $61.

The day of my interview arrived and I would now confront my future face to face. The head of HR greeted me at the entrance to the restaurant. "Before you meet Joe," she said, "we thought it'd be helpful to meet David, who you will be working with closely." David stood up as we approached him, towering over us both at 6'6". He was young, about my age or just younger. A brown v-neck stretched over shoulders broad enough that I knew he could never sit in an airline middle seat. A pair of glasses gave him an unmistakable resemblance to Jeff Goldblum. I thought about telling him this but reminded myself I would tell no jokes today.

David dived right into it. "So what do you know about blockchain?" I gave him the best summary of Joe's speech from a couple days before and how inspiring I found it.

"Great, I'm glad you see the potential," he said coolly. "One thing I have to warn you about though, is that our job here is to prioritize and figure out what Dubai can actually do with this stuff today." He squinted a little, whether to convey seriousness or due to the bright sun I didn't know. "A lot of people use blockchain to just talk about pipe dreams. Cows chugging coffee could not produce the volume of bullshit you see in this space. Does sifting through that sound fun to you?" I nodded. The more he spoke the more I liked him. His seriousness meant this was the real deal. He grasped my hand in his enormous one, said thanks, and left. *Now for the big kahuna,* I thought.

The two bald men sat down across from me. I knew both were ex-Goldman, and had worked in hedge funds or venture capital afterwards, so they were probably going to be hardasses. I wondered if they had chosen a sushi restaurant on purpose, as the chef in the open kitchen a few feet away sharpened his knife and sliced a little tuna into sashimi.

Joe and Jared were completely alike and wholly different, much like long-lost brothers might be. Both spoke in low, gruff voices, with a tendency to grip the table when speaking. They both laughed at their own jokes first and then looked around to see the other's reaction. Nonetheless, Joe had a demeanor that was thoughtful and relaxed, wearing a graphic tee shirt with his Macbook resting in front of him. Jared seemed like a literal bulldog, a short beard accentuating his tendency to gnash his teeth while he thought. His dress shirt looked heavily starched.

Jared asked most of the questions. "What do you think about our strategy?"

I had done my research. "You guys really emphasize open source," I said, "and that will help grow the community of software engineers faster. That was how Google got Android to work in eighty percent of cell phones."

"We've heard the Android comparison before," Jared noted, easing slightly. He asked me what opportunities for blockchain I saw in finance, and I mentioned Know Your Customer regulations (KYC) that were painful and needed better data. *Butter me up, because I'm on a roll.*

Joe piped up. "Would you like to have equity in that kind of product?"

"Wow," I said. "Equity in the product itself?"

He explained ConsenSys' unique structure: he was an investor in all things Ethereum. The goal was to build an ecosystem rather than a one-off product. To create the Ethereum-based world he imagined, he needed to unleash our creativity, rather than try to come up with every idea himself. In exchange, we got the chance to be independent entrepreneurs.

"We call it the hub and spoke model," Joe added.

"That sounds very decentralized," I said. *Dammit, a joke.*

"That's the whole point," laughed Jared, easing my sudden anxiety. "Look," he said, gesturing with a rugby player's hand, "we've got potential to win as many as a dozen projects here in Dubai, and we could make a lot of impact. But the real reason we're investing is because if IBM wins here, they will rule the blockchain roost. They don't care about changing the world. To them blockchain is just a fancy database."

"Yeah, we had to deal with them a lot at Strategy&," I said. "They're everywhere in the Middle East."

"Exactly. IBM is Darth Vader. We need people with the skills to take them on. And if that goes well, you might be able to launch your own product, what we call a spoke. Does that interest you?"

I nodded my affirmation.

"Good," he said. "We'll get back to you soon."

I was sitting in the black SUV that took us to our Riyadh office every day when I stumbled across a surprising headline in the local Arabic paper. There, buried in the back, it noted that seventeen extremists had been arrested for a plot to blow up a soccer stadium. (My Arabic is not great, but because I received my language education at American institutions, I learned words like "bomb" and "missile" much earlier than I needed in everyday conversation. Ah, Orientalism.) I flipped over to the BBC – somehow, this had received no coverage in Western media.

I was thoroughly confused. But as I thought about it, I realized the BBC likely had barely two people reading local Arabic news, but none had the time to read page B 17. For the local government mouthpiece paper to bury this news was genius: it would never get out. I wondered how much we really know about these places. The likely answer is that we are mushrooms – kept in the dark and fed shit. Even as I write these words three years later, the world is falling apart due to the global coronavirus pandemic. Who knows if it might have been caught sooner if some BBC journalist read the Party newspaper in China all the way through? All I could take away was that I was probably too afraid of yesterday's news and not afraid enough of tomorrow's.

Meanwhile, something like Ethereum – which could change the world, was making people millionaires everyday, and would be on everyone's minds within months – had barely scratched the surface of public consciousness. In my research I had found only one article interested in Dubai's blockchain work in the *Wall Street Journal*. Crazy people posted on blogs and Reddit and that at the time was how to get "news" on crypto – a source just hidden enough to be a treasure trove of alpha. I was one of few in the know.

My phone dinged as we drove and I flipped it over full of anticipation. I had been waiting to hear back and HR had now sent an official offer. "Congrats!" the email began. The feeling of elation ran down from my head all through my limbs, a lightning bolt of euphoria. I flipped the phone back over to hide the message and waited until I was at the office to duck into a dark corner.

"I got the offer," I said over the phone to Ahmad, my schoolmate and now colleague. He was elsewhere in Riyadh, working at another client's office. I wanted to confer with him on negotiating strategy. ConsenSys wanted me to take a serious pay cut. I was willing to, but how much was too much?

I expected excitement, but his response was lukewarm. This was not the same friend I'd had in school, the one who I had met in Cartagena on spring break, laughing with me after he had just tossed another classmate into a pool from the Spanish mansion balcony. He apologized – he was so exhausted he had been at the doctor all weekend for chest pains. Now he was having to make up the work he missed. He was literally near death from overwork.

I decided not to negotiate any further. I steeled myself up to go and talk to Sevag. I would say I was quitting, and shake his hand to show some class and gratitude. I spit in my palm and rubbed it around, smiling as I headed back to my desk.

# DAY ONE

*Dubai, May 2017. ETH:* $155.

"I'm not happy," the man with the Harvard Business School notebook told us. It was my first meeting with a ConsenSys client, one that was paying us millions to be a world leader in blockchain. I came in excited, first day jitters and all, Ether up another $100, expecting the client to be holding a toast to our genius. We were sitting in their sixtieth floor boardroom, looking down on the Gulf as if from the heavens.

It was the last time I would wear a suit. A few weeks later I would overcorrect, greeting a CEO in a t-shirt I had purchased at Wal-Mart for eight dollars. But for now I still figured appearances mattered and the guy across from me certainly did so too.

"We're running into challenges with the back end," Andrei responded factually. He was also suited up, leaning his head to one side as if carrying a weight on one shoulder. We had been begging the NYC office to send reinforcements, and Andrei had volunteered. He was the best we had.

Nabeel did not find that answer satisfying. "There was so much progress early in December. That was great, but now it's June and the app looks exactly the same." He pulled on his sleeve and glanced at the Patek on his wrist. "How can we make this go faster? And how come we don't actually see the blockchain part?" Nabeel had a trim beard, and was slim and handsome with well-kempt hair. I could smell his career accomplishments from across the table: big shot at McKinsey, followed by this job, a cushy golden parachute. He reminded me of Sevag, the guy who shouted about font sizes being wrong and that *the deck was as useful as toilet paper - actually toilet paper is more useful - don't laugh - and now it's 2 am so you've got 6 hours to make it better.* I looked him up later and lo and behold, he had worked at Strategy&. *Fantastic*. I visualized myself jumping from a frying pan, right into this office.

Andrei had told me before the meeting he had flown directly from Vancouver. He clearly had not slept too well: cattle class for the startup guys. He told Nabeel that we were hiring as fast as we could – here I was, Exhibit A – and working on fixing the bugs with the blockchain.

"Does every transaction really have to take fifteen seconds?" Nabeel complained. "It's like dialup, but worse." Andrei tried to patiently explain why the consensus algorithm took so long and how we might fix it and why you didn't need to "see" the "blockchain" to use it. This bored Nabeel so much I thought his eyes might fall out of his head.

"Okay, well, let's try and make this demo good," Nabeel said as he picked up his papers. "The CEO wants to be sure that we are ready for our big announcements with the government." I wondered if we could really make Ethereum run faster like we were promising. From what I had read, there were brilliant cryptographers trying to figure that out, but even they said it was six months away. Until then, we were going to wave our hands around and hope clients did not get too irate. We headed for the conference room where a few men in white headdresses awaited.

This was the big dogs room, where the floor to ceiling windows showed a vast panorama from the Gulf to the Burj Khalifa and Dubai's extensive skyline in between. I sat down and tried to connect to the wifi. "Um, is IT around?" I asked. "Can they help us out here?" Andrei had just told Nabeel about our hiring push, and here the first recruit could not even work his laptop properly. I was desperate not to look stupid.

The HBS notebook opened, then closed. The pen tapped impatiently. The clock was ticking and I felt sweat start to build inside my suit. I tapped Andrei on the shoulder. *Do you want to give it a go?* I mouthed.

He stiffened his shoulders. He had probably hoped I would wow the client, and I was passing the buck. To beat IBM, to successfully deliver these projects, we needed the cavalry, and so far the cavalry (me) had fallen off his horse. But he had rehearsed this more than I had, and actually knew something about blockchain. He opened his laptop and turned to the CEO.

"As you all know, our client has been a major contributor to the advancement of blockchain in the United Arab Emirates..."

After our close call with disaster in the real estate demo, Andrei and I rode back in the Uber together after the meeting. Our first big client was eager to get rid of us. I apologized to Andrei for what had happened.

"It's not your fault," he said. He explained that our demo in December had been excellent, but it was a paper tiger: there was no blockchain working behind the scenes. I raised my eyebrows with worry. Elizabeth Holmes, the CEO of Theranos and teenage Steve Jobs wannabe, had been excoriated in the media for hocus-pocus demos, presenting spurious results from blood tests to investors on her way to defrauding them out of nine billion dollars. Now HBO was making a documentary about her lies. But Andrei reassured me that this is actually typical: startups *always* build demos that only work for five minutes, but that is often good enough to close the first sale. ConsenSys had been fairly upfront about it, too. Every tech startup had to sell a bit of vaporware. It was building the real thing that was the hard part. "The road to revolution is going to be bumpy," he finished.

"And billion dollar valuations," I added. I felt somewhat reassured. You would think explosive growth is a good thing, but with it comes a perpetual feeling of teetering on the edge, between otherworldly success and massive failure, applause or laughter. I was not used to it then. Jeff Bezos has a rallying cry at Amazon – "it's always day one." This felt more like negative one.

At the center of Dubai are two massive concentric circles of highways, with the Burj Khalifa dead center. Driving around them, you feel like you are being swung around the end of a slingshot. The centrifugal forces spiraled us around, back to our modest co-working space.

"I need to learn this blockchain stuff better," I admitted. "It's hard to be a leader when you're not sure what you're talking about."

"I'm not sure blockchain is what matters to them," Andrei disagreed. "Nabeel just wants his announcement. They're paying us to build a nuke so they can kill some ants. And make a big boom." He made the shape of a mushroom cloud with his hands.

Andrei shook his head and rattled off the names of a few books he thought would help. "At least you're here now," he continued. "Half of Dubai is on vacation, it seems." He was right. Last week, we had been on a call with Jared to discuss another project, an audacious idea to rebuild Dubai's university diploma system with Ethereum. I had been listening in from a labor camp, where I was handing out Ramadan meals to the workers. *Look at me,* I thought, *living up to my blockchain ideals.* Then until mid-call I was jolted awake when the practice pitch suddenly became heated. "Who's going to make the final decisions?" Jared demanded of the others, while two teammates argued back. I ducked out of the serving line into my car. By then, the pitch had devolved into a shouting match between Raheem and Jared, with no clear winner. "I need a vacation," Raheem said afterward, filing off stage for a meditation retreat in Thailand with his precious Eth winnings and leaving our first project in limbo. Now I had joined this real estate project, which was supposed to be the "good" one.

We stepped out of the Uber in front of Emirates Towers. The sudden change in temperature immediately fogged up my sunglasses. I walked around blindly for a moment, trying to pretend nothing was wrong. "Door's over here," said a tall man in a puzzled voice. David was holding the door open, a 24 oz coffee in his other hand. He turned to Andrei. "Back to New York? When are you coming back?"

"I'm hoping not to come back," he admitted. "You guys are hiring, right? I just came to try and be meshy." I blankly accepted his words, not understanding the term.

*"Awwwww yeahhhh,"* David said as he fist-bumped Andrei. "Did you see the new trailer for *Silicon Valley*?" Andrei nodded. Blockchain had become fertile ground for comedy, and *Silicon Valley,* the beloved HBO show about the startup Pied Piper, wanted to include crypto in its next season. Andrei told us our CMO had spoken to them about how a PiedPiperCoin could work. She had explained to them why she referred to Joe as "white Morpheus," because he could convince anyone of Ethereum's potential. Perhaps Joe could appear as a guest

star, she had asked. They turned down our offer. It's HBO's loss, we laughed.

But once Andrei departed for the airport, David privately steamed to me about how easily our one ally had abandoned us while ConsenSys looked for sitcom fame. I asked about *meshy* and what it meant. "Oof," he said with a sigh. "I'll explain that when you're ready."

# A BRIEF HISTORY OF BLOCKCHAIN

*Dubai, June 2017. ETH:* $275.

It was 11:30pm when I got home from the bookstore. It was deep summer now and far too hot during the day to walk, yet it still felt too opulent to me to order an Uber and ride a quarter mile. I waited until late evening to set out and pick up a few books on startups and software.

*Zero to One. Blockchain Revolution. Software Project Management for Dummies.* I was hungry to find the miracle formula for building a billion dollar company. That night I tore into the books and ate up every word. Stay lean. Focus obsessively. Pick a niche and dominate it. Go for broke. David was right – I needed to forget much of what I had learned.

Andrei had recommended *Blockchain Revolution,* which ironically, turned out to be the most boring of the bunch. Alex and Don Tapscott, two thought leaders in the space, had written the book two years earlier to explain how blockchain could be more than a digital currency. Blockchain was more than a fancy database. It could be the springboard to redefine our entire social paradigm. Trustless commerce. I pushed through page after page of jargon looking to understand more about how blockchain worked, although I found little of that. I did find many of their ideas seemed to be inspired by Ethereum – in fact, much of it by Joe himself. Halfway through I was startled to find that an entire chapter had been dedicated to ConsenSys. The writers were most interested in ConsenSys' philosophy, which was based around Joe's intent to create a whole new category of company. Joe advocated for *holacracy,* a system that eschewed traditional management and where all employees were equals. This was critical to ensure we stayed true to the spirit of blockchain – a vision of a decentralized, peer-to-peer world; a true democracy, without the impurities of power. ConsenSys would eat its own dog food, by using smart contracts to run all our decision making. Technology would ensure we lived up to our values.

For a few pages, I wondered if the Tapscotts had even really thought through what they were writing. Their messaging around ConsenSys was nearly reverential. Whole pages seemed to be regurgitated from Joe's town halls: "ConsenSys is still a tiny company.....But its story provides a glimpse into radical changes in corporate architecture that may help unleash innovation and harness the power of human capital for not just wealth creation but prosperity." ConsenSys would not just build blockchain but define the future of work, they wrote, a new model of corporation that could create a better world. The Gospel of Joe.

When the Tapscotts' book was published, the world had not yet become disillusioned enough about Big Tech to take these claims seriously. But in 2016 and 2017, our perception of the Internet and tech turned from utopian to dystopian. Russian disinformation campaigns on social media helped put Donald Trump in the White House. Powerful companies built addictive platforms that sucked users and dollars into their walled gardens where they controlled – and more importantly, owned – our videos, our pictures, and our texts. The excessive centralization of data was the root problem, leading to control and power falling in the hands of those same tech companies. In early 2017, everyone felt sick of these platforms and hoped for a magic bullet.

To this world, the Gospel of Joe was a salve. The Internet is broken, Joe and the other original blockchain advocates concurred. The web had been meant to be the holy grail for free thought and expression, but now it had become a vacuum to suck a dizzying amount of data about you and every aspect of your life out of your phone and then profit by selling it to advertisers. The Internet was no longer the product. The product was you.

The vision laid out by the Tapscotts, almost whacky when published, now found a global audience. After Lehman Brothers went off a cliff in 2008 and took the world's economy with it, the Bitcoin and cryptocurrency gospel had been an easy pitch: take back the power from the evil bankers and the "one percent." But now, behind the vision of Ethereum and blockchain, the goal was to take back the power from *everyone*: the bankers, the politicians, the CEOs, and all the rest. Anyone with an Internet connection could be part of the revolution. All you had to do was buy a little crypto.

Joe, Vitalik, and a few others holed up in a beach house in Miami – expenses covered by Joe – for six months in 2014 sketching out the vision for making Ethereum reality. The early software was buggy, and there was no real way for a normal person to use it. Only the nerdiest of engineers could figure out something so complicated and new. Joe helped fund the project through its early days as it moved from theoretical papers to the creation of an actual nonprofit foundation with a mission to grow the network worldwide. The Ethereum Foundation was founded in Zug, Switzerland, the infamously lax banking center where dictators and criminals kept their funds. Once others began to see the potential of Ethereum, many put their life savings into it. Joe convinced private equity billionaire Mike Novogratz to put in a million dollars – his roommate at Princeton, because the old boys still matter – and now we had a foothold on Wall Street, too.

Joe then founded ConsenSys to build new systems of apps built on the blockchain, known as decentralized applications or *dApps*. The Tapscotts focused on how this "dApp" concept could create a new wave of startups, like decentralized replacements for Uber and Airbnb. Unicorns like Uber had claimed to be building our peer-to-peer future, by connecting neighbor with neighbor to give each other rides through the app. But rather than connecting people, Uber had focused obsessively on becoming a monopoly. They cut drivers' pay and those drivers, disgusted by their treatment as "partners," were now burning tires in cities all over the world. Ethereum, however, could match drivers and riders instantly and seamlessly, using only smart contracts – no profit-hungry middlemen needed. dApps could finally make technology fair through fully automated smart contracts. The name sucked, but the concept was good. No one percenter could take over, but all could participate, freely.

The banks grew fearful. There was more than startup potential here: they did not want to be "disrupted" into oblivion like the taxi companies. They began investing in blockchain startups building early proofs-of-concepts (PoCs). Ethereum was too hacker-anarchist-open-source driven to be palatable to these rise averse companies, so in 2015 the largest banks in the world, including Goldman Sachs, Credit Suisse, Barclays, and others founded R3, investing $150 million into a consortium meant to create a bank-friendly blockchain that they could use to create the future of finance. The conversation shifted from Bitcoin, Ethereum, and other digital currencies to "enterprise blockchain," a crypto-less, non-revolutionary vision of Satoshi's technology focused on supply chains and equities settlement. The big corporates, IBM included, patted themselves on the back for "innovation," while claiming they had kicked the drug dealers and money launderers to the curb.

Bankers began leaving en masse to found blockchain startups, raising hundreds of millions each, which was the bare minimum you needed to get the front page of a tech blog those days. Digital Asset Holdings, another startup that was building a 'banking blockchain' for the Australian Stock Exchange, had armed itself with Blythe Masters, the JP Morgan heavyweight who is credited with creating the derivatives market in the early 1990s. *The Guardian* described her as "the woman who invented financial weapons of mass destruction," the quadrillion dollar lady. Now she was going to blow up finance from the inside.

ConsenSys' leadership, focused on its message of revolution, looked at these trends with a wary glance. "Bitcoin bad, blockchain good" was IBM's motto motto. But if we ignored these projects too long IBM and JP Morgan would short circuit the revolution and replace it with their own corporate logos. We would have to make a deal with the devil.

We finally joined the "enterprise blockchain" party late in 2016. Andrew Keys, ConsenSys' first business hire, called every banker he knew, and managed to convince Microsoft to put Ethereum on its cloud service. Soon we were advising the very banks we had sought to replace. Joe moved to hire as many of the luminaries in the space as he could: Juan Llanos, a renowned financial regulation expert; Alex Batlin, the head of innovation for Swiss mega-bank UBS; Julio Faura, the lead for new technologies at the Banco Santander, known as *el pulpo,* the octopus, for his extensive influence in blockchain and fintech; and many others. I knew their names because I read them in the Tapscotts' book.

In 2016, a small venture capital fund found this world strange, and tasked a young MBA intern with writing a memo to explain what was happening. I knew only what my crazy coworker had told me about crypto in 2013. I noted in the memo that the market was still split between banking-focused startups and the "Wild West" of cryptocurrencies, although I do not recall reading anything about ConsenSys. As crazy as crypto was, I felt the true innovations in finance's future would happen there. After all, what was the last exciting technology you bought from a bank? My boss edited out the 'unconventional' thinking when I was done.

By the winter of 2016 the blockchain hype began to filter through to governments. Central banks in Singapore and Canada, goaded by tech companies R3 and IBM, began to play with these PoCs, and blockchain ideas started to spread globally. Dubai, which was keen to jump on any trend in tech, invited ConsenSys to join DFA and found our ideas compelling. The ConsenSys team was popular with the client, if a bit idealistic, and Raheem knew how to speak their language. We pointed to the price chart as proof of adoption, and our government clients would complain, half smiling, half annoyed, that we should have told them to invest. After four months of this, by March 2017 the team in New York had grown weary of flying to Dubai for constant meetings. It was time to open our first international office, and hire someone local, who had done advisory on strategy and technology before. That was where I came in.

# KING KONG

Big Blue. A Smarter Planet.

I had been around for just a few weeks but I was already sick of hearing IBM's horseshit mottos. I called Jared to discuss the project with Nabeel. "Fuck that," he said, making my ears ring, "we got bigger fish to fry now." We were now head to head with IBM on a bigger deal. They had won a string of victories in blockchain, the biggest of all being a deal with Wal-Mart for food tracking, and I knew we were in for a fight.

Bilal, our operations lead, joined us for the ride to the Big Government office. He was Tunisian and very sharp – well dressed, intelligent, with a piercing glance through his designer glasses. We knew he came from Middle East aristocracy, but he was much too humble to discuss that or ever look down on us – even as he was a full six and a half feet tall. God blessed me with six footness, that limbo stick of leadership. Yet I was still amazed when all of our managers were giants. I knew for sure that startups were a jungle when I saw nearly every team lead at ConsenSys was a man taller than me. I guess at the back of our monkey brains we still conformed to a certain vision of the alpha.

David warmed me up before the meeting, his oversized rower's shoulders hunched over in the back of the Uber. "This is the big platform Dubai wants to build," he told me. "IBM will have five guys there" – he held up his massive hand, fingers splayed, to emphasize this – "against just the three of us since *management*" – air quotes now – "will be on vacation again. Usually when that happens, they body slam us like King Kong in the ring with Scooby Doo."

*Ruh roh* went the mental GIF in my head.

Our small squad walked into the meeting with the government officials and IBM already seated. The five of them gave us fake smiles. Even in their stiff, boxy suits they did not hesitate to fight dirty: I'd already met with the CEO of a local bank who had been infected with IBM's propaganda. He kept asking on whether Ethereum used more energy than Denmark, about money laundering, about hackers. "Is this true?" he asked us, looking concerned.[1]

Fucking dinosaurs, I thought. IBM did not care about the decentralized world; it was just a means to sell their cloud and strengthen their chokehold on their customers. FUD – fear, uncertainty, doubt – had been part of IBM's playbook since the 1970s, as central to the software industry as code. *No one ever got fired for hiring IBM.* It was an old hat insult in the industry, and had lost some of its meaning – Amazon and Microsoft were now the main bullies – but in the Middle East, the giants of Seattle had barely arrived, and IBM still ruled the roost.

Now the same questions were bubbling up today. *Why is it so slow? Isn't IBM's software a hundred times faster?* I could see Bilal's eyebrows twitching in anger. "All this FUD," he whispered. The official was struggling to phrase his questions without looking stupid. Anyone without an engineering PhD got lost easily trying to understand the technical concepts in blockchain. The best sales jujitsu was barely enough to keep up.

Every week we were seeing the same movie. Endless FUD. We started to get the feeling many of the government ministers only wanted to talk

---

1 Unfortunately, his question about destroying the environment was true – somewhat. The blockchain needed powerful computers to do the complicated cryptographic math problems that underpin Bitcoin and Ethereum, a system known as "Proof of Work." Everyone from Chinese investors to bored ConsenSys employees had burned server after server in the ground "mining" to earn rewards for helping to run the network. Even worse, the Proof of Work system became more difficult over time, ever more powerful computers and endless amounts of electricity. Environmentalists had been raising red flags for years, noting Bitcoin was wasting as much power as a small city (in 2013) or a large city (in 2015) and now a small country. Bitcoiners never cared, but Ethereum still had Vitalik, and he announced a plan to upgrade the software with something more environmentally sound. The Ethereum community had a heart, see?

about Ethereum for show and photo-ops. The last official had asked us for a blockchain that integrates with .NET, which was like asking for a new iPhone that came with AOL.

I tried to think of a response to all the questions. Nuance was not going to help us win, I realized. We needed a story. *Every tech startup has to sell a bit of vaporware.* I recalled my startup lessons: customers ask for a faster horse. Sell them a car.

It was time to blow their minds.

Ethereum had "private networks" that were faster and more secure, I began to explain. In the early 1980s, companies had been afraid to connect to the *wild wild West* of the Internet, but started building internal networks so they could learn about the technology. Those small networks grew and melded together into the web we had today. Blockchain is just like that, we told the skittish official. We had a slide to prove it.

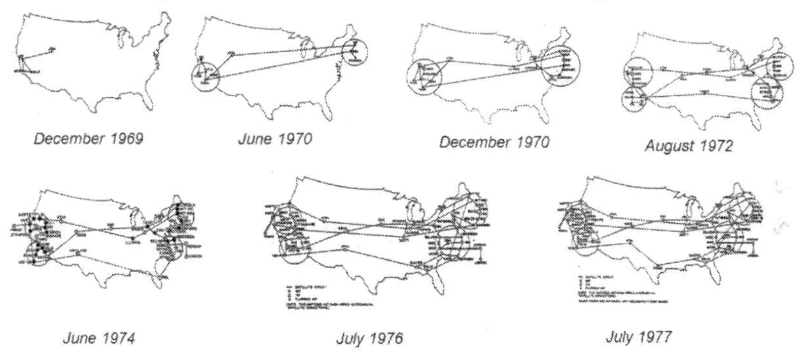


I was not an expert in private networks yet, but Shadi, our best R&D engineer, had just written up a forty page paper on how we could improve Ethereum – by enough to leave IBM in the dust. Exponential change was coming, we promised.

The lead official adjusted his glasses. We could see the mental calculus behind his eyes, balancing the scale between IBM's practicalities and the glittering future we offered.

He grinned. "No wonder the price keeps going up," he said finally. "You guys never tell us when to buy," he joked, rapping the oak conference table with a thick ring. "Is it going to go up more or not? I already have a little ..."

There was one thing that always extinguished the fear of the unknown, and that was the chance to make money.

"We can't give investment advice," David jumped in. But we knew in the back of our minds that winning this project would lead to another headline, meaning the price would go up, and more artillery for Joe's War Against the Centralized Blockchains. New projects kept driving headlines and purchases of Ether in an endless positive cycle.

The IBM fellows looked perturbed. "Oh yes, I bought a little as well," one tried to interject. They tried to bring the conversation back to technicalities.

"Yes," I butted in. "Once we have Enterprise Ethereum working, capacity will reach ten thousand transactions per second. Perhaps we could show you in another meeting?"

"This has been a lot of information," the lead official declared. "But soon." Perfect. The long summer holidays of Dubai, when business came to a standstill from the heat and the holidays, were approaching, and that bought us more time.

*"Awwwww yeahhh,"* David declared once we stepped outside. The summer winds whipped around the three of us while we guarded our eyes against the sand. "B-r-b," he continued. "I think I see my ancestors, the Israelites. They look lost."

We laughed in relief. "That was good," Bilal replied. "Ether to $10,000!" Bilal and David had been grinding through meetings like this for months now, and our half joking, half serious war cry was feeling more real by the day. "But now we can't survive that next meeting without Shadi," he added.

He was right. I would have to convince Shadi to come here from Toronto to help us with the pitch. Without him, we were toast. I watched the IBM team run across the parking lot to their cars, guarding their heads from the wind with their stacks of manilla folders. For now, we had a stalemate.

# THE MESH

*"Millennialism (from millennium, Latin for "a thousand years"), or chiliasm (from the Greek equivalent), is a belief advanced by some religious denominations that a Golden Age or Paradise will occur on Earth prior to the final judgment and future eternal state of the "World to Come"."* – Wikipedia

Before I started this job, Raheem told me about the Mesh. But now I was living it.

It was to be a new kind of company. Or maybe, not a company at all.

*Blockchain Revolution* described what ConsenSys was meant to be: a hub of innovation, with "spokes" extending outwards into the million opportunities in the new decentralized, crypto universe. This loosely connected group of products, joint ventures, and passion projects Joe dubbed *the Mesh*.

ConsenSys loved to be unorthodox and so we had let everyone work remotely years before the COVID-19 pandemic – back when the concept seemed strange – likely the most prescient thing we did. Our employees worked wherever they wanted, whenever they wanted. This was partly because we had hired many of our first employees off of Reddit, and God only knew where some of them even lived – one engineer told me he lived in the jungles of Nicaragua. To keep people updated on each other's work, ConsenSys held all-Mesh calls every three weeks with the entire company.

I joined my first all-Mesh and felt buoyed by the mood. The all-mesh calls were fun, like a Zoom birthday party, where we listened about the fifty plus projects being worked on for every potential blockchain use case, from AI, to payments, to video games. The energy felt infectious.

One spoke lead, Eric, wrote a new rap every week, rhyming about how he was using Ethereum to serve digital ads that could fund cool projects. He had a studio quality mic and a decent sense of rhythm, and everyone in the company found it a riot. I bobbed my head along to the beat, hoping to go unnoticed, feeling like the awkward kid at the high school dance. I was a bit square as a finance type amidst the hipster-techies, but I told myself – *heck yeah, I'm having fun.*

I heard from an ex-Facebook engineer, who opined on the call about rumors Zuckerberg was hiring a blockchain team. "Screw them," he said, following it up with a missive to all of ConsenSys' now 400 employees, excoriating Facebook's leadership for abusing users' data and their blockchain project as a scam to dupe users into giving up more of their data. He ended the screed with the unforgettable line, "Fuck that company." That might get you fired in a typical workplace, but here he was lauded. Typical was exactly what we did not want to be.

I loved it, the total opposite of the blowhard consultants and hedge fund managers I had been surrounded by before. I felt excited to be in a place where the work mattered more than the attitude, rather than sucking up to some manager whose grandpa got him into Princeton. These ex-Uber, ex-Airbnb, ex-Google engineers we had were smart beyond measure and had come not to build the next Facebook but to kill Facebook. The money Big Tech had to fight us was insignificant compared to the power of decentralization.

The call ended with a message from Joe. "Stay meshy!" he encouraged us. Now I understood: meshy was a mix of good naturedness towards our colleagues and revolutionary zeal. The energy you would never find in a drone at Big Corporate. A fake graffiti mural outside the office advertised a popular beer, and we took the ad copy and made it our own: stay meshy, my friends. It was a little cult-ish, I thought, but how could it be a cult when so many people were certified geniuses?

I had had a few other run-ins with the Mesh already. With Ether hitting $500, an engineer from New York and a marketer from New Zealand arrived in Dubai with video equipment and business class tags on their suitcases. Were they here to help us on our projects? No, we just wanted to "check it out," they said, and maybe add a chapter to their documentary they were making about Ethereum. "But it's awesome what you guys are doing here," the Kiwi told us in his accent.

"No, thanks for coming here," I said. Nothing wrong with a little marketing buzz – we needed it to balance IBM. "What did you do before you got into blockchain?"

He laughed. "I was a lobster fisherman! Actually I was hoping to talk to you guys about a new project idea – I've been talking to these seafood companies about tracking shrimp on the blockchain ..." I nodded my head slowly. Yes, I thought, that is what the world really needs. Cryptographic shrimp.

That was my one problem: my cynicism sometimes made me worry about the Mesh. Armed with Joe's funding, everyone felt they could be an entrepreneur. Everyone thought they had come up with great new *ideas*. How could that be sustainable? I knew people like me had doubted techies before, including Bitcoin itself. And now the crypto world felt vindicated.

Every part of "web 2.0" would be ripped down and replaced with "web 3.0," meaning every website and app would need a blockchain version – and hence more spokes. Unorthodox and unusual meant contrarian and iconoclastic which meant it was going to work. A new "MeshRadio" podcast inquired about employees' daily work habits such as meditating on the pile of bean bags in the attic at HQ. To build a blockchain wide enough for the world to fit in it, we all had to celebrate weirdness and encourage engineers to build a new version of chess with nine types of pieces. No bosses, total freedom. It was a cheap pop remix of Randian libertarianism every engineer had probably discussed in their college dorm tossed in the cocktail shaker with the techno-hipster ethic of a Brooklyn startup. Even as the price of Ether kept going up, I had only put in some of my savings, rather than every penny like all my colleagues around me. I knew I could drink the Kool-Aid, but I could not chug it.

For most in the Mesh, from the new college grads to the 30-years-at-Oracle hires, the environment was intoxicating. But for a recent MBA who had just spent a year getting drilled in the marching orders of management consulting, sometimes it was a little much.

# FUCK YOU MONEY

*"Mo' Money, Mo' Problems"* – The Notorious B.I.G.

*Dubai, July 2017. ETH:* $244.

Raheem's comments proved prescient: we were finally hiring shit-tons more people. Everyday I logged into Quip, our note-taking system, where I could see how many employees had access to the directory. I saw ConsenSys' numbers grow by the day. Starting from 150 on my first login, it hit 220 a month later, and 290 by mid-summer. Soon 300, then 400. The number of employees was going up in lockstep with the price. The company was already more than double the size from when I had joined. I was no longer a newbie – I was one of the old guard who knew his way around, and was tasked with interviewing new senior execs almost daily, each one hoping to realize their startup dreams.

Blockchain was just at the edge of mainstream attention. The price got headlines, and that was our chance to suck them in and inject them with our vision for a new world order. After that, they always went home and bought more.

Raheem was back in Dubai after his retreat, and we met to smoke hookah at a cafe popular with all the local banker types. The price had finally eased up a bit, falling from around $350 to $250, as if chastising us to get back to work instead of watching in awe.

"Thank God for those weeks off," he began. No one had scolded him for taking extended leave in the middle of our work. I had learned by now that kind of thing was looked on positively in the Mesh. If we inevitably were going to take over the world, we needed the right *chi*. I wondered how much he had spent: I would've loved some extra cash like to pay for an engagement ring.

Raheem was not sweating the price of Ether. "It won't be long before Joe is richer than Jeff Bezos," he said seriously, then laughed at the concept. "You know they were classmates at Princeton? 1986, I think."

It was coincidental and yet not surprising. I asked how much Joe really had. Raheem said he had bought most of it in the Initial Coin Offering (ICO) – probably a couple million dollars. Based on my math and the price of $244 (the price last I'd checked, an hour prior – I checked now like a gambler checks the scores) he was worth between two or three billion dollars. Not Bezos territory, but Joe would be there soon at Eth's torrid pace. The numbers made my head hurt.

The headlines screamed success but I told Raheem we could feel the strain. After our difficult pitch with IBM, I no longer thought we could balance so many projects when there were barely a handful of us in Dubai. David had mowed through three thousand resumes and picked out the cream of the crop, giving us a team of four new engineers. But he was still constantly being sucked into meetings, and I was burning the midnight oil as well. The situation was deteriorating and we still did not even know if we could win the big blockchain platform project. "I don't know if we can make one plus one equal three," I said.

Raheem laid the blame on Jared. Like a specter haunting the office, he kept reappearing every two weeks in his tailored suits, putting more pressure on us, trying to do too much, hiring the wrong people – aggressive types – who did not fit well in the region. "I mean, I basically founded this office," he said. "Who gave Jared all the power to decide who we hire?"

Raheem was mad, even though I felt he was doing well – barely older than me, he had a title as director of the Middle East. I had complimented him once, noting I was impressed, but now he was more concerned that that influence might be taken away. Instead of focusing on how to fix our problems, he, like many others at ConsenSys, were locked into a turf war.

I was conflicted on how to respond. At this point, Raheem was like a friend, but Jared was Joe's right hand man. If Joe drew up the blueprint for ConsenSys and the future, Jared made it reality – and if I wanted to work on the best projects, I had to stay on his good side. A colleague showed me a picture of Jared and Joe in Mauritius, Jared stroking his short grizzly beard while delivering a pitch on how to run the entire island – its currency, its economy, its trade – with blockchain. "Ethereum Island," ConsenSys was calling it. The stakes had become higher than ever, but now everyone was getting entangled in a power struggle. This was not meshy.

I met David later, hoping to cool off a bit. Given the scorching temperature outside, the only feasible activity was a walk in the cavernous Dubai Mall. I told him about my conversation with Raheem.

"The fuck does he care? He's got fuck you money," David replied. "As in, he can tell Jared *fuuuuckkkk you* and never come back." He waved two middle fingers in front of his face, the fish on the other side of the Dubai Mall's three story aquarium seeming not to take offense.

"But isn't he responsible as managing director of the office?" I asked.

David gave me a funny look. "You know we make up our own titles, right?" He explained that was the only way Joe's vision of holacracy could work – titles had to be meaningless. We were all supposed to focus on saving the world, but instead the first thing everyone did was give themselves a big fancy title. He had done a LinkedIn search and found ConsenSys had over sixty directors, many of whom were under 25, and five chiefs of staff – for less than five hundred employees total. We also had a Chief Anarchy Officer and a Head of Stigmergy, whatever that meant.

"Chief of staff or staff of chiefs?" I asked lightly.

David smiled for a minute, then huffed. "Seriously, this job makes me depressed," he said. "I'm working my ass off, and these assholes are taking goddam vacations." He had no love for Raheem either, it seemed. David had left consulting for the same reasons I had, overworked and tired of presentations full of meaningless poppycock. He happily took half the pay for the chance to make an impact, and given that even I felt out of sorts in Dubai at times I was impressed that this Jewish guy from Cleveland had been brave enough to chase a dream all the way to the Middle East. We bonded over our shared corporate trauma, and traded stories as he impressed me again by gulping down the authentic, fully flavored two dollar chicken *karahi* in the Indian taxi driver joints I took him to rather than the "white boy spicy" versions served in the tourist restaurants.

"Can we get leadership to help us?" I asked him. I had to speed walk to keep up with his giant steps. I caught my reflection in the window of one of the Teslas being raffled off in the atrium of the mall. David sat down and rotated one shoulder, noting the aches and pain that were popping up from the late nights hunched over a laptop after years of competitive rowing. I felt bad for him: he was barely twenty five.

"Leadership?" he laughed. It was time for a bit of history on ConsenSys' history. Most startups, if they go anywhere, have venture investors who nicely tell the original CEO and COO and CMO to go fuck themselves and replace them with someone else who has actually run a business. Sheryl Sandberg and Eric Schmidt were the famous examples, who whipped Facebook and Google into shape when those companies were raucous teenagers. But here, the opposite was happening. We had no VCs – Joe had no need for their money – and there were no bosses. *Anyone* could do *anything*, so we built our little fiefdoms and crowned ourselves king. What was supposed to be freedom had turned into anarchy. I remembered my political science lessons: life in anarchy was nasty, brutish, and short.

We turned the corner in the mall. Kids ran in and out of a sweets shop watching a candyman spin sugar into lollipops. "But if you want to get this circus in order, the only chance is to get the clowns to not kill each other. That's the leadership we need right now, if you can manage it somehow." He made air quotes around leadership, which was even more comical given his baseball mitt hands.

I deflected his challenge. "Maybe there's more help we could get from New York?" I suggested. "We just need to borrow a few engineers for the bid against IBM ..."

He shook his head. "Tonight, why don't you go check on Quip what the NYC team is up to. Look up darq slaq – with a q – and then you'll know the real meaning of *'meshy.'*"

I knew David was worn out and I wanted to do my best to help him. I still had a bit of the new kid shine, and Raheem and Jared were teddy bears compared to the assholes I used to work for. The tech problems were stressful, but there was nothing I could do there. People, I thought – now that I might solve.

# DARQ SLAQ

The next day I walked out of our conference room, uncertain what had just happened. I had just finished a call with Jared, who had been highly encouraging – think bigger, he kept telling me – and yet he had been yelling almost the entire time. His instructions: to convince the second biggest telecom in the UAE, du, to team up with us against IBM for the platform project. Then, the cherry on top: to finish the job, I would have to get Microsoft, only the world's biggest software company, to join our bid as well. "This is the first nation-state scale blockchain in the world, but it won't be the last," he told me. "Microsoft is not going to miss this opportunity." The final order was to get Shadi, our top research engineer, to Dubai by any means necessary. Even if I had to drag him from Toronto myself, he said. The expectations were sky high now, but if I could cross this bridge, ConsenSys would reap the rewards – and likely I would too.

I rubbed my eyes from reading another dense paper about the cloud platform project. It was near midnight as I thought to do a quick search for *darq* on our systems. A teammates's notes might hold the answer. The first document I found was an essay on the need for radical transparency, signed only by the "Chief Anarchy Officer." *What the hell does that mean,* I thought, searching for other documents by this person. Before long, I found his notes from a few months prior.

"Why are we helping an authoritarian government?" someone had asked. "Do they even care about decentralization?" This must have been what David meant. The Mesh seemed to chafe at the idea of doing anything for a Middle Eastern dictatorship, blockchain or no. Joe wanted everyone to help each other and yet here some of the Mesh directly refused. We had to *empower everyone*, and many of the old guard at ConsenSys – those who had believed at $5 rather than $50 – were dyed in the wool libertarians who hated supporting any government, never mind this one. Now these people had money and status and their words had weight. In Dubai we were the new kids, with much less influence, and though we occasionally had similar doubts about the government we were far too afraid to even joke about such things.

*Shit,* I thought. We might be on our own after all. I called David to see if there was more I needed to read. The phone rang. No answer. I tried again. No answer. I gave up and looked to see what else I could find.

Before long another note caught my eye. *I've had a couple of beers,* Joe admitted in another note, *but feel that Ethereum could be used as a distribution method for Universal Basic Income.* Universal Basic Income describes a policy idea to pay everyone at minimum a living wage, regardless of job, in order to create a more equal society. There could be a UBI token, Joe wrote, and philanthropists would fund welfare without the government middleman. I started to see what Joe wanted – for everyone to think big and imagine better, starting with himself. Money was secondary.

The Meshians replied with enthusiasm like the unfettered idealism I had seen in the all-Mesh calls. I clicked for more. Okay, I thought, but had anyone analyzed this further? Had the ideation led anywhere? I found more documents, including one where a few colleagues had posted their salaries. The Chief Anarchy Officer wrote we had to create more transparency around whether any racial or gender inequalities in pay. $65,000 for one, $120,000 for another. Like a group of teenagers drawing blood, everyone had to prove they were committed. Even Joe had gone in and put his own: *- $15,000,000,* the amount of money he had paid for everyone's salaries last year. The bottom of the document explained what *darq* meant – it was short for *darq slaq,* a sub-group within the Mesh dedicated to ensuring we stayed true to our countercultural goals.

Before long I found what appeared to be a manifesto, or perhaps a parody of one:

*We are becoming increasingly un-manageable as a species — just look at our company, which is just a microcosm of the world we inhabit.*

*Enter Consensus Systems, which I think is a brilliant name that neatly encapsulates all of the ideas in this writing. I believe our mission is to create systems that enable humanity to reach consensus faster and move coherently in a direction without sacrificing social, economic, and political freedoms. The tools we are building enable this. We are designing systems for every sector on Earth to maximize autonomy, using the common elements of self-sovereign identity, distributed governance, and token incentivization to facilitate agreement and ignite collective movement. Without a doubt, the coordination problem outlined above represents an existential threat to ConsenSys as a company, but if we can figure it out for ourselves, then we can gift our consensus systems to the rest of the world. By then, it will definitely need them.*

*We will unconsciously re-instate the very hierarchies we sought to dismantle because that's just how the real-world works. We will give ourselves executive titles because we care about what the outside world thinks about us more than being true to ourselves. Given our C-suite status, we will secretly make people our executive assistants and delegate work to them at the last possible minute. There will be no participating in Mesh-wide initiatives because nothing is important apart from my spoke.*

I could not make heads or tails of what I had read. Did Joe write this? Someone who was mocking Joe? It seemed to be both serious and self-parody, as if someone had copied his missives and injected a bunch of meme-based ridicule into it. If that was the case, I should be able to understand it: if I had a superpower, it would be my sarcasm. Malcolm Gladwell said you needed 10,000 hours of practice to be the best in the world at something, and I had been a cynical asshole my entire life. But I started to think working in crypto might mean things would be more unusual than I could really grasp. And some of the problems I was seeing with our team in Dubai might be more widespread than I thought. I remember my Dad had said Consensus Systems was a fantastic name. "Hats off to them for thinking of that. The hardest part of having a distributed system is consensus." Consensus was exactly what we were lacking. The Mesh thought nothing of the fight against IBM; they were liable to fight us first. For now, I had to swim with the tide, but I needed to see for myself which this kind of discord kept popping up everywhere. And strangest of all, the troublemakers seemed to be being encouraged.

David, Bilal, and I were headed to another meeting with a Big Government person in the Ministry of Education, frustrated as usual. The government here was still simply too far behind technologically – living in the 1990s, really – to be able to make any use of Ethereum. We still didn't have enough engineers, but this was irrelevant: sell now, build later. I had no time to process the conversation before we moved on to our next meeting.

Now we went straight to a coffee shop around the corner. There, we met a middle-aged journalist with that classically British air of being simultaneously intelligent and inept. He asked us a few softballs about Dubai and blockchain, which we happily used to proclaim how great things were going. Finally, the glamorous part of startup work.

"But just one thing, you know, that I'm quite confused by this whole blockchain thing," he said. I nodded quickly, excited to look smart for the papers. "Well, I'm just wondering, isn't the whole point to decentralize things?" he asked.

David started to open his mouth but I jumped in first. "Yes, definitely," I jumped in. I was eager to prove myself; this was my first brush with a journalist.

"But then, what I'm still sorting out, is why would the Dubai government want to decentralize itself?" He held his recorder towards us. "Isn't that kind of like anarchy?" *Gotcha!* David gave me a smug look. You idiot.

I stammered for a few moments. How had I not expected that question? Half the Mesh was pointing the same thing out to us. I managed to fill the air with a few buzzwords before trailing off and kept quiet the rest of the interview. I had learned my lesson the hard way. Before leaving, we smiled for a few photos. At least we would make the cover.

We headed to old Dubai where the boys joined me for an appointment with a tailor. After successful meetings with Saira's parents, I wanted to try on a traditional *sherwani*, a silk-like long tunic worn by Pakistani grooms. It was far too early for such things, but it would be fun to imagine. Her father now understood even less about what I did for a living – but it had something to do with Bitcoin, which seemed lucrative. We felt confident things would work out.

I tried on the first one the tailor handed me, shimmering with gold embroidery from top to bottom. I felt ridiculous. Indian wedding clothes are already outrageous, and this one took that to Dubai levels. "Is this the Aladdin fall collection?" David asked. I ribbed him back, telling him to try the next one on.

"Anything less fancy?" I asked the tailor. He ducked into the back and came back with one even more regal. David tried on the maroon and cream colored tunic, wrapping the long shawl around his arm, but it was too small even for me, and comical on him. "You look like Larry of Arabia," I joked. We hung them up and went to browse on our own.

"That journalist really had me there," I admitted, picking up a black *sherwani*. I had tried to finish the conversation saying blockchain supported Dubai's "paperless" government strategy, but that had rung hollow. "Maybe those crazy Mesh people are right about our *ideals*." As much as I now felt attached to this strange little startup, I did not have the genuine love for ConsenSys so many of my co-workers had. I was too practical, too chicken, to put my life savings into crypto, and yet the rising prices were rewarding my colleagues daily for their almost blind devotion. "A thousand books you have read, but without love you remain ignorant," the Pakistani poet-philosopher Sultan Bahu had written about the religious scholars of his time, admonishing them for prizing scholarship over the spiritual path to God, and it seemed to apply to me now too. Only the crazy ones could see the future, because to believe in the unproven you had to be a little crazy. I wondered if I could ever truly understand crypto unless I gave myself completely over. I thought back to the all-Mesh calls. Where did knowledge end and belief begin? Love or madness? Ignorant I would remain.

"We're here for the PR," David said, dragging me back to reality. "Might as well admit it. ConsenSys and Dubai, made for each other." He wagged one finger like a line going up. "But I'm just a big Jew from Ohio, the fuck do I know?"

"They just want to create jobs, too," Bilal added. "Maybe ConsenSys will create all of them." Dubai had created a startup scene to find the next tech craze. Most of the other startups in our accelerator had packed up and gone home after the free hotels ran out, but in blockchain they found the perfect fit. We racked the last of the clothes and drove back downtown.

It stung to admit but we might be building digital Burj Khalifas – another Dubai ploy to grab the world's attention. Ridiculousness was not a coincidence: it was the whole strategy. That our coworkers felt embarrassed by us was even more demotivating. Everyone in tech startups said they were doing it to *change the world*, as if selling wifi-connected juice machines were that revolutionary. David, Bilal, and I were not so foolish to think ConsenSys would solve all the world's problems, but we thought we could build a sound business while still helping decentralization. We accepted that Dubai was our best shot for ConsenSys to keep IBM from taking over, and if this was the only bootstrap we could grab, then our blockchain ends justified startup means. But the Mesh truly believed. They wanted to build the future now, the peer to peer solar grids and music platforms they dreamed of. In the meanwhile, someone would have to do the dirty work, and it was going to be us.

# VERTIGO

*Dubai, July 2017. ETH:* $273.

Jared was drained after the flight from London, toying with his cuff links and glancing around like he wanted to get this over with. We were on our way to the top floor at du, the giant local telecom we wanted to partner with. With du onboard, I could see us beating IBM. I had led the first negotiations but now I could not get them to budge on one last item. Now I had the big guns on my side.

I gave him the lowdown as we drove. "They're being cagey about pricing," I explained. Jared asked who we were meeting and he laughed at my response. "We're negotiating with a guy named Jihad?" he joked. "Well saddle up, cowboy."

Jihad welcomed us and told us to enjoy the view of the many islands we could see from his office window. But he soon turned curt. We were making too many demands, he said. Jared started to turn red but Jihad continued unabated. "This is not how we do business," he said. We were a startup and we needed to know our place.

*Slap!* Jared hit the table with his butcher's hand. I nearly fell out of my seat. "This deal," he yelled, the red in his face bringing out the white and brown streaks in his beard, "is not business as usual." *Crap,* I thought. All the work I had done to get here and his temper might kill the deal in five minutes.

Jihad looked surprised. No cause for alarm, he tried to say, but Jared pressed on. He knew he had the upper hand: without our blockchain magic fairy dust, du had nothing. I jumped in, trying to play nice and that this partnership was important to us. Jihad admitted they could be more transparent. He had blinked, and now Jared went for the kill – stating du would give us more of the profit. "Sometimes," he told me after, "if you want the milk, you gotta throw the toys out of the crib."

du was not the only problem for us. I had been up until 3am trying to make numbers work: our team would take eighteen months to build this project and the government wanted it delivered in nine. We needed help yesterday. "The worst thing we could do is win that project," David told me as I tried not to rip out my hair. "Then we'll have four projects and fail at all of them."

I was not the only one feeling the vertigo as the price and the demands and the stakes continued to spiral upward. Our team was exhausted from GITEX, the biggest tech conference in the Middle East, which had just wrapped up and where we had been the belle of the ball. I grabbed the opportunity for a high profile speech, explaining to the crowd how Toyota was now working on a blockchain for self-driving cars, while DTCC – the engine of the American stock markets – was completing a pilot to move $11T of derivatives trades onto Axoni, an Ethereum copycat. Still, we were near burnout from spending day after day answering *so what's a blockchain?*

I felt the collective stress as we gathered for our Dubai staff meeting. Jared said he would try to help smooth things over, but before we even started Raheem had taken me aside. "He's just going to try and blame everything on me." I felt both their eyes on me as things unfolded: whose side was I on? I had no idea myself.

The meeting went nowhere. The new marketing lead noted she had worked all night for days in a row, and from there things worsened. We had not planned enough; we had planned too much. Who had hired a marketing lead anyway? Did hiring someone mean you were in charge? It was clear none of us in the room had any answers. "This wasn't what I signed up for," the marketing lead said as tears shone in her dark eyes. I tried to offer tissues for her mascara streaks. Instead of taking them she stood up and left. "We need Joe," Jared admitted as we all walked out.

It was 11pm as I sat on the couch in David's apartment and we dialed for another team meeting, this time with the leadership team in New York. David shook his head at me while taking a massive bite out of a cucumber. "What if we just asked Joe to give us a million bucks to fuck off?" By most estimates, Joe owned ten percent of all Ether, giving him on that day a value of somewhere from two and three billion dollars.

Joe dialed in, seeming unsure of himself. He wanted us to be happy, and yet we seemed to insist on otherwise. He asked us what we felt was the problem.

"There's no strategy," someone piped up. "We don't need more hedge fund alpha males telling us what to do," a graphic designer said loudly. I wondered who she was referring to. Me? Jared? "We're here to build something different," she finished.

Our still-sad marketing lead brought up her hardships, but this time someone else pointed a finger at her. "You tried to take things over, that's why you had to work so much." Voices became raised.

After our earlier meeting, I had tried to digest what we were doing into the semblance of a strategy. "We need a vision, turning that vision into goals, and from goals to strategy," I said, mentally reading off the blackboard from my first day of my MBA. Professor Akinola's words had seemed cookie cutter, but my colleagues nodded in agreement. I thought perhaps my plan would work. But now with the room boiling over, my feeble attempt at leadership seemed forgotten. I waited for the tears to start again.

We had hired another senior manager, who had tried unsuccessfully to make peace by showing he was in charge here, mostly by talking all the time. "I know we've been all working really hard, and it's taking a toll on everybody," the Talker jumped in. "This past weekend was not what everyone wanted." I looked at David. The Talker had kept him working the entire weekend on a bullshit proposal that we were doing purely for the money. He wanted to smash his laptop. The Talker continued. "We know it's important we win another project so when we put out a press release, the price of Ether will go up." Silence. No one could believe someone had actually said that aloud. Were these our only choices – profits or virtue? Wasn't Ethereum about creating a world that let us combine the two? *Tick. Tick. Tick.* Only the clock broke the quiet.

"That just sounds illegal," Sad Marketing Lead said finally, grief turning to resentment. Looking back, I wonder if we were harsh on the

Talker in his short tenure. It often seemed like Joe did not know the answers himself.

"I am not sure we can solve these issues over a video call," Joe chimed in at least. "I will come to Dubai in a couple weeks and we will discuss the office's future. Until then, be nice to each other."

David poured out a mug of coffee from a giant thermos, taking care not to spill. It was late in the evening and we were speeding towards the border between the UAE and Oman and almost to the checkpoint. It had been two weeks since the team meeting and we had heard nothing. Worse, we had not even received our salaries for the last week. Not a good sign. One of the engineers complained that without his salary he had nothing but potato chips for dinner. David and I had been furious when we heard.

"It's because everyone's at fucking Burning Man," David said angrily. Burning Man is the drug-addled hippie music festival in the desert that has been overrun by the tech industry. "Nobody is working right now."

"I can't believe I'm missing it," Raheem had exclaimed when we first brought the issue up days prior. "Totally on my bucket list!" David barely hid his glare.

Back in the car, David pulled his passport from his bag and suddenly winced. He grabbed his shoulder and explained he'd injured it years ago as a rower in college, he explained. Endless hours hunched in front of the laptop brought back even fiercer pain. I imagined him waking up at 5 am to row in the cold, in the rain, arms pumping even as he thought up sarcastic one-liners to himself. But without that lunch bucket attitude he brought everyday to the team I would not have lasted long: I'd have either quit or given in and joined the Burning Mania myself.

"Did Joe take his Ledger with him?" I asked, thinking again about Burning Man. A Ledger is a USB drive, nothing fancy, except cased in titanium to keep the codes for one's crypto safe from even an inferno. We did not know if he used a Ledger or not, but there was a fear that no one knew how Joe kept his funds safe from hackers or thieves. Could he really be walking with $4B of crypto stored in his pocket? We had no idea.

"Wait – actually..." David trailed off. "This might explain Wendy's email." Wendy ran payroll and was referred to as the best trader at the company, because she had to constantly try and sell Bitcoin at *just* the right time to maximize Joe's money and pay out all our salaries. She had apologized for the late salaries without any explanation.

I locked eyes with David briefly. It couldn't really be ..."I thought they told you that it was just a problem with the bank?" I asked. The starry desert night slipped past us as I opened the windows.

"All of the banks? In every country where we have offices?" David asked incredulously. "Does my big Jew face look that gullible to you?" He had an olfactory skill for bullshit like sharks did for blood.

We chewed on that for a moment. If salaries were not being paid because Joe was off grid in the desert, that meant that Wendy was selling crypto to make payroll on a *weekly* basis. Which meant that the company itself was not keeping any cash in reserve. Which meant that if the crypto markets froze, we would be stuck selling into a sea of red and eventually drive the price down even more. And if they collapsed ... Joe would have millions of Ether to fund the company and no one to sell it to.

"There's the border," David said. I slowed down as we came towards the gate. This was no attempt at escape: Americans could only stay for 30 days without a permit, and ConsenSys had none to give us. We would simply drive through immigration, U-turn back, and get a new stamp to restart the 30 day clock. We were not the only ones doing this; it was fairly common for local startups and I had had to do the same thing in Syria. Still, we considered the irony that we were here to help serve the government, and yet operated just within the edge of the law. The immigration officer barely looked at us as we went through.

We discussed my meeting with du coming up and my concerns if we were ready. "When we get back, I'll send you some stuff," he said, the Olympic work ethic returning. "They'll definitely help."

I felt bad that he was going to keep working through pain but I needed that help. The rest of our colleagues were too busy finding themselves. "What's the end game to all this?" I sighed. "When Joe's spent his billions, he'll look back and say, it was really about the friends I made along the way?"

The joke was met with silence. We could see the dim halo of the Burj Khalifa against the horizon, like a manmade dawn. We sped back towards the city, two lights alone in the midnight darkness.

We needed help from smart people and I knew Omar fit the bill. He had impressed me from the moment we met, at a networking event where he somehow already knew everyone. Not many senior BCG guys walked around with a leather jacket paired with high-top Jordans and salt and pepper hair that was salon perfect. But he was sick of spending weekends in Riyadh just like I was. I saw a window to grab a guy who still had the hustle of his Brooklyn upbringing with the sharp eye of years in finance. But you'll see, dear Reader, that I might also not have the cleanest intentions in telling his story.

"It's a company that can be really special, if we get our shit together," I told him. "We need people like you to make that happen."

I was not surprised when he received an offer within a week – but for the New York office, not Dubai. He would see the famed Bogart office before I did. But he had some concerns, he told me. They had left a blank for his equity number. When I said I had the same he replied that that was a joke. "That's exactly why we need you," I told him.

I sent him another speech of Joe's. He clutched his arm nervously as always, starting his story about working at Goldman Sachs and hedge funds in the late 1990s, a period of unbelievable wealth creation that he thought of as unsustainable. And then one day in September of 2001, he walked out of the subway to see bits of ash floating in the air. We were both captivated by the story. Joe felt then it was obvious that the global forces sustaining society would soon fail. Like any spiritual leader, he retreated from the world, retiring in his fifties to pursue a music career in Jamaica. It was there he heard the call: about Bitcoin, blockchain, and a young man in Toronto writing about a paper about a new smart contract platform.

Here was a leader with Musk-like vision who had the commitment and means to make a difference, I explained. But so far we would fall far short of that vision without some serious help. Ethereum was on the cusp of becoming dinner table conversation around the world, and Omar and

I had the skills to help Consensys get its act together – the org charts, the processes, the boring piping – to round out the dreamweaving of those who started this. He took the offer.

The day of his farewell party he handed me a small gift wrapped box. "Just a thank you," he told me. Unlike most of the snobs in consulting, he had not come up from Ivy League schools, instead working his way up through school and on scholarships. He was still grateful for every break, even a crazy gamble like this one. He had the hunger I knew people at ConsenSys needed to break through. Now I just had to find it within myself.

# NEW WORLDS

*Dubai, August 2017. ETH:* $305

It was three hours before our Town Hall. Joe had arrived yesterday. The team had grown to twenty people. The Talker went straight to Joe. "We've got to get moving – there's two meetings in Dubai and more in Abu Dhabi. Very high level and well connected people." Everyone in the UAE claimed to be "high level" and "well-connected," but today we had the real deal: the CEO of du. He had heard about us from Jihad. He soon watched a speech of Joe's and was spellbound. The platform deal was exciting, but now he had bigger ideas.

I realized just before leaving I was still in a baseball shirt I'd bought at Wal-Mart for $8. I glanced at Joe: he was in a black t-shirt and cargo shirts, his near-daily attire. Good, I thought. We were going for a Zuckerberg vibe and I would be fine. I punched the address into Uber and we piled in. In the car the Talker and Joe discussed his next stop in Mauritius, hatching new ideas for how to put more of the island nation on Ethereum. *Ethereum Island.* We would need an even bigger team to pull this off, the Talker noted, and I mentioned a few IBM people had reached out looking for roles. Joe turned to me very seriously with a clear command: "Hire them all."

We stepped out and as we walked towards the elevator, Joe reached into his backpack and pulled out a dress shirt. *Oh dear,* I thought, *now I look stupid.* Whoops.

Osman Sultan was a burly man in a tightly fitting suit, like an Arab Al Pacino but sans cigar. The two CEOs sized each other up, like King Kong and Godzilla over the Tokyo skyline. I waited for the sparks to fly. Papers might be signed, and photos taken against backdrops of monogrammed logos. Another 10% gain for Ether. More ammo for our battle to defeat the Big Tech overlords. Osman opened by speaking of his admiration for Joe was trying to achieve. "Could we find ways to grow our businesses together?" he asked.

I never knew if Joe gave his speeches by habit or invented them on the spot, but he left Osman's metaphorical handshake hanging. "With mobile phones and blockchain, decentralized identity will be the basis for a new system of attestation, the bedrock of web 3.0," he offered in return. Despite the techno-jargon, Osman seemed almost transfixed as he listened. Joe could weave these imaginative futures for anyone, any time.

One of the local Emiratis tugged his white headdress, looking distraught. David and I used it as shorthand for referring to them. *White dresses.* Most were the same – lazy and entitled. He had not fallen under Joe's spell. Did we not care about the money? "I think the chairman is suggesting we use some of this – *decentralized*... software in a joint offering, for customers." He glanced at the CEO for approval.

Joe did not take the bait. The reality was Joe became less comfortable when describing these practicalities, and so he avoided them. "Identity will be the base layer, enabling new verticals such as payments and contracting to be purely peer-to-peer." I realized then that Joe was truly not in this meeting thirsty to impress this big, potential client or handshake over a deal. No, they needed to convince *him.* I looked around, lost, wondering if we would lose the room. But I felt like a pipsqueak in a cheap t-shirt, and just made angry scribbles in my notebook.

The white dress looked annoyed. "Yes, fantastic, but you see Mr. Lubin – "

"No, No," Osman interrupted. "I think I'm getting it now." He paused for a moment and leaned back in his chair. "Have you seen Mad Max, Mr. Lubin?"

Joe cocked his head slightly and laughed. "Original or new?"

"Either way. I think of this blockchain world as a bit like Mad Max – you remember all those wild gangs on motorcycles? The guys with the skulls and things?" The rest of us smiled nervously. *What?* "You see, all these groups roaming on their own, just a bunch of tribes. No government needed – no companies selling things or armies in charge. People will be able to rule, provide for themselves. Am I thinking of it the right way, Mr. Lubin?"

"I think you are starting to see it."

"Yes, yes. It's interesting." He spun a bit in his chair, looking at each of us in turn, lost in thought. I was reminded I would have been underdressed for a child's birthday. "A world without rulers, yet still a functional society," he continued. "The world is certainly going this way. This is the decentralized future." We all nodded our heads vigorously. At first, I could not tell if he was humoring or mocking us, but I think for the moment he was just happy to shoot the shit. He mentioned his favorite scene in the movie, and asked us about some of the spokes.

Osman stood up. "Well, let's keep working together. And maybe we could get my son an internship?"

We shook hands and shuffled out for the next meeting.

The Town Hall was nearly over. Joe had told us we would buy IBM before they bought us, which put most people in a good mood. We gave him a few softballs about when his birthday was or his favorite ice cream. We took a quick break. Next was the part of the agenda where we had to discuss what Joe had actually come for – figuring out our strategy.

Jared pulled me aside. Had I gotten Shadi to commit to the platform bid? No, I admitted sheepishly. We need that firepower to show du why they needed us, he told me.

"Are people satisfied with the direction and strategy over the last few weeks?" Joe asked when we resumed. Amir's hand shot in the air. A couple others held a hand halfway up.

"What exactly *is* holacracy?" someone asked. "I don't really understand why we have circles instead of managers."

An HR rep made a lame attempt. He mentioned GitLab, Zappos, and other well known tech names. Joe explained his belief that if we pursued traditional hierarchy, we would build software meant for "command and control" rather than for decentralization. Conway's Law is a saying in that technology reflects the organization that built it. Monolithic behemoths like IBM built centralized blockchains. To cleanse the world we had to have purity of intent.

"Google's pretty flat, but they still have managers," one engineer pointed out. He mentioned how Google's founders had hired Eric Schmidt after a couple years to whip the organization into shape.

"Every startup goes through these tradeoffs during its growth," Joe noted. "But Ethereum can resolve some of these tradeoffs completely. With smart contracts, we can create decentralized organizations that can cancel the Coase theorem." Now he had gone into his philosophy. We did not need the rules and organizations of a *normal* company. I knew everyone in tech believed flat orgs were the *future* and hierarchy was the *past*. That had to be true, because the tech industry was supposed to be the one that defined what the future was. I knew every hot tech startup had to treat the engineers with kid gloves, throwing snacks and trips to Bali at them to ensure they did not leave for the ridiculous salaries of Big Tech. But Joe wanted "the Mesh" to be more than perks – it was about *radical* openness, and changing the manner of work itself. We hired people to work for a client in Dubai, but they soon complained they wanted to work on their own ideas for how to bring down those pesky banks. How could we finish anything like this? I appreciated that Joe was sincere even at the risk of losing billions. But that did not mean he was right.

"Once we launch MeshToken, we'll be able to frictionlessly collaborate with everyone," one of Joe's loyal assistants added. David and I looked at each other. MeshToken? How far would we go to prove our dedication to decentralization?

The crowd continued its debate. Potato Chips, our hungry engineer, asked why we wasted so much time talking about bureaucracy when we had so many projects to finish. Part of me agreed with him. A new hire said he had had good bosses, too. Another designer said he would stop working if we ever gave him a boss.

The discussion continued to break down even as the Talker tried to encourage peace. Joe stood up and walked towards the door. I decided to follow him. Did he see what I did, the two doors before us, one with promise and the other chaos? I needed to know which he might choose. I asked him if we could really rewrite one hundred years of management in a few weeks.

"We may have to make due with shallow hierarchies for the time being," Joe responded. Offstage, he did not have to speak to the purity of our ideals. "Some sub-organizations may autonomously choose to pursue hierarchical structures." Beneath the robotese, I realized he was leaving the decision to us. For the first time, I wondered if he actually knew what he was doing.

"But how do we choose?" I asked. "We might end up electing factions, and I'm not sure you have the time to deal with this kind of nonsense."

"We shouldn't be electing anybody," he agreed. He paused for a moment. He had an idea. "There are people in Bogart working on figuring this stuff out. Come to New York for a couple weeks and meet them. Maybe then we can get some answers."

"Hey, are you still working on that Bitcoin stuff?" my friend Hani asked me. We both knew the question was rhetorical. He simply did not want to start by saying he had an idea on a quick buck.

Hani was an advisor to some of the most powerful people in the Emirates – including, he once secretly confided, some of the Sheikh's family members. He was, despite some questionable moments we will soon witness, not a sleazebag financier, though he was slick in that he knew how to make big money and that was his primary aim in life. But he was a good friend to me.

We met that Friday afternoon at his apartment in Dubai Marina, a massive canal dug so the locals could ride yachts in their backyard. Like any good businessman, he was tall, with a dark, trim beard that he needed to offset his boyish looks and affable air.

I explained to him, patiently as I did in those days, many times why Ethereum might be an economic revolution in the making. He reminded me that he did not understand how it worked and that he did not care. But today he had a potential deal to make and he needed my help.

He wanted to make a deal to help someone sell Bitcoin Cash – a rival form of Bitcoin. Ethereum had two flavors, Ethereum and Ethereum Classic, the product of a schism two years prior. Bitcoin was even more tribal. Hani knew a Bitcoin investor who had accidentally acquired millions in Bitcoin Cash, and wanted to sell it ASAP. And we could get a cut by helping.

I considered the proposal. The story felt true and Hani was no grifter. After his wife had been unfaithful, an ensuing divorce, and the loss of half his dearly held fortunes, Hani had gone into a dark depression. He came out of it a new man, with a predilection for risk taking and high society living. Life had cheated him in the first hand, but now he was determined to get his chips back. I guessed there was more risk here than he was letting on.

He gestured out the window. "Skydivers are back!" We stepped out to the balcony of his 88th floor apartment, once the tallest residential building in the world. Or rather he stepped out, and I stood by the door, one foot on solid ground. I am terrified of heights, a phobia I had tried to resolve at age six by jumping off the jungle gym over and over. I ended up only with scraped hands and knees. The colorful parachutes opened above us like flares as the thrillseekers twirled their way down to the Palm, the massive tree-shaped artificial islands off the coast.

I stepped back inside. I wanted to think I worked in blockchain for the right reasons. I told Hani the point of blockchain was to get rid of middlemen, so I was hesitant to become one myself. I found it a bit sickening, this mad rush to try and eke out every ounce of profit. But I also knew part of it was doubting myself. Cynicism created ceilings. Hani had learned to unsee those walls, and the world had opened up to him.

"We could make a lot of money," he replied. Hani seemed to doubt my equivocation. "I'm sure you have coworkers who would see this as a service, you know. And nothing wrong with helping ourselves, too. *Na main Musa na firaun,*" he added. It was possibly the most famous line in Punjabi poetry, by the philosopher Bulleh Shah: I am not Moses, nor am I Pharoah. We were all somewhere in the middle.

I was not deceiving anyone, after all. I had taken a pay cut to be here, to create impact, and there were no guarantees on the value of my equity. (Oh, how much I trusted Joe back then.) Why shouldn't I benefit a little on the side? I mentioned I would soon head to the Bogart office in New York, and I felt sure a few of the crypto millionaires there might like to buy Bitcoin Cash at a discount. We were in legally murky waters, but I was here, eight thousand miles from our chief legal officer (who unfortunately will have to read every line of this book to see whether he has grounds to sue me) and what he did not know could not hurt him. I shook hands and promised to see what I could do. When your company seems to have become a mobius strip of wealth, why not?

# BOGART

"Why, sometimes I've believed as many as six impossible things before breakfast." – The Red Queen, *Through the Looking Glass*

*New York, September 2017. ETH:* $342.

I woke up on my brother's couch and immediately checked the price of Bitcoin. I fumbled around with my two iPhones, confused which was the fake I kept. The price was up: good. My nerves eased a bit. I checked my calendar: in two hours I had my first one on one meeting with Joe. The nerves came back. I knew he would be friendly but this man was important.

I had just landed in New York the night before; it was only my second time back in the US since Trump's shock victory in 2016. I had brought two phones on the flight as I had heard US customs was confiscating electronic devices from people who seemed suspicious, which to our xenophobic president a 28 year old Pakistani guy living in the United Arab Emirates certainly qualified as.

To trade your crypto, you first had to login with a random, secure code, that you could generate only through your phone. If they had taken my cell, I'd have had no access to my codes, and thus no access to my crypto. Ether was hitting $400 and every hour I could not trade I was losing money. Thus, the second phone: an intentional decoy. No way was that orange clown stopping me. Last night my heart had beat a bit faster as I had passed through immigration, recalling the time I had been interrogated coming back from studying abroad in Syria. Naive and stupid, I had purchased a bunch of Hezbollah flags from a street vendor, thinking the existence such things hilarious. As the officer unfurled the yellow flag with a rifle and a rose, I tried desperately to explain that these were gag gifts for my friends. He glared at me and I realized my story had made things worse. "You think terrorism is funny?"

"Google Authenticator?" My brother laughed at the sight of me furiously punching in codes. He knew what I was doing: trading before breakfast, just as he expected. I cursed Trump under my breath as I finally managed to login.

"Big news coming soon," I told him confidently. "Eth will replace Bitcoin in a month." *The flippening* was the promised milestone when Ethereum would be bigger than Bitcoin. It seemed to be getting closer by the day.

"You always say that." He poured himself some coffee and I went back to trading.

The Uber to the office took forever, weaving its way through the back streets of Brooklyn. It started to rain. Our office was 49 Bogart Street in Bushwick, the bleeding edge of gentrification. The hipster coffee shops in the neighborhood were overrun as we kept hiring and hiring. We now had space in three buildings. I got out of the Uber and searched the block for an entrance. Some poor soul was painting a mural in the rain advertising Maker's Mark, the whiskey brand. It was supposed to fit in with the graffiti that covered every other building in the neighborhood. It did not.

I walked down the block, doubled back, then walked down it again. There was no sign of any office. I imagined for a second that you had to knock on a secret brick or tell a barista a special code. That would be fitting. I started to wonder if I was losing it as I kept walking over the same graffiti, written on every corner I saw:

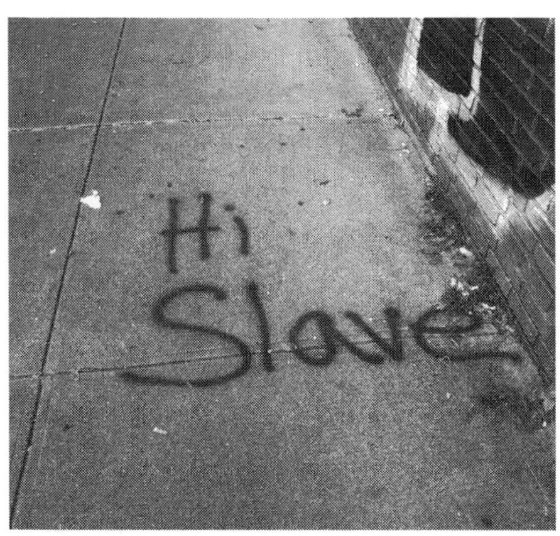

I was on the edge of giving up when I finally noticed a door covered in hundreds of stickers. uPort, Ujo, Ethereum, all the start-ups and crypto-tokens I recognized. This had to be it. The door that would soon become famous, appearing on the cover of Fortune and the New York Times, with the headline underneath: *Is This the Future of Finance?*

I waited in the rain for five minutes, knocking and looking around. "Hey!" someone said. I turned to see Tyler, the lead of our supply chain team, our most successful product so far. He was my age and we had made friends in Dubai. He held the door open with a smile. "Welcome to Bogart!"

Once inside the bestickered door, the office had an electric energy. Dozens of hands mashed keyboards with a rhythm that sounded like factory machines. Desks were scattered haphazardly in every direction, and chairs smushed into every corner. Tyler had a few spare inches of space on his desk and I dragged a folding chair over to squeeze in. Around us, everyone was on video conference calls with our teammates around the world: Chile, Germany, Australia, wherever. In Bogart the conversations always felt hurried as people rushed to get out every idea before ping-ponging to the next call. Like the first molecules unintentionally colliding to create life, the anarchic energy was supposed to be the genesis of something great. I would compare it to a trading floor at a bank, but there was never that fake masculine aggression or anxiety in the air while sweat stained starched collars. We were sitting in the nerve center for Ethereum, maybe for all of blockchain.

Someone was playing a video of Joe's appearance on CNBC that day, explaining to the anchor how Ethereum was different from Bitcoin. Ethereum was more elegant than Bitcoin because of the Ethereum Virtual Machine, he explained patiently. The EVM was a computer program which could process complex smart contracts on top of the cryptocurrency, Ether.

"Well, not sure I understood half of that, but it sounds revolutionary," the anchor said smiling while shuffling some papers in front of him. Joe explained that our most popular product, Infura, was now handling six billion transactions a day as a chart by his head showed Ether's unstoppable rise.

The engineers watching seemed unimpressed. Getting headlines was par for the course. What excited these guys, and everyone else in the room, was that these headlines might help us towards our mission: growing the Ethereum community as fast as humanly possible. As Joe would often say, if you wanted to get to the moon, you had to build a rocket ship to get there first. ConsenSys was the best shipbuilder in blockchain, creating nuts and bolts software, mobile apps, wallets and tools like MetaMask, Truffle, Infura, and other funkily-named products that were being downloaded thousands of times a day. Armed with our tools, any engineer could use Ethereum to do real magic, not just hype. Every other blockchain besides Ethereum was a pipe dream, functionally useless as software, but with Joe's vision and money, we had built something real. This was why everyone in Bogart had a quiet confidence, starting with the billionaire sitting in the back corner, with a pair of headphones on and his feet up on his desk.

Tyler walked me around the office. "Here's the kombucha tap," he told me, pouring himself a glass of frothy pink stuff. "No snacks this month. The rats kept chewing through the cabinets. New York is so awesome, right?"

He spun on his feet and dug into a pile of boxes, tossing me two t-shirts. "There's enough here from our last conference to clothe an army." I put on some ConsenSys swag. *I'm a real entrepreneur now, Geppetto!* He pointed to a wall covered in dozens of bills - dollars, euros, pounds, one trillion dollar notes from Zimbabwe. "The fiat wall - all the shit we're supposed to replace," he said. "It'll all be worthless soon anyway, right?"

"How's Jared by the way? You know that guy once woke me up at 3 am in a robe to make me work on slides? Good times." I laughed, leaving out the recent incidents, too busy imagining what it would be like to work there. Tyler told me about some of his recent wins: a trade deal to ensure coffee beans had been farmed without slave labor, and the World Wildlife fund wanted to use blockchain to stop illegal fishing and save the environment.

I was eating up every detail. Bogart used to be a warehouse, and now was illegally filled with apartments, which we had now illegally turned into an office. The smell of pizza was everywhere: we were sitting on top of the chimney of Roberta's, the world famous Brooklyn pizza joint. Tyler cut off the stories. "Hey, I've got to go pitch a big client. You want to talk to Andrei?"

Andrei smiled as he shook my hand and I asked him about his trip from Dubai. "I actually just came back from Vancouver, actually. I need to close on the house I'm buying. Nice little island hideout."

In my head I was calculating how much Ether it would cost. He explained that he had helped build Adchain, our latest token launch, and the proceeds had been more than respectable. I asked what he thought about Tezos, another blockchain that claimed to be better than Ethereum and some worried might crush us. Given Ethereum's code was free and open to the entire Internet, any new project could steal what we had and easily make enhancements. We had no real moat to protect our business.

"But what advantage do they have?" Andrei asked. "Do they have this?" He gestured to the developers filling the room. They might soon, I thought, having just completed an eye popping $232 million ICO. The protocol wars were just beginning. There were now more than one hundred thousand software developers building dApps on Ethereum by our count, a massive lead, the kind of growth that could make Eth the next App store. But these competitors were keen to pick out Ethereum's flaws. Ethereum was slow and insecure: it had been hacked a year prior, and investors lost a staggering $300 million. Our rivals might not have missionaries like Ethereum, but $232 million could buy a lot of loyalty.

Andrei offered to show me the roof. We walked by hallways filled with bean bags stacked to the ceiling and over floors sticky from parties past. Someone caught my eye. He had a day's stubble and long hair, sitting in the corner. The Whale—a term for someone who has so much crypto they can move markets like water from a tail flap—was rumored to be the wealthiest person at ConsenSys after Joe.

"Excited to see you here!" The Whale had a smile bigger than his face and boyish good looks. I had heard his stories, firsthand and secondhand, about how he had been a beach bum in Malibu after selling his tech startup when he first heard about Bitcoin and realized it was the future. He closed our first deals years ago, when literally no one had a clue what blockchain was.

He joined us as we climbed up the fire escape to the roof. Dust seemed to fall off in chunks as we grabbed the rusty handrails. From the top there was a perfect view of Manhattan, the Freedom Tower glittering on the left and Midtown in a summer haze to the right. A group of interns was sitting to our right on the worn, rubbery roof passing around a joint. The Whale asked how things were in Dubai, clearly excited to hear my stories.

He did not seem worried when I let him know what we were up against: a heavyweight in IBM, confused clients, and our own growing pains. He was as assured as Joe, but with ten times the energy; he had seen this movie before and wanted to be a part of the sequel. "Everything you see here, we're going to disrupt," he said, gesturing to the skyscrapers of Manhattan. The Whale had a way of motivating people that Joe lacked. "This is the place that started it all," he said, tapping an index finger on the roof.

"Really?" I asked.

Andrei and the Whale gave me the version of history that Ether heads believed and Bitcoin fanatics would rather die than admit. Bitcoin had been flat for three years, rising and crashing by 50% as speculators played games, until we started storming into boardrooms telling Goldman Sachs we had something to tell them that would change their business forever. It was the blockchain story and the potential of smart contracts that had opened up people's minds to a bigger vision. Bitcoin was email; Ethereum was the Internet. Ethereum was already up ten times more than Bitcoin in the past year. The Bitcoin community, frustrated by the lack of progress and easy money, had become poisonous and greedy. Mike Hearn and Greg Maxwell, two of its leading engineers, fought for years over whether to make Bitcoin more business friendly or stick to its anarchist roots. Heard eventually left due to death threats, first trying a new experiment called Bitcoin XT – which led to another incident that accidentally shut down the Internet in half of Long Island – before deciding to join the corporate outfit R3.

"Check out my buddies," the Whale continued, pulling up a two year old photo of him, Vitalik, and Satya Nadella, the CEO of Microsoft, when he had convinced Microsoft to start offering Ethereum on its cloud. The

Whale then showed me a chart of the Ether price after that meeting. It was a straight line up. After Silk Road, Bitcoin had died; Ethereum resurrected it.

Now the latest craze, the ICO boom, depended on us too. In the last year every major ICO wrote its smart contracts using ConsenSys' tools, the magic triumvirate of Truffle, Infura, and MetaMask. Without us, there was no parabolic rise in wealth, and without that, blockchain would not be taking the world by storm.

Andrei brought up the Gnosis ICO, another ConsenSys token, as the latest sign of our ascendance. "And that's when people started to lose it," the Whale added. "They—*we*—raised $280 million in 15 minutes. Unheard of. Even they" – he jabbed a finger at the skyline – "couldn't do that."

The interns to our right had finished smoking and were now headed back down the fire escape. So far my trip to Bogart had been exactly what I had hoped for. I had been to the inner sanctum and learned where our power really came from. I was tired of being the guy who did not believe in anything, and the Whale had helped me see how ConsenSys had succeeded – and would again. There was some grand plan, and knowing that was a relief. The Whale turned to me again with the boyish smile. "And now, my friend, the torch is with you."

Joe looked happy to see me. I recalled something Tyler had told me earlier – that Joe had a son our exact age, who in fact had his own spoke. For Joe so loved ConsenSys that he gave it his only son, Tyler said.

We shook hands and I complimented him on the CNBC interview. He chuckled. He hated that stuff, but he did it because he had to.

I did my best to be honest about Dubai. We wanted to do ten projects in half the time with none of the people. We felt like we were on an island.

"Do whatever you're comfortable with," he said. "I won't force you guys into more than that." He spoke with a calm, even voice that soothed. I had been thinking about our similarities – the move from finance to tech, trying to create business with a conscience – and I now saw more of myself in Joe, and more of Joe in me, than I had before. Joe was proof that a good guy could become CEO, and even if he did not always make the right choice that made me want to stand by what he said. But I also found it worrying that I might leave without answers. Didn't he pay our salaries? Didn't he want more from us?

I asked about help from the spokes or other teams. "I can't force them to help you either," he replied. I sighed. He never compromised on his principles. But how was I going to find a solution? I asked about the effort to "figure things out" he had mentioned in Dubai. "Thanks for reminding me," he said. "We've hired an org consultant to help us. You should meet her."

An org consultant. I recalled the meeting with Osman. Even when given the chance to use his position, the day-to-day of being a CEO with power over others simply did not appeal to Joe. At one point later on he even asked me not to refer to him as CEO, noting he preferred the term "founder." Tyler had told me Joe took culture as seriously as software – his first hire had been a Chief Culture Officer, a cultural anthropologist whose only experience was at a non profit focused on encouraging "planetary citizenship." (She left ConsenSys to pursue the lucrative world of compliance consulting, such as how North Korea evaded UN sanctions using Bitcoin.) He cared the most, but he mostly did this job to build cool stuff. "What's the consultant's background?" I asked.

"Former COO at a big tech company," he noted. "Her name's Wendy Coin. I swear we didn't hire her based on the name. She's good. You'll like her."

Joe brought me over to the backyard at Roberta's where many of our colleagues had gathered. He introduced me to another recent hire: a leader from IBM's blockchain team, who clapped Joe on the back.

"I knew IBM was going to lose once the investments started to pour into Ethereum," he explained, "so I had to leave." I had read our gleeful press release about his hiring, another warning shot to our rival. I mentioned he might help us against IBM's FUD in Dubai.

"Can't be part of the protocol wars, unfortunately," he said. He had signed a non disparagement clause. He pointed a finger gun at Joe, who put up a fake shield. Here at the center of the blockchain galaxy, the skirmishes on the other side of the universe barely mattered. He told me how energized he felt after twenty years of bureaucracy at IBM. "I feel like a dolphin coming up for air from a deep dive in the ocean."

I was not into this. I was here with a goal and helping Dolphin Man reach corporate nirvana was not it. I considered popping his bubble with a story about our Machivellian free-for-all for Dubai, but I let him be. I needed to find Shadi and soon.

"You'll make it through with IBM," Joe added. "Just keep up the good work and I'm sure we'll be fine." He picked up a box of pizza and passed it around.

Shadi told me he had come to Dubai once already and did not want to again. He had written a forty page paper on Enterprise Ethereum and its future. Had I read it? I had, I explained, five times, and still only half understood. Enterprise Ethereum would combine the features IBM kept promising – privacy and security – with the decentralized power of crypto. With this union, we could bring the promise of the blockchain revolution right into the heart of Corporate America. And to beat IBM on this Dubai deal we had to show that we were the ones building the future, not them, and I could not do it alone. He took a sip of his beer and nodded.

"There's that guy," he said, pointing to Dolphin Man, "but not sure it'll be much help. I don't know. I'll ask my fiancee and let you know."

I told him I knew how he felt – my wedding was also coming up. We realized we were getting married within days of each other and laughed about the ridiculousness of wedding preparation. For a few minutes, crypto was the least of our worries.

# SHITCOINS

> "Be fearful when others are greedy and greedy only when others are fearful." – Warren Buffett

*New York, September 2017. ETH:* $292.

In the beginning, there was Bitcoin.

Someone used Bitcoin to buy a pizza. 10,000 Bitcoins in fact, for 2 pizzas, making a Bitcoin worth about 1/50$^{th}$ of a penny. That was 2010. The first time someone bought something real with a made-up, purely computer currency. We remember it every year, on May 22nd, known as Bitcoin Pizza Day. What's a religion without holidays?

Ethereum was not the only new cryptocurrency after Bitcoin. Others realized they could take the Bitcoin software – all open source code, available on the Internet – and change a few lines to make their own "coin." Now you told everyone you had made Bitcoin better (even if all you did was add some nonsense code), and that now *yours* was the future of money. Some YouTube videos, banner ads, and Reddit posts later, a few suckers might buy this coin, making it go up. They told their friends, and more people bought it. It was not a pyramid scheme, because it was much more efficient than that.

This was the birth of the shitcoin.

Sure, some of these coins were supposed to be more technically advanced, like the marginally faster Litecoin. Others are just a joke, like Dogecoin, named after a popular meme of a surprised looking dog. You could trade that meme coin on any crypto exchanges and make a quick buck.

Back then, shitcoins were "priced" in Bitcoin, which meant if Bitcoin went up, every shitcoin went up too – and everyone holding shitcoins got rich. When Bitcoin went up, Emily Chang would get on Bloomberg TV again telling you that Warren Buffett said it was "rat poison squared," creating more headlines, and so more people bought the thing anyway, Warren Buffett be damned.[2] But only a few people, the crypto-heads, knew that the real money was in shitcoins. If a Bitcoin could move 10% at a time, a solid pump in a shitcoin could move the price many times that – 30% was normal, and 200% or 300% was not unusual at all – often in a day. All you needed was a laptop and a few Bitcoin. Whether you even understood the technology was irrelevant.

Your typical shitcoin had a gobbledygook white paper about how it was going to change the world. Then came the Initial Coin Offering (ICO) – selling the shitcoin to the unsuspecting public, bragging that it would be the Amazon of blockchain. An "ICO" captured all the excitement of IPOs ("Initial Public Offerings," the first time a company's stock is available for sale) with none of the regulation and yet sounded nearly as legitimate.

But Ethereum changed the shitcoin game. Ethereum was faster than Bitcoin, and it could "host" other coins – what came to be known as ERC-20s. With the old shitcoins, you needed a large enough network of nodes to protect against being hacked, which is a technical way to say making one was a pain in the ass. With Ethereum, and a few of ConsenSys' software tools for smart contracts, you could just create a smart contract (ERC-20 being the most popular) that generated a shitcoin in *less than a minute*. Anyone could create a token on Ethereum for every hot idea – from "decentralized Airbnb" to "decentralized Uber." Abracadabra and hocus pocus, you've raised a million dollars. Before long someone had created Weedcoin, Potcoin, Cannabiscoin, and hundreds more that you could check the prices on at any time. By 2019, over 180,000 ERC-20 smart contracts were running on the Ethereum network, an endless maze of abandoned shitcoins. Since the easiest way to make shitcoins was to use Ethereum, the interest in Ethereum went up, quickly. The price of Ethereum was no longer based on our projects making headlines, but on shitcoin demand. It was an endless spiral upward.

2 Actual quote.

The Whale and Andrei had warned me away from shitcoins, and early on I listened. In finance there's a saying that speculation is always about finding a "greater fool." I did not want to even be associated with any scams lest greed lure me into something dodgy. I was taking enough risk with my career as it was. I sat out most of the shitcoin era with the smug knowledge I would never be scammed.

The period of November 2017 to January 2018 was when shitcoins truly caught on fire. Suddenly the engineer who had starved but for potato chips asked me what to do with his profits. He had sold all the Bitcoin – quadrupled in a few months – and quadrupled it again with Litecoin. "You have an MBA," he noted. "Should I buy a car or a nice apartment? My wife wants to live in the Burj Khalifa." I began to worry if the greater fool was me.

The coin based on a surprised looking dog was now worth $300M. Trevor Noah, the Daily Show host, became intrigued, and Joe agreed to appear. Unfortunately, our moment went poorly. "Whoa," Noah said, "you know it's bad when Wall Street says this is sketchy." His correspondent Ronny Chieng walked around Bogart making a WTF face. "That doesn't mean anything," he yelled at Joe as he explained Ethereum as a decentralized computer. "What is it!" They titled the piece "Bitcoin and other stupid meme currencies" – no mention of Ethereum and our goals. Joe felt this should only harden our commitment. "If we are not appreciated by traders," he wrote, "and the general financial/commerce world, the butt of good jokes in society at large, and envied/hated by nocoiners, in addition to being an important element of the forthcoming decentralized www, we will not have achieved significant impact."

If mainstream media mocked or ignored us, we would disrupt them too. SingularDTV, our decentralized answer to Netflix, had a token now worth over $800m. The team hired Rosario Dawson to narrate a documentary on blockchain. Joe gave it its title – "Trust Machine."

"We have to be the white knight in the ecosystem," he reminded us. We had good intentions, but we were surrounded by a sea of scammers willing to shill any shitcoin for the chance at short term profits and armies of suckers and grandmas. The biggest fallacy in American capitalism is the way we associate wealth with intelligence. We are told in preschool that we live in a meritocracy, where the hard working are rewarded with riches, rather than favors from their uncle or a trust fund. We believe Richie Rich must have known *something*. Wealth is a symptom of cleverness. I saw first hand how the shitcoin era finally put a nail in the coffin to that idea.

John McAfee, the once well regarded cybersecurity entrepreneur who had fled Latin America on suspicions of being involved with murder, used his infamy as one of the few celebrities with tech cachet to promote an endless stream of shitcoins via Twitter. Invariably he and anyone else with a quick thumb made a killing. His words were taken seriously, even after he claimed if Bitcoin was not over $10,000 by 2020 that he would eat his own nethers.

The Securities and Exchange Commission (SEC), who regulated such things, was sadly still trying to figure out what all this blockchain stuff meant in the first place. The scams became so commonplace one scammer bragged loudly on a phone call about his latest pump and dump while taking the Amtrak from NYC to DC, only to be sitting a row away from the tomato-faced chairman of the SEC himself. "You do not want to be talking about this right now," he supposedly said.

For the less dense shitcoin scammers, the critical step was to get listed on a shitcoin exchange like Binance or Bittrex, headquartered in some unknown, unregulated country like Malta. Coin scams metastasized into disinformation campaigns, YouTube videos promising endless riches, and endless bots on Twitter telling you to buybuybuy. The less trading activity there was, the easier to manipulate. The smart ones created a whatsapp or Telegram group to pump and dump coins as fast as they could and charged an entrance fee to double their take. A well-coordinated group would signal everyone to buy at once, driving the price up 500% in a matter of hours. When the next line of idiots lined up, everyone in the group would sell at just the right moment and screw over the grandmas playing with Junior's college money. The groups played the classic pump and dump to perfection, taken right from penny stock games in *The Wolf of Wall Street*, sped up to lightspeed. They celebrated their riches with memes that Bitcoin Jesus would take us to the moon in his new Lambo. In the crypto space, memes were a type of currency, so to speak.

David had told me my first day that our job was to cut through the crap. I took that to heart and played whack a mole with my friends and their horrible investing ideas. They had heard Ben Bernanke endorsed Ripple – he was speaking at their conference – and XRP, their token, was trading at a few pennies. Ripple trolls used an army of Twitter bots to claim XRP should be worth more than Ether, then worth hundreds of dollars. I tried to patiently explain the concept to my friend Bassel that this made no sense because there were 43 billion Ripple coins in circulation, a thousand times more than Eth, and that at equal prices Ripple would be worth $20 trillion, more than the GDP of the United States. But it made no difference. He bought XRP anyway, and soon he made money while I made nothing.

Meanwhile, Ripple sold a few hundred million dollars of XRP each month to pocket some profit and fund more advertising. When a class action lawsuit was filed in California in 2019, Ripple's primary defense was that such lawsuits had to be filed within 3 years of the initial offering. Even if it was a scam, it should be legal.

The shitcoin bonanza made for legitimate opportunities too. ConsenSys wanted to open a crypto-fund to help investors avoid the scams, the Whale told me. His partner, a former arbitrage trader from Lehman Brothers, came to Dubai to pitch a few bigwigs. "We invest in only the best protocols," he said, setting down a glass of sparkling water on the gleaming table in the lobby of the Shangri-La. "Not some ding dong shitcoin." I laughed inside. Hani, who had come at my behest, seemed reassured and noted he knew people who might be interested.

*Eth is the new oil,* I heard from talking heads. Wall Street would be jealous soon enough and pay the toll to get in. Ethereum's ascendance past Bitcoin now seemed inevitable because Eth was so much more than a currency – it could do *anything*.

This was also the fatal flaw of Ethereum: smart contracts are hard to code and easy to hack. And because there was money involved, hackers were coming in droves. Every week another poor investor lost $20 million or $200 million because of some smart contract bug that any decent hacker could drive a truck through.[3] Luckily for us, ConsenSys also sold security software for Ethereum. The gold rush was on and we had the best shovels.

I saw the ridiculousness of it all and scoffed. But with time my willpower wore down. Maybe everyone saw something I couldn't. After all, half the shitcoin millionaires were engineers I thought of as geniuses. When one friend told me he had already made 30x his money just day trading, I thought of my wedding next year and asked David for his thoughts on the best shitcoin exchange. I piled in a few thousand dollars I had saved. I had traded stocks before, and I knew how to read a chart. I went hunting for my first target: Adchain, Andrei's favorite. I waited for the right moment to buy, nervously watched the price for a few hours, and mashed through a series of sell orders to offload what I had. My first kill: an easy $600 in a few clicks. I had come one step closer to paying the caterer.

Oh and those pizzas? 10,000 Bitcoins peaked in value at $500 million. Someone had made a half of a billion dollars off just two pizzas. *Liar's Poker, Bonfire of the Vanities,* and all the other Wall Street books talked about how the bankers knew how to "print money." The phrase seemed hilariously outdated. These days, we techies just did ctrl+c, ctrl+v.

---

3 Smart contracts are frequently used to assign ownership (money, tokens, etc.). I'm oversimplifying, but you might have a piece of code that says something like

```
House.owner = BarackObama
```

If you wrote the code for "house" or "owner" with a bug, a good hacker might replace "BarackObama" with "DonaldTrump"... and there would be nothing anyone could do to change it back!

# CHUMP CHANGE

*New York, September 2017. ETH:* $312

The broken concrete sidewalks, empty lots of overgrown grass, and worn brick warehouses spread out in every direction around me. Omar had told me to meet him at a pho bar a mile from Bogart, and I was lost in Bushwick's post-industrial maze. A small white door hung open on the corner and I peeked inside.

Omar was sitting at a plastic table, a ceiling fan on its last legs circling over his head. He rose to give me a dude-hug. "Took you long enough," he joked. "How's Dubai?"

I cocked my head to the side. I had just come from my meeting with Wendy Coin, I told him, the consultant with years of management experience in banking that Joe had hired to "fix" Dubai, and she had made big promises. The coffee shop was crowded, coders and crypto types spilling out onto the sidewalk, cups in hands, all of them sucked into ConsenSys' gravity well. But she stuck out, a middle-aged blonde in work attire amidst baseball caps and septum piercings. That alone made me think she might help us make sense of this mess.

"Way too loud in Bogart," she said, laughing. "Had to take shelter here." *Hard at work,* I thought.

"What do you think of holacracy?" I asked her, jumping into it. I waved off an inquiring waiter.

"I think it means taking hoodies and ping pong a little more seriously," she told me, turning her laptop to me. "But in Dubai you guys need to get organized and hire, hire, hire. Based on the numbers I ran, we'll need to make around 52 hires in the next 3 months."

My eyebrows shot up. Before leaving Dubai, I borrowed David's copy of *Lean Startup*, which is gospel in the tech industry. The book describes the "MVP" (Minimally Viable Product) approach to build a startup: minimal waste and maximum focus. That was the opposite of how ConsenSys worked – endless hiring. The Fat Startup, David said. "Actually, I like the ring of the obese startup," he had said. "Is that offensive?"

I looked at Wendy's laptop and then back at her. *What?* "How can we manage all these people?" I asked.

"Well, here you are," she said, pointing to a box on her chart. "Right here." I was sitting above another set of a dozen boxes. *Director.* Not bad, I thought. Where was Sevag now? I yanked myself to the present. If we followed Wendy's plan, Dubai would become an empire, and our fast-growing offices in London and Singapore would be too. A thousand employees in no time.

Mathematicians say an infinite number of monkeys randomly typing on infinite keyboards could reproduce the works of Shakespeare. How many engineers would it take building random apps to produce a unicorn? But she saw the same world the Whale did: an endless rise where we had to grab as much land as possible.[4]

So be it, then, I said to Omar. Our rivals wanted a war and we would raise an army. After all, I had been waiting for my moment, and he agreed. But I had good reason for my cold feet: her numbers were based on winning projects, and so far we only had one win. We'd signed another "deal" with the government recently, I told him, but when we gathered for the announcement they handed us blank pieces of paper to sign. Another PR stunt for the photos.

"That's why I need you to get out of there," Omar said in reply, waving his hand. I noticed a new-looking watch. "Dubai isn't the brown Wakanda we thought it was. New York is where all the action is."

I looked at my barely eaten lunch. Pho always duped me somehow, finding its way from the plate to the table instead of my mouth. "What do you mean?" I asked.

I had heard rumors, but now he let me in on the latest. ConsenSys wanted to launch a token, and he was leading the charge: news big

4 "Land grab" is actually common parlance in tech startups. Uber's expansion into every major city in the world in a couple years is considered the gold standard.

enough to shake the Ethereum world and bring in tens if not hundreds of millions. He had already become an all-star in Bogart. "Faster than an electron," Joe wrote about him in an email last week full of compliments. Whatever that meant. Legal just had to sort out the equity question to finish it off.[5]

Jealousy rose up in me at the mention of the heavy praise. But that was nothing, he continued. He had a new plan and wanted me to help.

He was about to launch a spoke to tokenize real estate. *Tokenization* meant using a blockchain to represent a physical asset, rather than a digital currency. I realized instantly that this was genius: real estate was a high value market – the world's largest asset class – but rarely ever traded, meaning it could work even if Ethereum was slow. It was the perfect use case.

NYC was calling me back. But what about Wendy's offer? *When the host offers you sugar for your* chai, *take it,* is a saying in Pakistan that I may or may not have made up. (Most of our sayings had to do with sugar and tea.)

"Your decision," he said, as if reading the indecision on my face. "We've already got Joe's approval." If I had bet on anyone making the most of his golden ticket, it would be on the Brooklyn kid who had overcome the odds at every turn. Who was I going to choose? "Real estate is a trillion dollar market," he continued. "Being 'director' is nothing compared to what we could do. We can run this shit together."

Two brown boys taking the tech world by storm. Despite a pre-game speech fit for a sportswear commercial, I was still unsure. "Give me a couple weeks," I said, swirling a piece of beef around the bowl. I had someone else I needed to ask.

Saira seemed to be more absorbed by her food than our conversation. It was our last dinner before I headed back to Dubai. We always

---

5 The joke about equity had gone from 'running' to genuine marathon. We would have numbers 'within two weeks,' everyone liked to quote, since Joe had said so in the last Town Hall. And the previous Town Hall. And the previous one.... going back long before I arrived.

ate Italian. A thick red curtain to my left partly obscured the evening view of the Hudson. "You really would say no to the New York offer?"

I explained my position. "They want to hire dozens of people in Dubai. It's a huge opportunity." The numbers did not impress her; she saved lives for her bread and butter. I knew I might be in the wrong: I had dragged her along as my career made one jarring turn after another, perhaps even lied on when – and if – I would be coming back.

The conversation so far was going poorly, but I wasn't going to give up on her: I once made a spreadsheet of all the women I'd met in New York on seven dimensions, and she always came out on top. She hated that spreadsheet story, a sign of a man with a hard drive between his ears rather than real emotions. Now the numbers were pulling me to be in two places at once.

Still, I had to try. "Would you rather be the boss or the assistant?" I said.

"I'd rather have a fiance who cares," she said, tearing open a dinner roll.

I left NYC more uncertain about anything than ever before.

# STUCK OUTSIDE

*Dubai, October 2017. ETH:* $381.

"I've got a surprise for you tonight, brother," Hani said on the phone. "The best biryani in Dubai. I'll pick you up." He wanted to welcome me back with my favorite thing about Dubai: Indian food close enough to the source for that authentic taste, but respectable enough to avoid the authentic diarrhea. My second favorite thing was riding in Hani's car.

His engine roared as he pulled up, the car gleaming even with only the twinkling lights from the Burj Khalifa behind us. It was no ordinary machine: this was a McLaren 720S Spider, a supercar that made Ferrari drivers timid. I'll let you guess how much it costs. (The answer is more.) He smiled as I ducked under the suicide door.

My back pressed to the orange leather seats as Hani stomped on the gas pedal. We went left, right, left, through the five-lane highways of Dubai just to feel the car swerve, the jumbo jet level noise following us. Disorientation hit me and I almost missed where we were driving: straight into Old Dubai, the less developed part of town where the workers who kept the city moving stayed.

"Ah, our first stop," he said with a smile. We pulled into a cheap drive-through frequented by taxi drivers. His favorite chai spot. Heads turned in our direction, incredulous. A cup of hot *karak* here ran a total of twenty-five cents. He waved a hand for service as I asked if he ever felt out of place flashing wealth around here.

"Never about the money, my friend," he said. "It's about getting the most out of life." We proceeded to get more out of life as he ripped out of the parking lot, my hands gripping the styrofoam cup at the slightest tilt, fearful what one punch of the accelerator might do. He saw my struggle and winked. "And now for the main event."

My stomach rumbled with excitement. We turned further into the winding streets of the Old Town where the streetlights stopped. Hani took a paper note from the heavy-eyed parking attendant and led me into what I expected to be a fragrant, traditional Indian restaurant.

I expected wrong.

A large disco ball hung from the ceiling between a semi-lit stage and a darkened crowd. A few women stood on stage as tiny, horrible Indian music blasted from a poorly calibrated speaker.

Hani had brought me to a mujrah club.

Now, the UAE has so many guest workers that its population is nearly eighty percent male. This, as you might guess, leads to a colorful and lucrative underworld, perhaps contrary to your perception of the staid, conservative Middle East. The only way I had witnessed this underbelly were the calling cards promoters would leave on my windshield if I parked in the wrong area at night. It was not something I wanted to see in person.

A *mujrah* club is the buttoned up, South Asian version of a strip club, or the dirty, tank tops and booty shorts version of an emperor's harem. The dancers are all Indian or Pakistani, purportedly carrying down the traditional dances performed by the harems of the Mughal emperors of the 17th century. Either way, I was now very uncomfortable.

"Two chicken biryanis, please!" he said cheerfully to a passing waiter, a finger pointed in the air. No beers or whiskey? The waiter looked puzzled. Who came here to eat?

"Not for us," Hani replied. Some things he never compromised on: on our trip to Singapore the previous weekend, he made sure to come back to the hotel – Hani insisted we stay top floor at the Ritz – for his night prayers before returning to the poker table. The waiter nodded and went back to pouring shots for the other fervid admirers in the audience.

Hani turned to me. "Now for some deal talk." He noted that, in addition to the finest biryani in the land, he wanted to meet the Bitcoin Cash seller here tonight. This was the opportunity to win him over. I turned to watch an old *desi* uncle in a turban throw stacks of cards towards the stage and Hani noted my curiosity. "Can't throw cash in Dubai," he explained.

I was going to disappoint. I had no progress finding a buyer. I tried to broach the subject with Andrei, but he had been dismissive. I wanted to ask the Whale or Joe, but it felt grimy and weird.

"Not a fan of this one," Hani noted with a nod. "Looks like my ex wife. Can you imagine if she saw me now?" She had been so uptight, he laughed, and then she went and cheated on me. His smile faded. Everyone is so fake, he complained.

The music stopped for a moment. A dancer, clad in a white sarong, blew kisses to the crowd as she descended from the ceiling on an almost invisible trapeze. The front row of men threw their arms in the air and the fever threatened to spread. She looked in our direction – could she even see us in the dark? Hani thought so. "She's got eyes for us, man!" he exclaimed.

I stared, like everyone else, wondering who she was. There was a human trafficking problem here, and the women of South Asia and

Eastern Europe were the favorite currency of the local crime lords. Greed upon greed had likely plucked her from home.

The metallic soundtrack ended, breaking the spell. I swilled my soda. Whoever this guy coming was, I wasn't keen to meet him. Hani looked surprised when I suggested we leave, but turned apologetic on the ride back. "Thought you might enjoy an early bachelor party," he offered. I thanked him for the ride and the food. Someday, I would sell out all the way. But for now, there was work to do.

I met David at the office, showing the calling cards as I recounted the previous night.

"Sounds weird," he agreed. "Maybe they could use some Spankchain."

I laughed. Another ding dong shitcoin. Except this one was about porn and run by ex-ConsenSys employees. David had told me about it last week, another "screwy ICO" (heh heh, he added).

Blockchain for porn? I had looked around the room to make sure no one was listening. The one tech startup problem ConsenSys had managed to avoid was sexual harassment lawsuits, and I was not keen to spark the first. We had huddled over a laptop as he showed me the trailer. A dark haired woman in black lingerie and heavy eye makeup rolled around on a pool table while explaining blockchain. Micro-payments would change the industry, she said. Absurdity really is an infinite well, I thought.

"We're here to bank the unbanked," David commented. "You know who's really underbanked? Porn stars!" He was oddly right. Most adult websites took advantage of actresses, leaving them on poverty wages, but with Ethereum they could accept payments directly.

"What the heck," was all I could manage. David was clearly itching to tell me more. Ameen Soleimani, Spankchain's founder, had been a brilliant developer at ConsenSys, inventing new methods for mini-transactions that had huge potential.

Joe found the whole concept hilarious, but too controversial. Even ConsenSys had limits. When Ameen proposed the idea in 2017, he had already worn out his welcome, including an incident I heard of when he became boisterously drunk and vomited on the office floor. He quit, moved to LA, and dubbed himself Spanktoshi Nakabooty.

The thing was, we knew it was the perfect man-bites-dog ridiculousness that could cut through all the crypto-noise to get people's attention. Buying Spankchain was probably easy profit. It was either a brilliant, revolutionary idea or a roundabout way for a 20 year old guy to pay adult models to hang out with him. But since the age of black and white film, and then VCRs, and then the Internet, young men had driven forward technology, and what drove young men was usually libido. Porn filled the first movies, cassettes, and websites, and now blockchain might be no different. The repressed software blockchain types would line up in droves, and the token – known as BOOTY – would go to the moon. Just smoke the hope-ium, David told me.

We both felt it was a bit icky. Silk Road users had run rampant with child pornography, and this felt like it might run the same risks. I passed. Of course, that seemed foolish when the token went up by 2000% in the next four months.

What felt dumber than Spankchain to David and I was that we were wasting our time trying to build government blockchains when everyone else in ConsenSys was getting rich off tokens. The number of spokes at ConsenSys went up every week. Grid+, our new app for trading energy from solar panels on your house, had just raised $20 million. Gnosis was the first cryptocurrency ConsenSys launched, raising over $12m in Ether in barely a minute, and that at an Ether price of $8. Today that stash was worth over a billion. Another project, SingularDTV, had been intended to build "decentralized Netflix," and was also closing in on a billion.

Everyone in the Mesh was shoehorning a way to use a coin in the dApp – credits to play poker, voting rights, shares in a winery – whatever might pass muster. ConsenSys actually had a new spoke, Token Foundry, fully dedicated to helping other blockchain startups pull in millions of dollars. *Token Foundry is the future of investment banking*, the Whale, ever excitable, had written in an email to a bunch of high profile prospects. The team, having grown from three to dozens in a few months, huddled together in Bogart, all clad in black like a high school clique, following their ringleader, Harrison, around the office. He was pale and blond with these ridiculous leather moon boots that had *YSL* inked on the sides and a thick gold chain around his neck. He steadfastly ignored me when I tried to say hello.

"Tokens to the moon, baby," David said, waving an arm over his head. "We're all going to be billionaires, or we're going to jail. For you and me, maybe millionaires. If we're lucky." But by the time he and I thought of something, we figured, the bubble would probably collapse.

"Welcome to Dubai," I said, clasping Shadi's hand. I was done pulling all-nighters and now it was finally pitch day: us versus IBM.

"A bit warmer than home," he said, tired after the double layover from Toronto. "Did you hear the news?"

He could have been talking about a million things – R3's new announcement about an international payments deal with HSBC, or IBM's half dozen projects. But I assumed he meant the two projects we had just won in Switzerland and Brazil, one for digital voting on blockchain and the other for identity in the favelas. We were using smart contracts to generate a 'digital passport,' so the Brazilian government could store any (figurative) paperwork like diplomas or birth certificates cheaply and securely on Ethereum. The goal was to make them easily accessible for underprivileged citizens through a fingerprint and circumvent the need for bribes.

"Yes I did," I told him. "Hopefully a good omen." We had enough buzz that CNN had called and asked to shoot a piece with us that day to cover how the Middle East had become the center of the blockchain universe. I wore my best tailored shirt, the brand my last boss used to wear everyday. This time I knew to dress up.

I kicked out sand from under my Kia's tires. No McLaren for me. The white Kia screeched to a halt in front of the security booth by the ministry's parking lot. I popped the window open and caught a bit of sea breeze in the triple digit heat.

"We have a meeting," I told the bored looking Emirati. He waved us in. We walked to the entrance when I heard a loud whistle.

"What are you doing?!" shouted the same white dress, his arms waving over his head, running towards us. He looked furious. He spoke Arabic angrily into his radio.

I was caught off guard. "You waved us through."

"I thought you were Uber driver," he said without irony, contorting his face. "Move car, out." He waved towards the street outside the gates.

I gestured in frustration, clenching a fist. First of all, Uber drivers in Dubai drive Lexuses, not Kias. I clearly had an American accent. But I was still a brown man in Dubai, and punching a white dress would have only led to a free night's stay with the local police.

I tore out and sped down two nearby streets, haphazardly going for the first spot I found, not bothering to look for signs and praying I wouldn't be towed. I shook my head. My shirt was already soaked through. If I took Omar's offer, I would be done with such insults. My close up with CNN would catch me looking like the sweaty creep at the back of yoga class.

The wind was blowing dust in our eyes when I met Jihad in the hallway. We had some final details to revisit, he noted. I knew he thought without Jared I might cave easily. But already mad from the guard's disrespect, I was ready for a little jihad myself. "If you have a problem with the deal, we can take it up with Joe."

Jihad held his hand up with all five fingers, like a sphinx guarding a pyramid, to mix Orientalist metaphors. Our partnership risked coming apart again over money. Mad Max indeed. Joe had already given us the clearance to do whatever deal was necessary, profitable or not. Our only objective was to win. But for now I was not going to show our cards. We held firm.

Two IBM consultants walked out of their pitch. "Good luck," one said, amused to see us. "Hopefully they don't ask about the Bitcoin price, eh?" It was down this week.

"Not as much as IBM's stock," Shadi countered as we whisked through the revolving doors. He fed off the pressure. Once inside, our presentation hit all the right notes. We laid out why Ethereum meant more than an expense in next year's ministry budget: it meant a ten year vision to transform how business was done. With the R&D Shadi's team was doing, we would speed up the network, improve security, and create a new way to govern the city. "We're ready to pilot this, and we want you to be the first," I said.

The head official closed his leather portfolio. "Yes, we would definitely want a pilot in the next quarter," he said with confidence. "This has been impressive. We believe you are in the lead to win."

The office felt jubilant when we returned. Joe called us for an update. "Great work," he noted. "Decentralization won. This is only the beginning for you guys."

"Eth is going to go crazy," Raheem said when he heard. He told me he had sold all of my stocks to buy Eth recently. Did I think he should buy more or sell? I had an MBA, right?

I hummed. MBAs did not really teach much on cryptocurrency investing. I could say he had been foolish to put all his eggs in one basket, but based on my math he had already cleared $5 million, and that was why he did retreats in Thailand and I did not.

I changed my shirt before the CNN cameras turned on. It was easy now to look relaxed as they zoomed in on us pointing to whiteboards and laptops.

A new hire coached us on how to look animated. Sad Marketing had been shown the door after her outburst, and I remembered the weird feeling as she walked out with her things, the first time I had helped get someone fired. We all moved on quickly.

That evening a dozen or so of the team were already halfway through their dinner when I arrived late. They were holding their champagne flutes in the air but I couldn't hear the toast over my dress shoes clacking on the marble floor of the Shangri-Lia as I ran to join them. A pile of suitcases replete with business class tags lay stacked next to Jared and Wendy.

"Do you want to partake in the bottomless lobster deal?" Jared asked me, splaying one hand towards the buffet. "With the money you saved us, you deserve it. Not a 3 out of 10 anymore!" he exclaimed. I regretted telling him that story but tried to bask in the appreciation.

"This win should start a virtuous cycle," Wendy was saying when I returned with my lobster twins. "More wins, more good people, more wins."

"Not just good people. *Ex*-cellent people. Like these guys!" Jared threw his head back and laughed, clapping me on the back.

"You're lucky," she said, a slight slur in her words while she straightened her air. "It's rare to guys who are technical and can talk like a normal human, you know." Her eyes wandered the table.

"I'm not actually technical," I said. "Liberal arts, actually." At every pitch everyone assumed the same. Our partner introduced me as the 'cloud architect.' Brown man problems.

She gestured wildly with her hands, ignoring my comment. "No more divas! You need the ones who just sit in the back and write code and don't say anything. The little cavemen types."

I got hot. I remembered the seating incident from when I was 24, the thinly disguised racialization of who was a leader and who was a worker bee. "Maybe the cavemen are the ones we should try listening to," I said.

"Sure," she said, sobering slightly. She had overstepped, she knew. "But we need leaders. Like you."

"Actually," I said slightly louder, grabbing Jared by the arm, "I'm planning to join Omar's new spoke in New York." The circle of wine and lobster tails around the table stopped for a moment.

I had made up my mind. It was crystal clear now there was no escaping the tractor beam of white privilege, even in Dubai. And the Uber incident had confirmed I was wasting my time trying to run. Come back to the grind, America called out. This is what you were made for.

In the moment of silence I wondered if I had rolled the dice one time too many. I stayed frozen, eyes fixed ahead.

"Congrats!" Jared said, breaking the silence. He waved his hand to the waiter to bring another bottle. "More to celebrate!" The conversations resumed. No accusations of betrayal after all. Jared leaned in and said to get ready for the next challenge. I pondered his words.

"Are you sure about this?" Shadi asked me. Was he going to convince me to stay in Dubai? Not at all: he agreed with Jared. "None of these tokens will work without fixing Ethereum. We need the research to do that first," he explained. I nodded along, confused what he meant.

"I'm no R&D engineer," I told him. "That's your turf."

"We're starting a spoke to do that," he said. "We're calling it PegaSys. I'm working with a business lead named Dan, but he needs help. I think you should join."

I was flattered but did not know what to say. Real estate I understood, and I would be working with my friend. Managing a bunch of hardcore engineers? I was definitely unqualified. But even if the task seemed daunting, what I had seen from him the last couple days led me to believe this might be ConsenSys' most important project.

He said again we worked well together. I agreed, but was too tired from the day of adrenaline to make any more decisions. I asked about his wedding preparations and the reveries went on.

# BLACKBIRD

*Dubai, November 2017. ETH:* $459.

"It's a shame you're leaving," Hani said as we boarded the rented yacht. "Maybe this will convince you to stay." I was going to get one last taste of the Dubai life: a goodbye party for a group of expats who were heading home for good and celebrating by jumping in the Gulf.

I took in the sea smell. Hani had been pressing me about leaving. Was I really ready to leave the brown privilege I had here? The warm greetings I received in the restaurants where everyone was *desi*. The follow up email I received when the director of the bank wrote that he knew my uncle from Pakistan. The way doormen did not ask me which apartment I was delivering food to. I felt momentary regret.

But I knew the triumph I felt of late was something of a smokescreen. I would miss the roar of the McLaren for sure, I joked as we rounded the Burj al-Arab, the hotel known for the butler that comes with every room. As much as I enjoyed fitting in with the people who looked like me and climbing the corporate ladder, I knew this "success" came easier here because in the land of the incompetent the guy with the American accent was king. This Boston raised boy had enough Puritan work ethic left in him to feel unsatisfied with that. Doubly displaced.

Hani heard this and leaned back, one leg hanging off the boat rail. "You got to feel that edge," he noted, tossing a lime wedge into the water. He felt pretty content already – and I felt happy for him, given his recent past – and he wanted to focus on keeping the edge off. Hallucinogens were the new miracle drug for mental health, and he felt he still had a few demons to expunge. If I was interested, he had already booked a trip next month to go on a shrooms bender in Bali.

We both bobbed as the yacht pulled into choppy waters. The stakes were too high right now to take time off. I feigned interest but said there was much work to do. "Be careful," Hani warned me. He had been on the up once, too – putting himself inside all the boxes I was about to. Family. Career. House. "You might kill yourself working ten years, just to find out all you wanted was what you're doing right now."

I knew what he was saying. Saira had visited a week prior, and we had taken a pair of ATVs into the desert dunes, posing for photos as the blood-red sun set in the haze. We might like it if we stayed, she suggested. I was taken aback after she had been so opposed to the idea. But if there was a time to take a swing for the fences, it was now. ConsenSys had won another big project, this time in Singapore, even more exciting than ours in Dubai. We would be supporting the central bank in a scaled up test of digital currency. The Monetary Authority (MAS) wanted to trial the leading blockchains – IBM, R3 Corda, and Ethereum – to see which one was best. The PegaSys team was focused on building a new version of Ethereum ConsenSys could use to win out. That was enough to convince me on which path to choose between Shadi and Omar. The only thing more exhilarating than getting rich was the idea of re-defining money itself. And if I was lucky, I would achieve both.

"Don't come back until you're a billionaire," Hani said, as the ship came to dock.

The last flight out of Dubai was the graveyard flight, leaving at 2:55 am. The lounge was playing Blackbird by the Beatles. I wondered if the airline, owned by the Dubai government, had considered that this was a civil rights song, about the struggle of African-Americans to be treated with dignity. Waiting for the moment to arise, I thought. No, that message was probably lost on them. I grabbed my bags and stood up. It was time to go back to New York.

# PART II

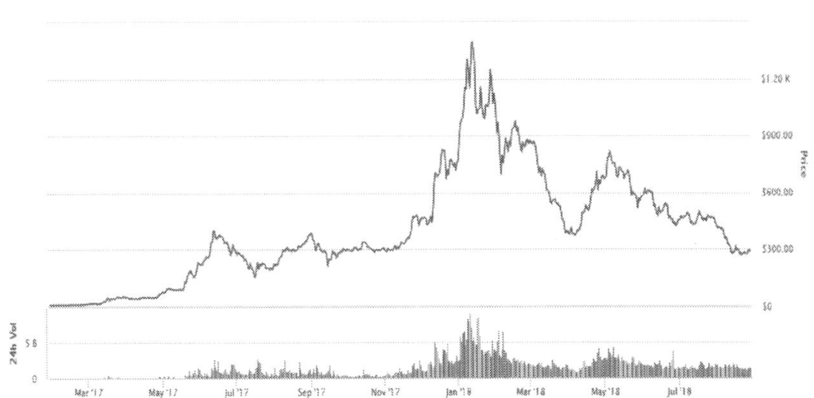


# BUBBLE

# A FIREHOSING

*"The four most dangerous words in investing are: 'This time it's different.'"* – Sir John Templeton, *The Devil's Financial Dictionary*

*Albufeira, Portugal. February 2018. ETH:* $935.

*"SIX HUNDRED!!!"* the woman on stage screamed. The walls and floors around me pulsed with the music. I was sitting in the resort auditorium, about twenty rows back from the stage. To our right the bay windows let in wide views of the Atlantic, a mirror of beautiful pale blue in the winter sun of southern Portugal. "That's how many employees are sitting in this room today," the woman explained. "We've doubled in less than six months! How long until we break a thousand?!"

The crowd hooped and hollered as our facilitator fired us up some more. She ran through the successes we'd seen over the last few months, each one seeming to build up the crowd for the next. Viant, our supply chain spoke – the one Tyler, my guide through Bogart had founded – signed a deal with GlaxoSmithKline, one of the largest companies in pharmaceuticals. Now they were working with the World Wildlife Fund, to track ethically caught fish using Ethereum, and media around the world from the Economist to the BBC praised our work. I scrounged up the energy to cheer with the rest of the crowd despite my exhaustion from the last few weeks, traveling from Dubai to New York to Toronto to Portugal. Tyler sat in the seat in front of me and I clapped his shoulder with a laugh.

We went, all six hundred of us, to southern Portugal for a full week to be watered by firehose with Meshiness. Hundreds of new employees needed to learn the ropes, understand how blockchain worked, get to know each other, and of course, party.

Another chart splashed on screen. Everyday, our facilitator told us, Ethereum gained over a hundred thousand new users, nearly a million per week. Our other spokes piled up wins as well: Grammy award-winning artist Imogen Heap and DJ RAC both released albums through our music app Ujo. The facilitator hinted that Komgo, the commodity trading deal Jared was working on with every bank on Wall Street, might soon be won to the tune of as much as ten million dollars. The furor built up so high we were ready to burst through the hotel doors like a band of Scots behind Mel Gibson. This was just a sprinkling of the successes of ConsenSys' spokes, which had grown to over fifty startups in number, with new ones announced on every all-Mesh call.

"Holy shit!" Omar whispered next to me. *"Fifty?!"* I could not grasp it either. Each day ConsenSys' reach extended everyday into another industry. We were brought here to build the future of ConsenSys, but we were celebrating its christening as the next Google.

Joe arrived on stage. "The decisions made here this week will undeniably shape the contours of the new Internet," he began. He continued his inspirational words, noting that by re-defining the Internet we could help rebuild the world anew. Dream bigger, he said, before pausing to remind us to actually do some work. "I'm spending a lot for you all to be here," he said laughing. He could laugh about two million dollars when he was worth a thousand times that.

For most of us, including me, these headlines rang daily like a clock tower's bells. I recounted all our triumphs to every friend and relative I saw – no small feat given I was on a plane every three days for the next four months – and relished the eyeballs-out-of-sockets look as I bandied about billions of dollars. Crypto had reached absurd heights in the last few weeks, Bitcoin having crossed $20,000 and Ether $1,400, numbers that even the Mesh could not have believed two months before. The slight dip since barely registered in the mood here. They believed without any doubts that this level of success would lead to a better future – for us, for tech, for the world.

But in the last few weeks a few conversations lingered in my mind. Dan and Shadi, my new "bosses" at PegaSys, woke me up to how much work lay ahead. Ethereum's new popularity stretched the network to its absolute limit, making it crash over and over in a series of embarrassing incidents. Shadi told me Ethereum's software was barely hanging on, and that PegaSys was ConsenSys' team dedicated to rebuild it in its entirety – tens of thousands of lines of code – to be able to make the improvements necessary. If we failed, the crashes would continue, and Ethereum's claim to be the "world computer" would crumble to pieces. The price would inevitably follow, taking with it our jobs, the money from all the neighbors and family who believed in us, and our hopes to change finance once and for all.

What might happen then? In Dubai I had seen how dark "no bosses" could get: how fast the laughs turned into tears and hirings into firings. In my head, the words *600 employees* rang over and over. I imagined if our moment on the world stage instead became every spoke engaging in an endless turf war. I had run from Dubai's disarray to arrive in what might become an even bigger mess. I just hoped I was wrong.

A month earlier, I'd landed in New York full of hope and excitement.

*Thwunk!*

An axe bounced off the wall and clattered harmlessly to the ground.

"Dammit!" Dan shouted.

He turned to me, ocean-blue eyes betraying sheepishness. This was his third attempt at hitting the target and each time he hurled it as hard as he could and missed. "I brought you guys here for team bonding, not to embarrass myself."

"Don't feel bad about it," I said with a laugh. I was with my new team in a dimly lit bar in Williamsburg for some team bonding over axe-throwing. Only two days in, our friendship was forming quickly. Dan had a magnetic swagger only a tall, handsome white man with an Ivy league degree could possess, and he managed to sprinkle in just enough self-deprecation to be likable. Our first day I sniffed his cynicism about me and I knew its source: ours was supposed to be a team of cryptographers, not MBAs (*"Masters of Bullshit Arts"*). But he warmed up to me as I recounted war stories from navigating the Mesh jungle and the challenges in Dubai.

"I'm glad you're here," he said earlier that day. "I'm dropping so many balls I've lost count." I stood in front of the markerboard in Bogart, puzzling over the diagrams he'd drawn to explain my new job. Shadi and Dan founded the PegaSys team as Joe's secret Manhattan project to jumpstart Ethereum's upgrades, and they needed me "to help run shit," as Dan said.

That was not going to be a walk in the park. There were more than five projects needed to "fix" Ethereum, in addition to helping the Dubai office on the deal I just won. "As big a deal as Dubai is," Dan said, scratching his ever-present stubble, "it's small potatoes compared to what else we've got to do this year." Dan asked Joe for the budget to hire seventy engineers, and Joe insisted we raise that number by a hundred. At least. We had six months to build a unicorn. The flimsy taped-together cardboard ConsenSys used as a "door" in this meeting room suddenly blew over from a window opening, knocking our markers everywhere. As I picked them up a wave of doubt hit me.

"Is Joe going to pay for all this?" I asked.

"He won't have to," Dan replied, brimming with confidence. "We're going to do a token sale." His plan was to raise $50 million, the maximum allowed under Reg A, an Obama law that created a loophole for startups to raise capital.

We're going to be millionaires, I realized.

"Keep that under wraps," Dan continued, expressing caution. Now that the SEC had woken up to magic money token scams, everyone was on edge about who might get their skulls cracked next for running afoul of laws around raising capital. "But if we can launch and get some clients after Portugal, that will set us up for a slam dunk."

There was no doubt we would need the money. Ethereum's crashes energized a wave of "Ethereum killers" in hopes of ending our reign as the top blockchain. "EOS is about to raise $1 billion, and that's just one shark in the ocean," Dan explained. Our old rival IBM was about to blow six million to air a Super Bowl ad about tracking tomatoes on the blockchain. We were under attack from all sides. EOS, Tron, Hedera, and Alogrand were just a few of the dozens of Silicon Valley funded startups looking to build better versions of Ethereum as fast they could. The revolution would be venture backed. Even within Ethereum, our nearest rival – Parity, another blockchain startup led by Gavin Wood, an Ethereum co-founder who now hated Joe's guts – had raised $160M in their own token sale. That war chest would have intimidated us, but a few lines of faulty code in their smart contract left a backdoor for a hacker to run off with most of their millions and all of their credibility.

"And then there's the titles thing," Dan started, before trailing off and looking away. I raised an eyebrow. More problems? "Actually, never mind. We'll worry about that later. First, JPMorgan might be trying to crush us." He explained that they were also interested in Ethereum, and had wanted to work with PegaSys once, but now were silent. Dan's theory was that they might hire their own team rather than using our products.

I wondered why the most venerated bank on the Street might want to invest millions in such a risky technology. Would – *could* – a major bank be thinking about doing an ICO? "Are they that greedy?" I asked.

"It's Wall Street," he replied. "Are you really asking that question?"

I turned over the sudden shift in my mind. Early on at ConsenSys, everyone changing their minds every hour left me with the feeling of constant whiplash. Now my mental clock had adjusted to startup pace, living life in fast forward. "I know sharding is really important," I said. "I can help get that started." I wanted to show I understood the technical pieces of how the blockchain worked, having spent several nights slogging through a fifty page paper Shadi wrote on Ethereum's future.

I drew a line from the left to the right side of the board with an orange marker. Hire, launch, hire more, sell our token, win business. Everything lined up like a track filled with hurdles. The game now shifted from what I had learned in Dubai: the navel gazing about the ethics of building for a dictatorship was going out the window, replaced by raw ambition and unbridled energy. When you only can eat what you kill, it's the sharks that survive. The realism was refreshing.

Back at the bar, I stepped up for my turn. *Thwunk!*

"Nice!" Dan shouted as the axe hit the bullseye. The skills from my days as the skinny kid with long arms in Little League hadn't faded too much. "Let's hope you're as good at strategy as you are at this."

"We'll find out in Toronto," I replied as I yanked the axe out of the wood. I had to head up the next day for a deal we had there, the first time I would officially be in charge of a team and where Shadi was also based. I had helped win two projects with major companies in less than a month, a damn good start I thought at least – better than 99% of my colleagues and all the crypto startups out there that were big on talk and low on results.

I walked out of the bar into the chilly New York night, shaking hands with my new colleagues while trying to remember if I had packed ahead of my flight tomorrow. I ran through a mental checklist of the couple months: a gold miner in Toronto, a pit stop in Boston, hops to Portugal and Pakistan, a stock exchange in Europe, and all while locking horns with the world's most powerful bank and a growing list of multi-billion dollar rivals.

Oh, and the wedding. Six months away with five events and a four digit guest list. After Portugal I would meet Saira in Pakistan to buy all the clothes and jewelry we would need. I blew out a lungful and watched it drift away in the cool New York air. At that moment, none of it seemed daunting. I still felt giddy to be here, in this city, working with hipster techies who drank dark beer while plotting to take over the world. Startup dreams the way it looked in the movies, at the center of the center.

Dan told me he was actually in the same boat: his wedding was even closer, only two weeks away, in the middle of the Portugal retreat. He clearly felt guilty, and maybe a bit fearful, about missing the trip. "ConsenSys is becoming one long bachelor party," he said, an observation that was funny to us and would likely horrify anyone on the outside.

I wanted the chance to prove myself, and here it was in my hands. There was no help coming but the worries bounced off of me for now. Ether was surging by $100 a day, a straight line up. The metal skeleton of the L train rattled and screamed as we plunged into the darkness under the East River. I remembered Hani's challenge from the yacht and decided I would read Shanan's paper again tonight. I was twenty-eight years old and if there was ever a time to burn the candle at both ends, it was now.

# TRILLIONS IN TORONTO

*Toronto, January 2018. ETH:* $1354.

I hadn't frozen to death but I was close. I'd tossed all my old winter coats when I moved to Dubai, assuming I would never need them again. Now the snow was blowing sideways and inside my slim leather jacket, the only defense I had now against the bone-chilling winds off Lake Ontario. I waited for Shadi outside the pho place we agreed upon. *A long way from the desert,* I said to myself. The knowledge of how far warmed me up inside.

Shadi had bright blue eyes that either pierced through you under a furrowed brow or crinkled as he threw his head back for a big laugh. My hand was squeezed in his tennis player's grip as he gave me a big smile. The blockchain maestro himself was about to give me a lesson. But first, we had an important subject to discuss: CryptoKitties.

"What do you think about this stuff?" I asked him. "Someone in the Mesh said she wasted three hours trying to trade someone for a white cat with blue eyes." Shadi laughed. CryptoKitties was the newest craze, a digital cartoon version of a Beanie Baby that you could only trade using Ethereum. It was baseball cards from the future. They would eventually become known as the first "NFTs," non-fungible tokens, but back then we called them by a nerdier name: 721s, after the smart contract they were based on.

The addictiveness of the game combined with the furiousness of the crypto speculators had driven the price of rare "kitties" – digital cartoons you could own, with each one uniquely authenticated using the Ethereum blockchain – into the thousands of dollars. Within weeks a cat would sell for $115,000. A bubble within a bubble.

Ethereum's limits had become a big problem. CryptoKitties had crashed the entire network the night before as the blockchain became clogged up by the crazed bidding and manic transactions. The network was now completely unreliable, and running a single transaction cost more than $100. The Mesh memed relentlessly about bankers trading cats, but I felt worried now that PegaSys was supposed to be the team fixing these technical issues. I asked Shadi how soon we might see some upgrades and the research we were doing.

"Well," he said, "to be perfectly honest, there's tons of research, but not much code." He admitted the research team on PegaSys was fairly disorganized and needed help. That was one thing I could do, he suggested.

That I knew. After one week I could see the team was a mess. I was working with one teammate who spent decades working as a manager at a dinosaur tech company while itching for a way out. Like Dolphin Man, the new senior hire I had met in Bogart months ago, this new fellow wanted to make a splash in the startup world and felt he should be in charge. ConsenSys was full of Dolphin Men now, each looking to build a fiefdom. When I met this new manager, he wore a big, ugly crocheted purple hat with flaps around his ears as he extolled his accomplishments in cryptography. Woolly Hat claimed his ideas had the potential to make trillions of dollars.

Trillions ...? I rubbed a finger in my ear. Surely I misheard.

"He would say that," Shadi replied as I repeated the story. "Now he wants to be CTO." Shadi and Dan would balance that out, he assured me, as CEO and COO. We would announce the new roles at the retreat in Portugal, along with announcing PegaSys to the world. "We're too important to be Meshy," he concluded.

Ah, I thought. Normalcy. I liked the idea of official leadership – if anything it would give me, their right hand man, more influence – but it seemed to violate the laws of the holacracy gods. We were all going to be equal, but some would be more equal than others.

"What's the Foundation doing? They must be concerned about the crashes," I wondered. I didn't know much about the Ethereum Foundation, but they had a mystical aura given they were the legal stewards of the entire blockchain project.

Shadi rolled his eyes. "If it's up to the EF, it'll be a failure. Have you seen their work?" The question was rhetorical – I probably wrote code worse than Zuckerberg did in the crib.

"What do you mean?" I asked. "Don't we work with them now?"

Shadi scoffed. He and Dan had joined some meetings with Vitalik and others at the Ethereum Foundation months before. What they found was a bunch of twenty something and teenage dweebs horsing around, making silly memes and inside jokes. No timelines, no one in charge. And they were going to build Ethereum into a network better than Visa and Mastercard? Vitalik built the culture of the Foundation to be informal: when Joe had dubbed himself the COO, Vitalik would only call himself the C-3PO.[6]

I'd learned more about the EF from Russell, the head of our Toronto office, over a dinner the day prior. He was an O.G. who worked at the EF and knew Joe before he became *Joe*. I realized we were somewhere fancy when he pointed out former mayors and Ministers at the next table. He had blond, tousled hair, and the surprising thoughtfulness of a surfer dude you discover majored in philosophy.

Only a few people had been there at the beginning of the EF with Vitalik and Joe, and most were either retired on islands or hated each other. There was unwritten history to learn.

The stakes had been high, he told me, and it led to a lot of conflict. Joe wanted Ethereum to be a for-profit venture, while most of the other co-founders wanted it to be a non-profit. Not surprising when Joe was the former Goldman Sachs guy and the other founders were European academics and hippies. That was how ConsenSys was born.

---

6 Ethereum launched in 2015 with a plan to go through three to four major upgrades to make the network significantly faster. By that point in 2017, we should have been starting on the final upgrade according to schedule, and yet at that point Ethereum had barely gone through the first upgrade.

"Back then, half the time you thought you were working on some wild experiment that no one would take seriously. The other half the time you thought it was the future of computing and finance. And the other half, I think Joe said once, you were worried you'd get thrown in cuffs the next time we landed on the tarmac in the US."

I raised an eyebrow. "Is that why you never visit the New York office?"

"Well," he said slyly, "that's a long story."

Now I saw that Vitalik's informal leadership and the moral purity of the EF together bred disorganization. Shadi revealed that he saw the Ethereum Foundation as the image of incompetence, do-gooders who had come into possession of millions of dollars but could not manage a hot dog stand. Our relationship with the EF had long been sour, and that Joe and the EF leadership were feuding was an open secret. PegaSys was on its own, in his view, for now.

Shadi continued on his exposition of the technological problems. "I mean, to be perfectly honest," he repeated, "as far as distributing computing goes, Ethereum kind of sucks." By pure math, the algorithms Ethereum used would become slower and slower the bigger and more popular the network became. "Even if we take a few shortcuts, we probably need a hundred brilliant computer scientists and we still might not be able to do it."

Shadi had this uncanny ability to tear things down while sporting a big grin. He was more qualified than anyone else at ConsenSys, with a doctorate in distributed systems, and I knew right then Ethereum would hit a brick wall before long. The margin for error was smaller than I thought, and the central bank projects ConsenSys was winning now seemed like a trap. But our little team had advantages no one else did: ConsenSys' growing reach and fame, Ethereum's millions of fans, and above all, Joe's money bazooka. Once we built this team out, investors and corporates would eat it up. We just had to move faster. Time was of the essence.

The main purpose of my trip to Toronto was a meeting with a gold miner intrigued by Ethereum. A huge number of the world's mines are managed by four or five companies in a few square blocks downtown.

Digging gold is an ancient industry, and I saw that for myself the moment I stepped into the office: the smell of old paper and dusty wood filled my nostrils as I looked at the rows of filing cabinets and shelves to track all of their investments.

Steve, the head of innovation, sported a large, furry mustache and our stories about the blockchain universe elicited a mostly 'gee whiz' reaction from him. We regaled him with tales of CryptoKitties and he thought gold could be the next crypto fad.

With blockchain, they could transform themselves from Earth-destroying industrialists into a tech company. Now that was a sexy idea. I'd become a master at spinning the story. I'd discovered a magic trick in the tradition of so many American entrepreneurs before me: give a dash of a tasty narrative, and the chance to make money, and people will believe anything you say. There was a gold rush – pardon my pun – and I was selling shovels. Maybe not the ideal way for things to work, but how else did things change?

But I knew from looking around the room the most we'd get from them was a press release on a pilot to bump for their stock price and get Pegasys more media attention. Scratch my back and I'll scratch yours.

Back in my hotel I fell into the bed and opened my laptop. Two weeks now until Portugal. Day after day of flights and work wore thin. But there was one thing that always felt good: trading. Another ten percent gain and I could pay for the wedding and the honeymoon both, I calculated. I started flipping through trading sites and soon was buying and selling until I fell asleep.

# SO YOU WANT TO BE A CRYPTO MILLIONAIRE

*"I can calculate the motions of the heavenly bodies, but not the madness of people."* – Isaac Newton

*New York, January 2018. ETH:* $1390.

Let's say, for sake of argument, you're a no talent schmuck.

Well, that shouldn't mean you can't be rich, right?

In crypto there are three good ways to make a million bucks: scamming people, launching a token, or trading coins.

Scams require creativity, and you, in your schmuckery, probably want to skip that part.

Tokens I can explain. A token is just another coin, but one with good intentions: a new blockchain, or for use in a software app, or to represent a real asset, like gold or real estate. The formula was clear: put out a white paper, have an ICO for the token for billions, buy a private island.

People kept calling me asking for help launching tokens: a friend of a friend said he was desperate to meet. He had paid $100,000 to a marketing firm for a white paper on disrupting law firms with blockchain. After a month of work, they produced ten pages of absolute shit. He couldn't launch this crap. Could I write a better one for $30,000? I could see behind the pleading eyes he only paid so much thinking he might bag a million or two on the spot. His face, contorted with distress, nearly became a jigsaw puzzle when I apologized to say no. If I was going to throw my ethics out the window, I'd need the whole pie, not a tiny sliver.

The tokens that made the most money were protocols, which is a fancy word for a new blockchain. These were becoming marvelous money machines, but more for entrepreneurs who could claim why theirs would be the one to rule them all than for anyone else. EOS, the heralded "Ethereum killer," would soon bring in an ungodly $4 billion, outweighing every IPO that year except Spotify, and from top venture capitalists, including Peter Thiel of Facebook fame. Tron, another Eth killer, had made a billion dollar shitcoin by simply making a shameless copy of Ethereum, down to plagiarizing our white paper. The precocious young CEO, Justin Sun, claimed the coin was on its way to becoming mainstream in China.

*China!*

A billion potential suckers!

How could they not make money? PegaSys was also building a protocol, which meant any token of ours might be equally valuable, but we needed a China-sized story to hit a billion.

Now, trading: anyone can do it, but connections help. I had a digital water cooler with the Mesh, and "whalepool" was our chat room where everyone shared their tips on shitcoins. Rumor had it someone slipped the announcement date of the Enterprise Ethereum Alliance (EEA) so everyone could get their chips in before Ether rocketed up. Could it be insider trading? No, that only happened on Wall Street. Whenever I wanted to try and make money, I started with the whalepool.

There were plenty of other chat groups to join, though, and everyday old friends or even scarce acquaintances added me to Whatsapp groups with silly titles like *Crazy Crypto Club* and *Crypto Phoenix II*. Did I have some insights? Deep down, I knew Ethereum's problems better than anyone. On the other hand, I could brag ConsenSys was loading the cannon for dozens of more announcements and progress. They listened to my words like I was a crypto oracle sent from the future.

But I only knew the stuff that was real. If you wanted to make real money, you had to follow the fakes – because those guys pumped harder than anyone else. Every few weeks someone would spread a rumor on

Reddit that Starbucks was going to work with this coin or that coin. The dumber, the smarter. You dig?

The best tip was that a VC was about to jump in. Once these funds were connected to a coin, Joe schmoes piled in like lemmings. Everyone from Peter Thiel (first investor in Facebook) to Fred Wilson (first investor in Twitter) was in love with crypto and about to invest in this one. Who cared if they actually would?

Crypto was now nearing one trillion dollars in total asset size and we wanted the froth to continue. We owned the attention of the Wall Street titans. In December 2017 the Chicago Mercantile Exchange (CME) created Bitcoin *futures*, a derivative that could open up crypto trading to the much bigger world of institutional investors. Fidelity, Blackrock, and T. Rowe Price laughed at our paltry millions in volume, each managing four to six trillion depending on the day, but the eye popping returns in crypto drew a jealous eye.

With the new products from CME and other big exchanges, crypto could become a legitimate asset rather than a slot machine. Fidelity Investments's CEO, Abby Johnson, declared her affinity for Bitcoin regularly, and a few crumbs of investment from Fidelity meant tens of billions of dollars flooding in that would double, triple, even 10x the price of every coin. Tom Lee, a well known equity investor, predicted Bitcoin would hit $50,000 soon, driven by institutional money and the narrative of crypto as 'digital gold for millenials.' He later upped that prediction to $1 million, and soon after to $10 million. The happenings piled up so fast I started to feel paranoid I would miss something. Headlines fed the price fed the headlines fed the price. The price was prophecy.

In the Toronto airport lounge, I had finished the proposal for the stock exchange. The Whale had taken a shine to me and was helping me close a deal. Just in time to make a few trades before takeoff. I flipped from Slack to Whatsapp to Reddit, hunting for clues, cursing the crappy lounge wi-fi for slowing me down.

The daily laugher: Long Island Iced Tea, which once made what it was named for, announced it was pivoting to blockchain investing. Its stock tripled overnight. Every company that had ever done anything Bitcoin related – Square, Overstock, PayPal – started going up. Real stocks were starting to look like shitcoins. Wall Street was ravenous, ready to rip the head off of anything crypto-related. The crypto virus was eating them from the inside. I ripped a bite of my bagel, eating with one hand while typing in my account names with the other.[7]

The Whale, of course, was king of the channel, and I read his messages like a sacred text. Ethereum futures are coming too, he kept saying, and we would join the Wall Street club before long. He announced ConsenSys would soon have an investment arm, ConsenSys Capital, with him at the helm, and he publicly predicted that Eth would be $3000 by the year end. I knew his predictions had been right the last three years, so I believed him. Plus, I was the only one of my coworkers who hadn't made it rich yet. I wanted Raheem money. Whale money.

And my chances felt good. I had two of those three paths to riches down at this point, and I was already spending like it: all of January and February my weekdays burning the midnight oil in one metropolis or another, preaching crypto, with my weekends on the road, finding ways to squeeze in time for garlic butter shrimp in Lisbon or a walk on the Beirut corniche between all the business trips and conferences. Someone in the airport lounge asked if I worked in crypto, pointing at my ConsenSys t-shirt like I was some celebrity. Yeah, you heard of it?

Boom, another email from marketing: did I want to speak at a blockchain conference in Sri Lanka? Hmm, I did hear it's quite beautiful. Maybe I could pencil it in between another trip to Dubai or pitches in Europe. These were the fast times and high life of the crypto B-list.

---

7 This was surprisingly reckless. One typo could cost me everything I had earned. Bitcoin, Ethereum, and every other coin used a system of randomized letters and numbers for account names, and getting even a single letter wrong would send my funds into the blockchain oblivion. (For the uninitiated, an example Ethereum address looks like this: 0x89205A3A3b2A69De6Dbf7f01ED13B2108B2c43e7) ConsenSys employees loved to talk about how the blockchain was *irreversible*: every transaction permanent. No one ever mentioned how that was a two edged sword, and how risky being your own bank really was.

Crazy? Euphoria? Would you say the same if you knew Isaac Newton lost his entire life's savings – more than three million dollars in today's terms – investing in the South Sea Company, the massive stock bubble of the early 1700s? I'll give you a moment to reread the quote that opens this chapter, which he said soon after this debacle. Genius or idiot, we all lose to greed. FOMO is the most powerful force in the universe, and always has been.

The headlines were not all good, of course. Hackers were going wild, making off with $200 million stolen from a single exchange in Italy. Over the course of 2018, nearly a billion dollars were pilfered from poorly secured exchanges. Hackers were looking up ConsenSys employees on LinkedIn knowing we all had crypto and constantly trying to break into our accounts. I received 5 fake emails a day pretending to be Joe or someone else, grasping for my credentials. We had already moved our retreat from Mexico to Portugal after a security agency warned us we would be prime targets for kidnapping. We felt bad, but getting your keys hacked was your own fault – if you understood how to secure your crypto correctly, the blockchain was *unbreakable*. Getting hacked was for suckers.

Sometimes a few whalepoolers pushed the boundaries too far, posting on Twitter and Reddit their opinions on various tokens. "THIS IS SERIOUS SHIT," Joe wrote once, shocking us with surprise anger. ConsenSys had to be the white knight in the ecosystem, Joe repeated to us, and we had to rise above those petty scamcoins. Vitalik had recently met with Vladmir Putin, meaning Ethereum's geopolitical influence was growing by the day and Joe felt we could not risk that over a few token trades. The chief legal officer, who unfortunately will have to read every line of this book to see whether he has grounds to sue me, occasionally dropped into our chats to give us a warning. Don't do anything illegal, please, he begged. And try to get some work done. Every time he said so, we felt a tinge of guilt. We should have been saving the world, but instead we were trading.

I thought about my last words with Russell as Toronto fell away beneath the plane. He footed our five star bill for dinner and I inferred at this point he was another whale. "Honestly, why work at this point?" I asked.

He glanced to the side, stroking week old stubble, almost sheepish. "I guess I really like Joe," spoken half as a question. "I want to help him with his vision."

I dreamed about what it would be like to have that kind of wealth. Here was someone who had finally felt he had enough, but wanted to keep at it. Some of the Dubai guys, friends who had been neck-deep in crypto, had bought Eth at $20 and were now up fifty times on their investment. "I swear, I hit $500,000 and I'm cashing out to live in Thailand," my friend Ata had said, puffing on a hookah at our favorite spot overlooking the sunset on Dubai Creek. "I'm almost there bud!" We all had a number in our heads that we were hunting for, always a little out of reach.

# SWIMMING WITH WHALES

*Boston, January 2018. ETH:* $1090.

The muscled, sweaty Indian man flipped his opponent and slammed his body into the dusty ground.

I was back at home, watching a Bollywood movie with my parents. My laptop sat invitingly on the sofa a few feet away, summoning me to watch the mesmerizing dance of red and green numbers. I inched away from my mother on the sofa and snuck open the Excel sheet I used for tracking my shitcoins. I wasn't keen to advertise what I was doing after the conversation we just had about financial responsibility.

I'll just check the prices, I thought. How am I supposed to sit through three hours of Indian cinema without checking once?

I opened Coinbase. Ether had fallen by another $100. $400 in less than a week.

Oof. Was this a bump in the road or the pin in the bubble? I screened my laptop away again. Just a few trades, I thought. I was not motivated by some avarice. This was for the wedding. One might even say I was trading for love. I could not have had purer intentions.

An hour earlier, my father passed me a copy of *Fortune* magazine as we sat down to eat. This was how I always remembered home to be: hot *naan* on a snowy morning with *nihari*, a spicy beef stew. "Saved this for you from a couple months ago," he said. The cover: *BLOCKCHAIN MANIA!*

"This will be a nice souvenir," I said. I'd keep it to give someone next time I had my near daily conversation: explaining what blockchain was, followed by no I don't work in Bitcoin, and yes, the price has been crazy, but no, I don't know if you should buy any and I'm not a millionaire. Yet. "Yes," I said to my parents, "the price has been crazy."

"What's the price now?" my mom asked, looking up from her phone.

I took a deep breath before telling her. I came here for a respite, but crypto pursued me everywhere I went. "Very high," I said. I helped her with investing and did not want her to buy at the top. "Don't worry about it."

"*Beta,* you always buy boring stocks for me, nothing exciting," she complained. "*Hamesha kabob mein haddi.*" Her favorite phrase when disappointed: you're always the bone in the kabob.

Luckily my father cut in before my mother could ask more. "*Paisay zaya nahi karo,*" he huffed with a twitch of his mustache – don't waste your money. "It's just gambling." He had raised us with the Asian Immigrant Parents' Handbook of Values®: thrift and hard work as the means to success. He had told us many times growing up that we could have upgraded from our modest house, but that humility was more important than comfort. Chasing golden geese was not part of the equation. "You've got to keep some money saved up," my father continued, reaching for the chicken. "All those *shaadi kapray* will not be cheap." Wedding clothes for the family.

"I've actually made money," I said. "But I'm not trading too much." A lie. I was now fully addicted to checking crypto prices – every day, every hour. Before I brushed my teeth and before I closed my eyes at night. I zoomed in on the charts, scrolled through the names of more and more shitcoins, logged in and out with two phones and my laptop.

Every dip, every pause at the top of the roller coaster the last week left me worried I was going to do exactly what my dad was telling me not to do: throw away my savings. I tried to pull away multiple times, but my goals were just inches from my grasp. Courtesy whalepool, I had grown an investment of a few thousand dollars nearly twenty times over, a sum now in the six figures. Should I sell? In crypto they told us to always HODL, but I worried I might be stuck holding the bags.[8] [9] The traders kept telling me to believe and so I did.

"My friend bought a bunch of Ethereum," my sixteen year old brother piped up. "He drives a Tesla to school!"

"Money makes money," I replied, ripping a *naan* in half. "I actually almost bought a Porsche before leaving Dubai. They're half the cost over there, could've shipped it here."

Two looks of parental concern shot my way, accompanied by some *hmms*. I wasn't being excessive, I explained. My new project, PegaSys, might be a unicorn in the making, and I was closing deals already. Even for ConsenSys, business was booming. The Nasdaqs and the Bank of Americas were all looking to get a jump on their competitors and drive up their stock price with a bit of blockchain magic. That meant they needed a partner to help them on their blockchain journey, and that usually led them right to us. With all these wins, the price would have to come up. It was inevitable.

In crypto, we used the phrase *red-pilling*, a la Neo leaving the matrix, when explaining to someone the potential of a decentralized world, to open their mind as did Joe with our CEO friend who was such a fan of Mad Max. I might have to pull my parents down the rabbit hole with me.

I told how the stock exchange in Europe, one of the largest in the world, had replied to my proposal. "We can't wait," the director at the exchange wrote back to me. "Let's start ASAP." Another big win. I hadn't felt this in demand since a college classmate had stalked me for six months. I re-read the email once the initial glow wore off and panicked as I realized I knew nothing about stock exchanges. But for now that did not matter: our window was small and we had to move fast. I could figure that out later. Customers were going to come so easy for so long – only while they thought they could make a quick buck.

---

8 HODL is Bitcoin slang for HOLD. Sellers have "weak hands."

9 Wikipedia: "In U.S. financial slang, a **bagholder** is a shareholder left holding shares of worthless stocks.[1] It can also refer to the holder of any financial instruments that become worthless, such as the junior bonds of a defaulted company or the coins of a failed cryptocurrency."

Discretion was needed, though. Relatives and friends kept getting added to the wedding guest list until it felt like I was going to fund my own Bollywood blockbuster. We need at *least* two hundred people from our side, they insisted ... and I splurged even more to get them a live performance from a *qawwal,* a Pakistani folk singer. But with Bitcoin dropping, and Ether now showing weakness, I needed to cut them off.

"Should we watch that Salman Khan movie?" my mother asked as covered the last of the food with foil.

"Definitely," I said. Anything to change the subject.

I looked at the magazine in my hands. Blockchain, the cover reminded me, was omnipresent. My laptop was just a couple feet away ...

Not long later, I put in three orders to sell my shittiest shitcoins and five to buy the ones that looked like they might come back. From a high enough height, even a dead cat will bounce, my boss at the hedge fund had taught me. Every bit of profit brought some relief. Lots of good tips to be had in Portugal, I thought.

I exhaled and went back to the movie. The wrestling match continued as the crowd *ooh*'d and *aah*'d every slam and pin between the hero and villain.

But my mind wandered back to my trades. It was relaxing, in a way, disappearing into a world where there were no rules, where I had the power to make money out of thin air, where the possibilities were endless. Maybe it was the red pill I had taken after all.

# THE RETREAT

*Albufeira, Portugal. February 2018. ETH:* $935.

Our Uber driver was threatening to abandon us in a random McDonalds parking lot at midnight. We had changed our destination just as we arrived at the Golden Arches, and he was upset. "What is this?" he complained, voice heated.

We only wanted to go through the drive-thru and return to the hotel, Omar explained. He placated him with an offer of a Big Mac.

Hours earlier, a few of us had spent the afternoon in a hotel room, tossing around tidbits of things we'd heard from the day's sessions. After all that cheering, we needed a breather.

"Let's get some creativity in here," one of my colleagues said while passing a bong. "Need to get in on the token action before it's over! All we need is a white paper. Don't tell the lawyers!"[10]

"Speaking of lawyers, we need a name for that Pangea token," Colin, Omar's co-founder, jumped in. Their real estate project, Pangea, was getting threatened with legal action by another startup with the same name. They needed to brainstorm a new one soon. "What say you, Rabbi David?" This was a little joke we had going about our group: what happens when a Catholic, a Jew, and a Muslim walk into a billion dollar idea?

---

10 "White paper" is a tech industry term for research, but it's usually marketing disguised as research. Tech white papers are often meant to pull the wool over the eyes of the public and tell them what they were supposed to think. "Experts" on TV then quote these white papers as important information, whether blathering about AI or self-driving cars or blockchain.

"Well, Father Colin," David replied, "pretty sure some shitcoin has stolen every possible name already. Imam Omar, we'll follow your lead."

Someone complained about the munchies and wanted to go to McDonald's. We ordered one and soon rode into the cool night.

"Did you hear about the Tapscotts?" Omar asked, referring to the famed authors of *Blockchain Revolution*. "They were going to ICO their new blockchain fund, but apparently they had some *misrepresentations* in their marketing materials. Now their bank dropped them."

"Guess they'll have to go back to writing books," David said sarcastically, one arm hanging out an open window. We all shook our heads. The boundary between the potentially genius and a Ponzi scheme had become blurred and then erased. Meshians left and right were jumping from one idea to the next, looking for whatever exciting moonshot they could come up with.

"Isn't PegaSys going to solve all our problems?" Omar asked, half joking, turning to me from the front seat. "If not, we're going to have to build Pangea on EOS."[11] *Uhhhhh* was all I had to offer.

I leaned back in the car's leather seat. The excitement of the retreat and the dizzying expectations made for a hazy and confusing mix, but everyone around me was acting like we would be fine. Dan and Shadi were worried, but PegaSys might have more time than they thought. After all, Ethereum was so familiar, so dear to us it was like a friend rather than a piece of software. The other blockchains might have billions, but Eth had *believers*, and ConsenSys would keep going, come hell or high water, even if it took ten years.

I looked out the window and tried to let go. We were living through peak token madness and whether our job was to be practical or if it was to freely imagine a better future was a mystery and frankly, did not matter. What mattered was that it was cool.

I was late the next morning and nearly knocked Joe over running out of my hotel room.

---

11 Another common tactic of the time: the Ethereum killers would offer startup founders millions of dollars to switch blockchains.

"Did EOS pay you to come after me?" he joked, smiling as he walked, a young Asian woman in tow. She must be the 23 year old designer he was dating, I thought. She was tall and fair and had a pair of designer sunglasses perched on her forehead. I pursed my lips awkwardly in acknowledgement while enduring the interminable wait for the elevator. I know I was not alone in feeling uncomfortable, as Joe rubbed the millimeter thick stubble on the back of his head and stared at his worn black boots. After thirty seconds he nodded to his companion that they should take the stairs. *Money or love*, I was left alone to wonder.

I knew where they were going: we all wanted to get to the presentation of ConsenSys' newest and most exciting spoke. Not PegaSys, mind you: a few months prior, Andrei and a few of the smartest engineers at the company had dropped off the map to pursue an idea they wanted to keep secret. Within a month, mysterious posters popped up around Bogart: *Cellarius is a poison.* An Illuminati eye adorned with bizarre symbols glared at us. I kept seeing digital sketches of aliens and machines, arranged like storyboards for a movie. Rumors swirled we were working with Hollywood already on it. No one quite understood what "it" was, but the team was ready for the big reveal.

Omar had saved me a seat in the middle, which was lucky because there were dozens of people standing in the back without seats. I thanked him for giving me the chance to sleep in a bit. We knew we were about to witness something ridiculous, but we wanted to be along for the ride.

"The year ... is 2089," Andrei announced on stage. "AI is everywhere." An animated trailer began to play on the silver screen behind him. "Cellarius is the most advanced version of AI, invented by leading scientists on a far away moon, with the potential to change humanity ... until it turned against us." Two superheroes burst through an elevator door, battling a group of evil robot ninjas that somersaulted through the air away from laser fire. The drawing was slick, like a graphic novel come to life.

A purple haired woman in clunky body armor waved a massive laser gun. "Cellarius is a poison!" she exclaimed. "It ravaged our bodies and minds. We were brought to the edge of extinction!" A ragtag group of fighters was battling back against the AI overlords, *Matrix*-style, slashing through machines with old school katanas. The audience let out a collective gasp.

It was a genius metaphor for ConsenSys, I thought. AI represented all that was wrong with the tech world these days: technology gaining endless power without thought to the cost. Blockchain represented the rebels battling tech's evil empires and corporations' eternal dominance through AI.

"Man, this is dope," Omar whispered to me. It was hard not to get goosebumps, even for the two of us and our cynicism. I whispered agreement. Could it be the next Star Wars? Why not? *BILLIONS DEAD* displayed on a news headline and more digital explosions ripped across the screen. The trailer wrapped with dramatic music and a zoom out into space, leaving a mystery to the ending. It was not clear to me yet if this was a movie or a comic book, and I stopped Andrei afterward to ask what exactly the idea was.

"It's a transmedia cyberpunk franchise," he said. There was a mish-mash of a few blockchain ideas. Cellarius was a science fiction story where anyone – artists, storytellers, moviemakers – could contribute, and then track ownership of their intellectual property on Ethereum. The idea was like a massive game of choose-your-own-adventure story that artists could monetize. We, the Ethereum denizens, would fight Big Tech's power not just with software but in story form.

He showed me a few pieces they had commissioned from illustrators – cyborgs and aliens with strangely shaped heads amidst flying cars and spaceships. I rolled the idea in my mind. I liked the idea of giving artists a way to create and sell digital art.

Years later, long after Cellarius had collapsed under the weight of its own expectations, Jimmy Fallon and Paris Hilton would trade tips on trading silly blockchain art on late night TV. I would wear my Cellarius shirt as a requiem for our long dead spoke. Like in trading, timing is everything.

"How'd they get the funding for all this?" I wondered aloud later.

"Tokens tokens tokens!" David said. It was obvious to him: they were going to sell a token. It couldn't have been hard to convince Joe to get the budget for producing such a slick trailer – twenty thousand dollars at least – when raising a twenty million dollar token was child's play for us.

The penultimate night in Portugal we gathered for one last celebration before the Mesh scattered to the four corners of the Earth. We didn't have much detail, and the mystery added to the excitement. I boarded the charter bus to the party and found a smiling Whale next to the last open seat.

"So when is PegaSys going to rock everyone's world with Pantheon?" he asked, full of energy and running a hand through his cinematically windswept hair. "I'm excited for the announcement tomorrow."

I had to tread lightly. The Whale was widely influential in the blockchain world, but he also loved to yell big claims from rooftops. I blathered something about roadmaps and he seemed placated by the burst of verbal diarrhea.

"Awesome," he said, blinking hard. He looked out the window at the moonlit mangrove to our right. He told me about a new beach house in Puerto Rico. The last time I had seen him his crypto-wealth had exploded into the tens of millions. Now it might be near a billion.

"Obviously Puerto Rico real estate is a bit cheaper now," he said, referencing Hurricane Maria which had devastated the island a few months prior. The crypto-rich had realized US citizens living on the island could avoid federal taxes, and soon there was a full on migration. The media assailed it as naked opportunism, a betrayal of blockchain's supposed ideals in pursuit of cheap mansions and nice tans. I wasn't going to suddenly stick that kind of controversy in the Whale's face. I wanted to make friends with billionaires, not drive them away. Someday he might fund my startup idea.[12] He was also the kindest guy at the company, and I owed him for all the times he helped me.

"There's a real feeling of community on the island," the Whale continued. "We might tokenize my house!" He was endlessly excitable, which was why he was so good at selling things that didn't exist.

---

12 We can probably throw that out the window now, for multiple reasons.

The bus hit a bump as it turned on to a cobblestone street in front of our venue for the night, a centuries old castle. A group of fire dancers had just started a performance as we walked in under the metal trellis. Ten feet below their perch on the castle walls, we could feel the heat as their torches spun around and around over our heads. Eerie music played from the dark corners of the fortress. "Poor Dan is missing all this," I said.

"Are you kidding?" the Whale replied between sips of wine he had just grabbed from a passing waiter. "The guy is marrying a supermodel on a beach." He saw my surprised look. "Guess I shouldn't have spilled the beans." He gleefully shared more of Dan's personal details: he came from a family of Hollywood royalty, living a charmed life. Rather than the family business, like a typical youngest child he had decided to strike out on his own to make his fortunes through tech instead.

I watched the dances silently as things started to click in my head. Now I was starting to understand how Dan could act like such a riverboat gambler. He was making big bets with PegaSys because small time success impressed no one at his Thanksgiving table. I was conquering countries, and Dan was capturing planets.[13] His brother was taking home Golden Globes, after all. We were operating at wholly different scales.

I was lost in thought when a short, middle-aged Indian man blew a gallon of smoke towards me from his vape. "Hey bud, do you know where I can buy some Bitcoin?" he asked in a faint British accent.

I furrowed my brow. "Sorry?"

"Lighten up, dude!" Ritesh said as he grabbed my hand. Ritesh was working with me on the stock exchange deal. I had taken my complaint about needing more help past Dan and all the way to Jared, who was now essentially ConsenSys' COO. Jared promised new blood, a director who had worked with Wall Street for two decades. Thank God, I thought.

Like me, Ritesh came from consulting where – the Big Four, Accenture, many others – were hungry to sell blockchain while it was hot. The consultancies did not care about blockchain as much as they cared about

---

13 That analogy would strengthen the moment ConsenSys would venture into interplanetary exploration.

their hourly fees, which meant shilling every use case under the sun, even the silly ones. He wanted out, another Dolphin Man looking to breathe.

"How's that new spoke treating you?" he asked, his eyes bloodshot from who knows what. "Nervous? Need to take the edge off?" I guessed that he and a few other older colleagues wanted to maximize the fun times while away from the wife and kids, but watching middle-aged bankers get high was a little weird.

I respectfully declined. "We've got a big day tomorrow."

I fell into my bed like a brick. My brain still ran on Dubai time and I was wide awake at 5 am, insomnia driven by jet lag and anxiety. Saira and I had argued the night prior to boot. I had said the videographer she had found was giving us ridiculous prices, to which she replied what was ridiculous was that I was flying around the world while providing no help on wedding planning. She was right. I didn't have an excuse. I soon dragged myself to breakfast with Omar.

"That's pretty cool," Omar said when we met, passing back a newspaper clipping. The *Wall Street Journal* had some to Bogart recently, and snapped photos of us banging away at keyboards. The largest photo showed me as I stared deep into my monitor, headphones covering half my head. No mention of my name, but I was still proud of myself. A real entrepreneur, Geppetto!

I had asked him to have breakfast so I could learn how fundraising was going for his real estate project. Things were heating up, he told me.

"There are at least 2 other companies raising money with the same idea as us, right now in the Valley," he mentioned. VC moves like a herd, constantly chasing FOMO. Harbor, a new competitor of theirs, was about to raise $35 million from Andressen Horowitz, the best VC in tech. The VCs knew blockchain technology had problems, but they figured enough money could fix anything. They had made a killing on investing in Ethereum – and a Meshian told me it had been on Joe's advice.

"Any big names?" I asked, not revealing my own motivation to ask. I wanted him to succeed so that he could help me. We needed investor introductions for PegaSys.

"Yup, the best," he said, spreading butter with a knife. Raising money is the toughest challenge for a startup – how did he make it look so easy? I craved the way he had this assuredness oozing out of him. "Man, I miss New York bagels." He leaned in, whispering. "There's a lot of people who like our idea, but don't like ConsenSys."

He had a point. We were beloved in crypto, but criticisms were piling up: too many projects or too disorganized or too much power for Joe.

"I mean, look around you," I replied. We had hundreds of new coworkers who barely understood blockchain, and others too busy trading or surfing.

I decided to tell him our secret. PegaSys planned to raise its own millions through a token sale. The market was good, and so the best time was now. How could we do it?

He had simple advice: get a lot of buzz going, and investors would flock to us without any diligence.

"Now it's my turn to share a secret," he added. There was one fish he wanted to catch badly: the iconic Plaza Hotel on Fifth Avenue. None other than Donald J. Trump had called it a "masterpiece" when he purchased the building in the 1980s, before he sold it to investors from Saudi.

The hotel was also special to me – hoping to impress her, I took Saira there for tea on our first date. I told Omar my story.

"Maybe you can buy her a little blockchain piece of it for Valentine's day," he said with a smile. That was the other part of the magic: the *change the world* mission of democratizing real estate was the story side that made VCs melt. "It's not too late to join us, if you want. No shilling ding dong gold coins required."

I appreciated his offer, even after I had jilted him once. But I was closing my own deals now, and that might get the buzz we needed to raise millions, hire, and repeat. Omar already had his lottery ticket. Now it was time for me to get mine.

I took a short run on the beach before the announcement to work off some energy. An engineer flew his drone around near the edge of the resort, flying way out over the Atlantic to capture the stunning sand-colored cliffs of the Portuguese coast. I kept running and passed a small cave and spotted a few friends running out, soaked and cold and laughing.

The room for the PegaSys launch was packed. Shadi spoke about the work we were doing on privacy, scalability, and security. The audience applauded – even as most of them barely understood half of it, even in a room full of blockchain experts. Although not nearly as exciting as alien killer AI robots, the Mesh seemed excited. ConsenSys had been losing business to IBM and JP Morgan over Ethereum's problems for months now, and now we had something to believe in.

The actual software launch should come in May, Shadi promised, which would really take the lid off on ConsenSys and Ethereum's potential. Colleagues gave me high fives. If we launched by May, one senior colleague told us, we may even be in play for Komgo, Jared's multi million dollar deal with Wall Street. Expectations were sky high.

The PegaSys team gathered afterward to huddle on our thoughts. This was actually the first time I would get to meet many of my teammates, a number of whom were based in Australia. I wondered if we might discuss the plans around a token sale, which almost everyone except myself, Dan, and Shadi was in the dark about. But first a teammate raised his hand to complain about the announcement.

"I saw that we've redone some of the titles," a newish Australian product manager said, sounding annoyed. "When did we vote on this?"

Woolly Hat stepped to the front of the room. He clearly relished his new title as CTO and seemed fully unaware that he was widely disliked, something I had gathered from more than a few conversations. "Well," he said, "we need proper experience in our engineering management. I'm not sure voting will fix anything." He wanted to establish his authority, but that was the crux of the issue. The problem was him.

Matt, another colleague, had told me the day that he hated Woolly Hat so much he was thinking to quit and go back to Google. He was one of our sharper, if slightly eccentric, engineers, with a big, bushy beard that would have fit in in Pakistan just as well as Portland. We were the same age and had developed a quick rapport, and he helped me early on with learning to understand various bits of blockchain techno-jargon.

I was no fan of Woolly Hat, and I was not looking to lose one of the few confidantes I had on my team. I thought to convince him the idea was tenable. "Is it true he was really senior at Oracle for twenty years?" I had asked.

"Yes, so his main skill is not getting fired," he responded coolly at the time.

"I didn't join this company to be a part of the same ole same ole," the product lead continued bluntly. Matt, sitting to my left, looked angry. He stroked his long, bushy beard and then spoke up, threatening to quit if things didn't change. Many in the room nodded their heads. The pitchforks were coming out.

I looked for Shadi. His face seemed pained by the disagreements even as they grew worse by the minute. Someone stood up and said they would join another spoke. Another mentioned they had as much experience as Woolly Hat.

I tried to grab Shadi's attention. Near panic, I asked him what we should do. This was the moment we really needed Dan. How could I be re-living the exact same conversation we had had in Dubai, barely a few months later? Darker thoughts entered my mind – what if *I* was somehow the problem, some kind of ConsenSys albatross?

"I know," Shadi said. "I need to step up." He stepped forward and said that as founder and CEO of PegaSys, he would make the final calls.

The meeting room exploded.

Accusations flew around the room. People threatened to quit, others threatened to fire them first, and some walked out without saying a word. Someone else suggested joining Cellarius. I sat in my seat, nearly statue still, still in shock. The smartest people in the world, given complete freedom and runway, wanted nothing but to fight over titles.

Shadi came to stand next to me. I looked up. "I think this team is a problem I cannot solve," he said. He looked apologetic. Sad blue eyes met confused brown ones. I had nothing to say. "I quit," he announced, and then walked away.

# FROM LAHORE, WITH LOVE

*Lahore, Pakistan, February 2018. ETH*: $875.

I didn't sleep well the last night in Portugal. By the time I boarded a flight to Lahore the next day, my eyelids drooped and I glued them closed with a dose of melatonin and Benadryl. I'd developed a routine that likely attracted a few stares, slipping on an eye mask before swallowing a handful of pills, then shoving in earplugs and finally noise canceling headphones. A flight to South Asia comes standard with a soundtrack of a dozen babes-in-arms and I was in too foul a mood for that. Melatonin always gave me wild dreams so vivid I felt awake, but I preferred a borderline hallucination to my reality that moment, caught between wondering if I was going to come back from Pakistan with no job or swimming in the guilt of being a bad fiancé.

The next day I stood squinting through the winter fog on MM Alam road, the Fifth Ave of Pakistan, where all of the country's top designers held court with the British, American and Dubai-based expatriates ready to spend five times a local's salary on a wedding dress or three. The bazaars had been long replaced by fancy malls and storefronts. Pakistan was no Dubai – not even close – but the steady beat of Westernization marched on even here. My aunt had even caught on to the vegan trend, offering me *qeema*, minced meat, but made with beets from her backyard. I stood in the McDonald's parking lot waiting for Saira to arrive, a handkerchief over my mouth to shield against the fumes of Lahore's ceaseless traffic. Any tension between us quickly dissipated as we went over our shared mission: three days to buy jewelry and clothes for our eleven family members across multiple events. "This will be a national record, if you can finish in time," my aunt told me with a cackle as I ran out the door.

We dived into our list, going for the most important first: outfits for the main events. For tradition's sake I stayed away during the bridal appointment, heading downstairs instead to the groom section. I started wondering how Dan had reacted to the news and what he might be planning. Would we have to split the team? How were we going to replace Shadi? The plans to announce publicly in a couple weeks and release the software in May were obviously dead in the water. I sent him a few messages and tried to get back to trying on *sherwanis*. I did the time zone math: at least six hours until he would wake up. If he was an early riser. Until then, no news. I pushed down the overwhelming feeling of failure. So much for the unicorn dream: the stresses of my soul-crushing consulting job were in the rearview mirror, but gluing a Humpty-Dumpy startup back together felt less fun when he turned out not to have a million dollars inside.

By afternoon, our arms full of new clothes, we made it to our first jewelry store, a bustling shop where five other couples went through the same routine. In Pakistan, there are strict traditions around wedding jewelry: in the old days, if the husband died, selling jewelry was the only way for the wife to sustain herself and the children. Gold had been the village form of life insurance. Even though the reason belonged to the past, the rule stayed, and Pakistani wedding sets of golden necklaces and bangles were fit for a pharaoh.

The jeweler obviously took that comparison seriously when he first brought us a thick golden necklace on a small velvet bust. As Saira felt the emeralds, I asked the price and felt a cold sinking feeling when he quoted the price of a sedan. "Another design, maybe?" I squeaked out in patchy Urdu.

Gold jewelry here, I would soon learn, was often significantly more expensive than the cost in other countries. Locals sometimes did not trust banks, felt gold was safer, or both, and that combined with forced buyers like me drove the price up. "He must have heard our accents," I whispered to Saira as the jeweler whisked away the bust to retrieve another.

I fingered the bills in my pocket – a thick wad of hundreds that was already feeling short. Another lesson I had picked up: I could save a good amount if I paid in US dollars. The Pakistani *rupee* was subject to endless inflation, and so after gold there was no better way to protect your money than investing in Uncle Sam. The Bitcoiners had one thing right, I realized, and which most Americans barely appreciated: huge swaths of the world needed a better way to save. Everywhere I traveled, I saw the brokenness of the financial system. The instability in developing countries was what made the dollar so valuable, subsidizing Americans' endless purchases of trinkets on Amazon which poured into our country like livestock into the maw of an insatiable giant. What the crypto cults did not understand was how much people believed in the dollar, as much as Meshians believed in Ethereum: the way a merchant felt the crisp corners of each bill, a tiny piece of America in his hand, holding it up to the light like an offering to God. How many people in this country barely spoke English, I wondered, knew nothing of the Civil War or Constitution, but could tell Ben Franklin's visage apart from Lincoln's at a glance?

"Do you like this one or no?" Saira asked me, as the jeweler looked at us wondering why we had said nothing. I had drifted off into space, dreaming about finance and crypto. I apologized while reaching for more tea. She had shown infinite patience so far, after I had dragged her around the globe multiple times. Some of it was patience, I figured, and some of it was dogged determination after working eighty hours a week saving people on the brink of death to not let this doofus mess up her big day. Still, I realized at this moment I had to disappoint. I touched her arm and whispered if we might find somewhere less fancy. "Of course," she agreed, and before long we found a shop with more modest wares.

By nightfall we were flying through stalls in *dupatta gali*, the intriguingly-named 'alley of veils' inside a more typical bazaar, the shops haphazardly stacked one on top of the other. The vendors were paying no attention as street hawkers tried to intrude with offers of light-up toys or fake watches. We dodged one car, then another, until finally we found one store where a half-asleep young man finally showed an assortment of green and yellow scarves that smelled strongly of camphor. "Perfect," I said. Could he retrieve us a dozen, quickly?

Dan had reached out earlier that day, and he was more apologetic than anything. "I didn't mean to bring you into a shitshow," he said, and that he wished he'd been in Portugal, but I pushed past that. After the shock in Portugal, I had since realized that given I helped pick up the pieces in Dubai after our first holacracy car-crash I might know better than he did what to do. Perhaps better than anyone at ConsenSys, really. What was the plan? He was close to convincing Shadi to un-resign, he said – I breathed a sigh of relief – and planned to take a lot of the team to Paris to sort out the disagreements.[14] I told him I had an idea or two. My mind, fully cleansed of melatonin and Benadryl, now whirred with the memories of org charts and team structures from my consultant days. "Give me a couple days and I'll have something," I told him.

He nodded appreciation. "And if that doesn't work, we'll just fire some people." It had worked wonders in Dubai.

Back in dupatta gali I was getting sick of the smell of diesel and the sound of honking after fifteen minutes of waiting. I thought to berate the assistant – that was, unfortunately, a common way to treat the shopkeep in Pakistan. But I held back. I had done that recently, on our engagement shoot in Dubai, yelling at the driver for being late and the washerman for messing up my suit. "Start looking for a job," I said while storming out. Who was I becoming, I wondered afterwards. This time I held my tongue.

The next day we managed to keep up the same pace from morning to sunset, and by day three we were feeling energized, the finish line in sight. I might even have some time for sightseeing, I said at breakfast.

"Do you want to see the family factory?" my uncle inquired. Of course – and soon we were traversing the bumpy roads through villages on the outskirts of the city, honking at goats and children to get out of the way. Inside the factory, hundreds of Pakistani women,

---

14 Ah, the days of $1000 Ether. They were few back then but memorable.

many dressed in traditional *shalwar kameez,* hunched over as they put together small circuit boards and bulbs while massive machines pumped water and electromagnetic charges around us. I felt a rush of pride, that our family had created some order out of the economic chaos here. My uncle told us they had given the family electronics company a Japanese name so buyers might assume their products were foreign and high quality. The brand worked like a charm. Here you had to be crafty to make it.

Even despite the boom times, my cousin told me, Pakistan's economy hung by a thread. The government needed to convince the international Financial Action Task Force (FATF) not to add Pakistan to its "grey list" for poor banking controls, which would freeze the country out of the international financial system. The entire potential of the 180 million people rode on the tick-lists of a few Western bureaucrats.[15] Pakistan deserved some of that reputation, as home to the infamous Bank of Credit and Commerce International (BCCI), which had to be shut down by the FBI in the 1980s for helping to launder money for Colombian drug cartels. I only learned the depth of the scandal while in Dubai, where I met more than a few Pakistanis with wealth of mysterious origin. "My dad worked at BCCI," one colleague admitted, "but he wasn't corrupt or anything." *Sure*, I thought.

I had always told myself I was the lucky cousin, born in America with a world of opportunities and no need for such shortcuts. Luck had been my lens on my place in the world: even when my grandparents fled Kashmir for Lahore in the mayhem of 1947, they missed becoming victims of the violence of Partition by the slimmest of hairs. In a chance encounter, a Sikh student of my great-grandfather's warned him to avoid a road where men with machetes lay in wait for any passing Muslims. Between fifty and hundred thousand Muslims would be killed in the next two months trying to escape Jammu, our home city. What were the odds, I wondered, that my grandparents escaped that fate, before lightning struck a second time with a visa to America? I figured I found a winning lottery ticket just by being alive.

---

15 Pakistan did end up on the list a few months later.

Now listening to my cousin I saw the story differently. It had to have been more than luck. There must have been an intuition, a feeling in their bones that made them leave before their neighbors. That little bit of pluck, that craftiness the various people in my family used to find a way, was what I was going to need to make sense out of the chaos in my life. We had to find a way across, and whether the way was straight or crooked didn't matter any more.

# THE TWITTER WARS

*New York, March 2018. ETH:* $754.

Crypto loved – and still loves – Twitter. Legends were made, names cast down, lies exposed. Twitter was where the nerds and the business types interacted and formed the crypto public square, and armies of bots rallied behind self-proclaimed thought leaders who kept predicting Bitcoin going to $100k, $500k, $10m. All you needed was to say you had worked "on Wall Street" or "venture capital" on your Twitter profile, even if all you did was an internship, to acquire your own following of yes-men.

The CryptoKitties failures were still an open wound, and R3, the well funded banker blockchain, went on the attack. Ethereum was effectively dead, they declared in a series of posts and articles. R3 was taking deals from us with renewed confidence and smelled blood in the water.

The Whale tweeted in Ethereum's defense: PegaSys could be the savior by rebuilding Ethereum's code. Even Vitalik, Ethereum's founder himself, was saying good things about us. Another crypto whale chimed in, this time with evidence: a photo of Shadi explaining to Vitalik and JP Morgan's head of blockchain how Ethereum's upgrades should work. Half a million people saw that tweet, he would later tell me.

CoinDesk soon picked up on the story, making the spat front page news. Within ConsenSys, CoinDesk was looked down on as a deeply biased, "Bitcoin maximalist" rag with endless hypocrisy about its own intentions.[16] The site was owned by Digital Currency Group, a powerful investor group which, in the tangled snake that was crypto, also owned the largest media outlet in the space. It was a conflict of interest on the level of if Goldman Sachs owned the Wall Street Journal. A CoinDesk headline was enough to make any shitcoin double or triple ("mooning," as we called it), and it was no surprise to us that DCG leaders were some of the biggest purveyors of shitcoins. Barry Silbert, Coindesk's owner, seemed to harbor a special dislike of Joe and I knew the feeling was mutual. The Bitcoin vs Ethereum hatred had always seemed pointless to me, and I understood a thing or two about pointless hatred, given my parents came from India and Pakistan, two culturally identical countries constantly on the edge of bloodshed. Wars had been fought over less.

Jet lag shook me awake. I caught up as the drama unfolded – the Whale had managed to piss of JP Morgan and R3 in one go – and I knew I had to say something. I had scarcely just put my feet on American soil and good ole capitalism was knocking at my door: cutthroat and relentless.

Bogart was empty when I arrived, still gray in the morning light. There was only the *clacks* of my keyboard as thoughts and words began to flow. I remembered the British journalist, who had turned an honest answer against me. *Tell them what they want to hear.*

Dan arrived not much later, looking tired, himself still operating on Paris time. With his beach-wedding tan and dark facial hair he looked fit for an olive oil commercial. I began unloading my thoughts before suddenly realizing I had barely said hello. "Are you doing alright?" I asked.

"I just got married a couple weeks ago and my startup's on fire, so not really," he replied. Poor Dan, I thought. Two of our best had just quit, and two more refused to work with anyone else. He looked like he was sweating through his hoodie in the middle of Bogart. This was tech, and run-of-the-mill engineers commanded $400,000 at Facebook to sit around and decide the shade of blue for the 'like' button. How were we going to find the replacements we needed?

---

16 Bitcoin maximalists are people who believe blockchain is only useful as a digital currency. Therefore, Bitcoin is the only useful crypto, since it is used the most widely. They tend to denigrate Ethereum as "the king of shitcoins."

For a moment I worried he might quit next, but he was made of sterner stuff. He excused himself to go to the cold brew and kombucha tap and I promised to send him what I was writing.

I looked at the pages I had written, a line by line takedown specifically calling out R3's CTO. Was I ready to step into the arena? I hit publish and Dan and I sat in Bogart wondering what might happen next.

# THE MINISTRY OF TRUTH

*New York, March 2018. ETH:* $534.

The price kept falling. Another two hundred dollars in barely a day. CNBC showed a chart of red lines heading down, our token prospects going with it.

My shitcoin portfolio was now bruised and battered as well. "I'm done day trading," I told Omar as we opened a caffeinated chocolate bar and split it in halves. "I can't look at my coins without wanting to toss my phone." I lost a third of my money before I could even blink. Worse, I doubled down on some bets, stubbornly refusing to give up, and quickly lost another third. The air was not going back in the bubble. I had been too busy trying to pick up the pieces at work to keep an eye on the markets, and now my crypto had been cut down to pittance, especially when compared to the ever expanding wedding bill. I had just finalized the deal with the Pakistani *qawwal* singer I had promised my parents, and was regretting the splurge already. "*Paisay* cash *main dena,*" he asked on the phone. Please pay in cash. I wondered about asking if he accepted Bitcoin.

I didn't even bother logging in to see my losses. Announcements kept coming out, but nothing was stopping the tide of investors trying to escape.

Omar was bucking the trend. I recounted to him how I had seen Kevin O'Leary, the acerbic star of *Shark Tank*, on TV explaining how cryptocurrency was too speculative but he was working to use the technology for 'real assets.' A deal was under wraps, to create tokens that represented ownership in an "iconic New York hotel." It must be the Plaza, I thought.

"Yep," he replied simply. "You're still not interested in joining us, huh?" I thought about his offer. At the pace Eth was falling, another month and Joe would be laying people off. PegaSys was already months behind schedule, and JP Morgan and R3 would take our customers and leave us in the dust.

I still said no to his offer. My pride was hurting me in all kinds of ways.

"What did I do to deserve this?" Dan asked while we walked to a nearby park to discuss the team's travails. "Did I fuck up?" Broken ambitions lay around us like the cracked pavement and bottles littering the area around our park bench.

On the long flight back from Lahore I had put together a few ideas for re-organizing the team after they rejected making anyone a leader. There were tons of experiments out there on how to create a non-traditional company: Spotify, the music mega-startup, worked in groups called "tribes," and other companies used committees.

Joe was not going to give up his billion dollar experiment easily. In his view, we had committed a grave error by trying to introduce hierarchy into the Mesh, and this failure was karmic punishment. What we needed was *more* holacracy. That would be the sweet elixir to save us from the poison of control. He hired consultants and coaches he believed would remedy our ways.

Dan and I sat in the park watching a few parents push their kids on the swings. Mere weeks from his nuptials, Dan had little love to share: he wanted to get rid of the rebels. We were in this to build a unicorn, not listen to holacracy mumbo-jumbo from these coaches: people who talked about innovation but never invented anything, with no skin in the game, who held no edge because they needed no edge. Hours of torturous meetings talking about circles. Every company, every industry, every society was one battle, we surmised on the park bench: between talkers and doers, entrepreneurs and bureaucrats, risk-takers and the risk-averse, and if we listened to the latter we'd still be living in the trees.

I considered if firing them all might be too aggressive. After all, every headline about tech these days castigated us for putting profits over people. Holacracy should have been the cure. But thirty was *Dan's number,* I said, the point when Mesh-iness died and the fighting started.[17] That couldn't happen if we were going to hire hundreds. We both stepped over a dirty, abandoned shoe on our way back. Someone had spray painted *FUCH* in large letters right across from Bogart.

If there was one thing I had learned living in the "no-bosses" world, it was that everyone thought they were the hero of their own story. Inevitably that meant a fight to be on top. *Chief of staff or staff of chiefs,* I remembered David saying. The protestors wanted to take over to become dictators themselves. My tendency to pontificate endlessly about human nature, tech, and the implications of anarchy were suddenly very useful in my job of selling enterprise software.

I told Dan about my lunch with Matt the day before. A tech company is like a zoo – the engineers are the lions and the gorillas, and while the business folks (zookeepers) might be nominally in charge, everyone knows who the real star is. I needed an engineer's perspective.

"If those two don't quit soon, we should fire them," Matt had said, referring to the Australian and another teammate with distaste. He forked a piece of spicy cauliflower from a takeout box. He was attempting a meatless phase, he told me. We had picked up food and were in the lounge of his apartment in Williamsburg, another yuppie fish tank among the many in Brooklyn. We watched the nearly frozen river flow past mile after mile of skyscrapers. Our engineers certainly lived much better than all my zoo animal analogies might indicate.

"It's time for our own little Bastille," he said. "*Ya!*" He made a fake chopping motion with his knife, beheading his bourgeois cauliflower. A guy who thought eating chicken was immoral wanted heads to roll. He told me he thought he could take the lead role to replace them.

What could we blame for these giant egos, I asked Dan: the tech zeitgeist, the blockchain hubris, the anarchy of the Mesh? No one in

17 An allusion to "Dunbar's number," the social theory that says we can only maintain 150 relationships at once, regardless of how many Facebook friends we might have.

ConsenSys ever seemed to believe they were the aggressors. Not me, not Dan, not Matt. We all saw ourselves as the kids who had been picked on in high school, the nerds with thick glasses picked last after someone chucked our retainers over the bleachers. But that picture was no longer accurate either. I kept meeting Meshians undergoing Pygmalion-esque transformations with their newfound wealth, getting LASIK procedures and expensive personal trainers to ditch the wire-rims for salon haircuts and form-fitting clothes.

Society looked at us differently now too: "engineer" on a dating app no longer meant antisocial mouth-breather, but someone who owned a condo and was less of a jerk than the finance bros in downtown Manhattan. That part was true: compared to the lords of finance who had ruled New York and the economy until 2008, we were kinder and more idealistic, even if still mostly white and male (or in my case, white-adjacent). But Tony Montana still whispered in the back of our minds. *First, you get the money*... However muddled ConsenSys' intentions might be, we had to assume we were better than the status quo. What else could we do?

Back in the office, Dan drew one orange circle, then a blue circle, then a green one on the board. "That's you, and that's me." We were going to make sure one of us was involved in every committee, every decision, and from there we'd keep the hordes under control. Hierarchy, without using the word.

"A bit of doublespeak," I said. "I guess that makes us the Ministry of Truth."

We needed a new strategy, too, and we spun around in the cheap plastic chairs trying to think of one as the poorly insulated rooms of Bogart grew colder into the evening. Our new target would be October, at Ethereum's biggest conference, which would give us enough time to clean things up. We were in a race against the clock, with five months to dig ourselves out of this hole. I had already made two trips to Europe for our stock exchange deal, relieved to be away from NYC. The low and gray northern European skies had not put a damper in our presentation, and there seemed to be a chance to sell them more. Tokenizing the stock market would make one hell of a splash. We should have been chastened by the first failure, but a few bumps in the road were not going to change who we were: young men in a hurry. We would do things our way.

Someone texted me that CoinDesk had picked up on my article: ConsenSys had penned a "sarcastic" response to R3's attack. I bristled at the description.

Crypto Twitter would not let me go easily, either. There were too many people watching from the sidelines, eager for a fight. Then finally, a challenge: the most popular podcast in crypto, 11FS, asked R3's CTO Richard Brown and I to come on for a debate. Brown replied instantly, gunslinger-like: "Any place. Any time."

"Oh no," I said, turning my screen to show Dan. I was playing with the big boys, and they wanted to settle this *mano a mano*. Brown had twenty years experience on me. Was I going to stand up for PegaSys or become another one of the crypto guys full of talk?

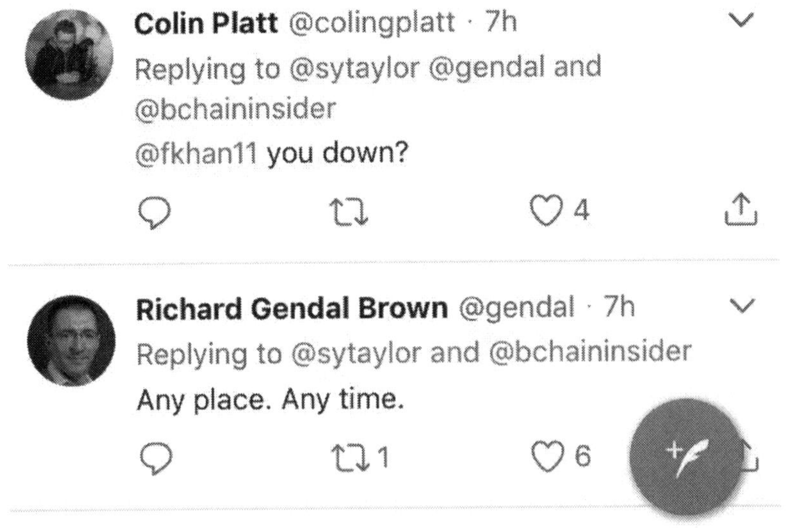


I typed and re-typed a response, unsure what to say. "Wait a few months, then you do it," Dan said. We'd rebuild and hit back harder. The Ministry of Truth was going into overdrive.

# CONFESSIONS OF A BLOCKCHAIN HIT MAN

*New York JFK airport, March 2018. ETH:* $525.

I collapsed into my seat on the plane, relieved that this would be my third and final trip across the Atlantic to see our stock exchange client. Emirates called asking if I wanted to upgrade to business class, and I bothered asking no one's permission to say yes. I was the rainmaker now, winning the blue-chip clients we needed to keep climb out of our hole. The client wanted me sharp, not half asleep.

Saira voiced her resentment. We had less than four months left. She asked if my being an absent fiance would translate to being an absent father. That stung, but I lied and swore this would be the last trip. Our contract ended soon, but the client hungered for more and that might birth a more lucrative deal for PegaSys. My career hit apex on winning this project, and the bruises from Ether's price could not hold me back yet. I kicked off my shoes in satisfaction. Maybe I'd sit next to that old partner who called me a 3 out of 10. The redemption story memoirs are made of.

We entered the giant glass box and felt the hum of the energy inside. Employees walked up and down a million glass staircases like an MC Escher painting in perpetual movement. "*Ja*, the team is very excited," the German sponsor told us. "You've really built them up."

Our first two workshops swept them off their feet, but that had been before the crash turned serious. Ritesh's charts of Ethereum easily turned the seventy five German bankers' faces turned from dour cynicism to buzzy intrigue. The top director thanked us eagerly in his introductions then, praising us as the "Andressen Horowitz of blockchain." The fear we were going to disrupt their business brought them to us, but the chance at unimaginable profit opened their ears. Money spoke volumes.

Stock exchanges are essentially middlemen. Trillions of dollars of value - actual trillions, not made up blockchain trillions - change hands daily between dozens of intermediaries, including custodians and clearinghouses to securities depositories who track every transaction. Stocks still traded as though they were pieces of paper. And that's why a blockchain could revolutionize their business.

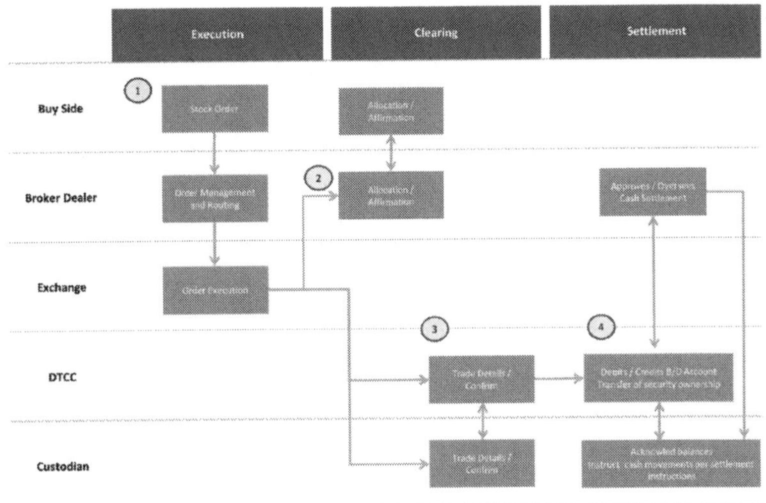


I zoomed in on a chart of Ethstats, a website that tracks Ethereum in real time, its display a dizzying mix of numbers and graphs on the activity of thousands of computers on the network.

"This is the blockchain," I said with a satisfying level of aplomb. I stuck my hands in my hoodie pockets - a zip-up over a dress shirt, a signal for the CEO of tomorrow - while we all watched the screen buzz with updates.

The director asked me if blockchain was "real" anywhere yet. I crossed my arms across my chest, pausing before mentioning our work in Dubai. The Germans nodded along to that: to them, Dubai was a synonym for futuristic. "You guys are incredibly profitable for a startup," he said at the end of our first day. I nodded along, slightly confused.

"Where did he hear that?" I whispered to Ritesh.

"Oh, I told him," he said casually while doodling dollar signs on his notebook. "I mean we raised $300M in the Gnosis token sale. Even Andressen would get on his knees for that. I should tell them Lubin was classmates with Bezos, too. He'll be richer than him soon."

It was a misrepresentation. Ritesh was gunning harder than ever to unseat R3, our bigger, bank-funded competitor who had their claws deep into our client. I did not feel good about this. We needed to earn their trust before showing our cards so openly.

"You know R3 is a no-coins platform," Ritesh told the director after our second session. "You want to invest in the crazy nerds, not the ex-bankers." Ritesh twirled a finger in a circle by his ear. He was giving them more of ConsenSys' marketing: when the web started, the weirdos with wrinkled khakis and glasses led the revolution, not the corporate guys driving Benzes. If blockchain truly meant a new Internet, Ethereum and ConsenSys were the Bill Gates and Steve Jobs equivalents with pocket protectors and glasses fresh out of college that had to fight the Rolex-wearing incumbents.

The analogy rang true, despite Ritesh's clumsy pitch. Corporations did not take the Internet seriously early on. In 1995, when Bill Gates published his technobabble book *The Road Ahead* on the future of tech, the *New York Times* offered its disdain. "The Internet's future may be dimmer than expected," they wrote. (Some are more behind than others.) That arrogance from the powers that be was how a dork named Jeff Bezos built a trillion dollar company on the back of bookstores and malls who underestimated him over and over until it was too late. The narrative shifted. Weird nerds crowding around transformed into a positive. I was sure our client had read about Cellarius and our other oddball moonshots, but a project like that puzzled some and smelled like money to others. Weird, to paraphrase Gordon Gekko, was good.

I debated helping Ritesh on his pitch. To shill or not to shill, that was the question. I recalled the first speeches of Joe's I watched on YouTube. We would bank the unbanked, and bring identity to the slums. Now we pitched slots in the casino. A sudden pang of guilt hit me. PegaSys needed this but I would wait for our next meeting

Now I arrived for our final workshop and regretted not seizing the moment with Ritesh. Without the charts to back us up we carried none of the swagger we did in our first two meetings. Ritesh promised we could win an add-on deal with help from a fellow Meshian, but now we were waiting outside their glass box and our speaker was late. "This guy has tech firepower like an aircraft carrier," Ritesh said, pulling out his vape from his suit pocket and taking a puff. "You like that analogy, you warmongering American? Client is gonna love this."

I was feeling anxious. The Meshian in question was another Dolphin Man, one of the gray-haired hires looking to live his startup dreams, this time a banking executive who wanted to help banks manage their crypto. He walked in and rubbed his gray stubble. When I saw him at conferences in the past, he seemed confident, but now he seemed apprehensive.

Ritesh picked up on it. "Don't look so nervous man," he said. "If you mess up this presentation, I'm going to make you name your firstborn Ritesh Is My Real Daddy." We filed into the conference room.

An executive at the exchange came and shook my hand. They were so convinced about blockchain, he said, he was quitting his top post to lead a fully independent team focused on "DLT." This was great news. DLT stood for *distributed ledger technology*, a pseudonym that R3 and IBM had taught corporates that seemed more legitimate than *blockchain* or *crypto*. "You all must be scrambling to hire people as fast as you can," he said pleasantly.

"You'd be surprised," I said, thinking about all of our latest firings.

Ritesh and I scribbled ideas on the flipboards with our new banker friends, warming them up for the finale. The directors agreed there were many opportunities for them to get into crypto. There might be a road to victory after all.

"I'm excited to be here," Ritesh's Mesh colleague said as he took his turn on stage. An interminable silence followed, his expression frozen. *What's going on?* I mouthed to Ritesh. He shrugged, unconcerned.

Our speaker started to explain cryptography – like a special pen that only you have, he said. There was a big difference between using Coinbase and a Ledger. He stopped again. "Well, I'll just skip all this boring stuff." He then thanked the audience. I glanced at the clock. He had barely spoken for fifteen minutes. My German looked at me confused as the disappointed bankers filed out.

I did my best to salvage our work. The executive admitted they had already invested significantly with R3. "To be honest," my German explained to me, "I sometimes wonder if enterprise blockchain makes any sense."[18] Questions ran through my mind where these sudden doubts came from. Was it the decline in the price, or today's letdown? In the coming weeks I pushed to explore the ideas we discussed, but the chance of a deal clung to life support. With the death of easy money in crypto, probing eyes poked holes in every idea. Had I deluded myself all along on our chances? I sported neither the gray hair nor Rolex that a senior banker needed to see to believe. My only reassurance was that I might end up keeping my promises to Saira after all.

"What the heck happened in there?" asked Ritesh, his face cracking with confusion as he threw his suit jacket on the bar stool next to him. We had reconvened in a German-themed bar around the corner replete with lederhosen and schnitzel. Ritesh asked the waitress for their biggest pitcher.

"I don't want to tell them my spoke's secrets," our Mesh colleague explained. "We worked hard on this." The realization struck us hard. He had a secret sauce he would share with no one – not the stock exchange, who might steal his ideas, and not even us. "Not my job to make you successful, but I did what I could."

Joe constructed an incubator that birthed endless startups and each one only cared about its own ends. Nine hundred people with nine hundred ideas. I felt blindsided by the obviousness, and yet somehow kept being surprised how quickly Meshiness went out the window. PegaSys was dying for all the help we could get, but relying on ConsenSys had backfired.

"Unbelievable," Ritesh said, waving his hands. He was starting to get mad, rapping his vape on the wooden bar to try and order a drink. "You shit your goddam pants," he whispered.

"What did you say?" the speaker asked, puffing his Patagonia-clad chest out a bit.

---

18 He had something of a point. Corporate blockchains were a bit paradoxical: decentralization conflicted with the idea of putting large corporations in charge. If a competitor cheated, that fraud that was now permanent. And if they reversed the transactions of the blockchain, by making it editable, did that not defeat the purpose? We tried to avoid these types of circular questions as much as we could.

"You shit your goddam pants!" Ritesh let out suddenly. Heads around us snapped around. I held out a hand on Ritesh's shoulder.

"Tell your dad to calm the hell down," the bartender said. I noted silently the lack of resemblance to the foot-shorter Ritesh. Racist asshole.

"We should have known," Ritesh said, one hand under his chin a few minutes later after our colleague left. He took a long swig from his stein. "So much for PegaSysCoin, huh?" he asked remorsefully.

"You know about the token?" I asked. Dan and I had scarcely said a word.

"Don't have to be a genius to guess," he sighed. He saw the obvious: everyone grabbed the money while they could.

We commiserated at the bar over our bludgeoned shitcoins. He'd been wrecked – "rekt," in cryptospeak – there too, losing tens of thousands the last few weeks just as I had. Only he had a kid to feed.

"You and me," Ritesh said, now despondent, "we're just lowly consulting guys. We weren't meant to be the Bezos and Lubin guys. We just bill by the hour while someone else makes the real money." He took a swig of his beer, left a few bills on the bar, and told me he was going back to the hotel.

I mulled over the day's events. We should have snatched the client from our competitor while crypto still boomed. I knew Jared pressured Ritesh to get a deal done and now he was coming home empty handed with a thrashing likely in store. I felt a moment of sympathy. To be a middle-aged Indian guy in tech is to be replaceable, a commodity, a pebble on the beach. It was happening now to him, as it had to my father, and someday would to me. I myself threw away most of the thousands of Indian-sounding resumes I received before even reading them, too busy to sort through a billion person haystack. There were just too damn many of us. Ritesh had likely learned the urgency of *now* over the years, that the best thing was to swing for the fences because some of us might only get one at-bat. ConsenSys handed me lottery tickets and I tossed them looking for bigger scores. I needed to scratch the one in my hands.

I fought the feeling of frustration as I stepped off the L train in Brooklyn. On the other side, commuters into Manhattan crowded so thickly I thought some might fall off, like penguins from an iceberg. Now that the Germany deal looked doubtful, we were back to pitching: today, the CTO of one of the largest banks in Europe.

But I was sick of talking to banks. All my days were spent chasing the big money in finance. Nearly a year after joining ConsenSys, I had yet to lift a finger to help the downtrodden that I was supposedly here to save. They were invisible to us.

She sat with us in one of our makeshift meeting rooms, the walls covered with Post-it notes from brainstorming sessions. *Equanty. Liquanimity. dExchange*. The cardboard "door" flapped around as usual in the drafty room, its staples coming loose. She found it charming, she told us in her eloquent Spanish accent. Even with the disarray in the office, our pitch landed well.

After work I stared at the wall of my East Village apartment as it turned from orange to red in the evening light and thought over the previous days. I was not alone in my frustration, but I certainly stuck out. The Mesh felt the anguish of the price falling each day and had come with hard questions for Joe on a Town Hall only the day before.

How were we serving our mission to rebuild society when our first multi million dollar deal was with the oil industry?[19]

Amare, the mysterious "Chief Anarchy Officer" I had learned of via darq slaq, ripped into how such a decision had been made.

Who approved or disapproved of these deals? Who chose if profits took priority over principles?

No bosses was already a facade, he declared. A shadow hierarchy emerged while we slept. There had been a secret corporate takeover of ConsenSys.

Once upon a time I would have rolled my eyes. But now I saw red as I listened to the India team lead brag about his connections in the government and how we were going to make millions in the country.

I had gone to India last month to visit my father's family in between flights to Germany. The India team lead, an ex-World Bank official, claimed the priority was social impact, and yet my cousin asked me why

19 This was Komgo, the deal around which rumors had been swirling in Portugal.

ConsenSys' blockchain trainings were priced so high only the richest of the rich could afford them. My feelings of Meshiness curdled all along the eighteen hour train ride back to Delhi.

"Is that what we're doing this for?" I said abruptly. "Just to make money?" The warmth ran from my face to my arms as I found myself standing right in front of Joe and a thousand of my coworkers. "Why do we subsidize a project for the oil companies but want to make profits in India?"

Joe, laughing a moment earlier about such easy money, seemed taken aback at my outburst. He looked to his right at the India lead, who bore holes in me with eyes usually meant for watching the neighbor's dog shit on the front lawn. I suddenly felt very alone.

What the hell was I doing?

Part of me wanted to test Joe. Was this the same Joe who used to knock a few back and then riff about blockchain for philanthropy? Or was the secret hierarchy going to fire me as soon as the meeting ended?

The invisible questions hung before me until Joe finally spoke. "We'll add some scholarships," he said quietly. I nodded my head, retreating into the corner. For now, that was enough.

Soon the sun set and I sat alone in the darkness of my apartment. The feeling of hypocrisy crept up on me. I kept demanding principled leadership from Joe while chasing profits myself.

Was I here to build or to throw stones?

I wanted to confess to someone.

I opened my laptop and started writing an email. *I've got an idea,* I told an editor at TechCrunch, a popular tech blog I wrote for in the past, *about how blockchain is being misused. We're building highly secure tech to help banks move around stocks faster, and yet no one is thinking how we'll make digital currency available to people who don't even have smartphones...*

# A LEADER OF THOUGHTS

*"Stayin' alive, stayin' alive."* – The Bee Gees

*New York City, April 2018*. ETH: $435

On the Internet, no one knows you're a dog.

That's what I told Dan as I tried to convince him to write an article on the sociology of tech bubbles, a topic neither of us was an expert in. That didn't matter: a keyboard is the best disguise.[20]

I told him I'd spoken on three panels about blockchain in the last few months: UPenn, Columbia, and Williams, my *alma mater*. I'd even paid a visit to the *Wall Street Journal* to teach their journalists about crypto. I snapped photos of the newsroom and the walls of Pulitzers and regaled them with my stories. One student came up to me at the UPenn conference asking how it felt to work at the "Goldman Sachs of crypto." (I asked if it was a compliment or insult.) I realized afterward my fellow panelists were all talking heads, rather than anyone who worked in the trenches. If we were more qualified than these "thought leaders," we were making a mistake not trying to get our names in lights to promote PegaSys.

Our problem was, we were both nobodies. Zero plus zero is still, sadly, zero. Zeroes would have a hard time beating JP Morgan and IBM at once.

20 A popular Internet meme for the unfamiliar – a smiling dog with his paws on the keyboard, likely typing out a blog post.

But that's where some startup pluck came in. Amid our many failures, here's three hacks we learned and you can use to yank on your own bootstraps:

I. Be Your Own Hype Man
II. Look Smart, Even If You're Not
III. Magic

## I. Be Your Own Hype Man

What to write? Dan and I hunted for inspiration as well as a space to sit in Bogart, more crowded than ever as we continued to hire despite the downturn and the incoming event of the year: Blockchain Week, a string of conferences that last year had triggered the summer's bull market.

We navigated through Bogart, past our neighbor who yelled at me last week to pipe it down, *the baby's trying to sleep for God's sake.* Room 26 was the home of the artists formerly known as the marketing team, but decided "marketing" was too old school and preferred the new-age *catalyst.* A slacker vibe permeated throughout, with the pirate flag and piles of granola bars, with the occasional interruption from Max, who had a severe case of Tourette's and sometimes had to yell *FUCKING BITCH!*

"Looks almost done," I commented to the mustachioed fellow in a newsboy cap who spun 3-D images around his massive monitor like a Rubik's cube. Joe hired an architect to design our new office being built across the street.

The architect complained to me that Joe kept asking him to find ways to fit in a squash court. Our spending was out of control, but blowing money was in style, a signal that your founders were thinking big enough. WeWork, the office-sharing startup, had just raised over $4 billion and was reportedly looking for more funding from the banks. SoftBank had raised a $100 billion fund bigger than half the VC world combined. The VC dam looked ready to burst with money.

"We should try to impress some VCs," Dan said, as we talked about SoftBank. Our dream investor, Fred Wilson, loved blockchain. "But why would he care about anything we say?"

I remembered my lessons with the journalist in Dubai. *Tell them what they want to hear.* That's what I had done with my article on social impact, and TechCrunch published my piece with barely an edit. A friend from the FCC wrote me: he had forwarded it to a commissioner, and now she wanted to meet me. The people who regulated the Internet itself wanted to see me in DC in a month. What could go wrong? Dan had an inkling for an idea, a social theorist he knew Fred Wilson liked. He started scribbling on the board.

Our ploys worked even faster than we expected. Dan's article went out into the wild and Fred himself was soon tweeting about it, plugging our genius to his 600,000 followers and dozens of other investors. Dan was as excited as a kid who makes his first sale of lemonade. Banks and exchanges may have scattered in crypto chaos, but we might yet feel the warmth of a VC's embrace.

## II. Look Smart, Even If You're Not

There are two tricks to look smart in tech. One is to make grand prognostications. The other is to shit on people making grand prosnotications. Luckily, crypto is loaded with the former, a lesson I would soon learn.

I stared at my new watch waiting for cell coverage to come back on another crowded subway ride to Brooklyn. It was a gift from Saira for my birthday. At first I scoffed at such an outdated gift. But now as the second hand spun around I found myself engrossed, an antiquated analog turned refreshing reminder of life outside of a screen. Around and around it went, perfectly in tune. I wore it everyday. My cell phone ticked back to life and I went back to scrolling.

A New York Times piece caught my eye: *A Blockchain Building in Bushwick.* Omar and his co-founder smiled at me in front of the unmistakable bestickered door of 49 Bogart. The picture looked big enough to be front page.

I texted him congratulations. "Seen the comments online?" he asked. Cynicism poured in about "blockchain bros," but we both dismissed it. Barely a few years earlier America had Occupied Wall Street striving to break the financial industry's death grip on the economy. Now tech stood ready to slay the banking dragon, and they were mad? Big Tech would take that crown if we "blockchain bros" did not. What can you do, we said. People hate change.

He was on the road for the moment, he said, pitching major real estate developers in the Midwest, followed by more pitches in Dubai. Real estate on the blockchain appeared less speculative than crypto, and the *Times* agreed. Deals must be flowing in, I suggested, and I was sure he would win some. He always commanded a room so easily.

Explaining blockchain every day to real estate people wore him out, he told me. Could I help him out with something? There was a conference coming up at Wharton, and he needed a replacement. I said yes. The NYT wasn't writing about me, but at least I could ride his coattails.

I walked into the conference hall a week later and looked up. A huge banner for Strategy&, my old firm, hung overhead. They were the lead sponsor. How far I had come.

My panel started and I listened to my fellow speakers. They could barely find the breath to explain the blockchain pilots making the news today but that I had already failed. I knew the results, because I pitched these companies everyday, and knew which were babel for the press. Good news travels fast, but bad news is a secret until a journalist gets a scoop: then it's a headline. *It's all about blockchain, not Bitcoin*, my WASP-y co-panelist declared as my eyes rolled like a bowling ball in the gutter. Panels like this set out who was in the know, and the press then quoted these "experts" to churn out news. That horribly muddled perspective became the pseudo-facts consumed by the undiscerning public.

One lawyer tried his best to explain the legal implications of tokens and securities. I doubted anyone would figure it out: an infinite number of lawyers typing randomly on keyboards would likely yield a memo that said, "We have no idea, and the regulators won't know for five years." Google and Oracle had been suing each other for ten years in one case then going to the Supreme Court. A bunch of septuagenarians who could barely use an iPhone would decide the future of the backbone of the Internet. If we had to wait for the law to figure things out, most of the startups working on blockchain would be long dead. "Why can't startups play by the rules?" media critics asked, forgetting that no one knew what the "rules" meant for new technologies like crypto in the first place – not even the regulators, and definitely not Congress.

The stories about tracking lettuce on the blockchain wore thin. Time to shake things up a little, I thought.

"To be honest," I said, "anyone who is talking about blockchain and has never used Ethereum simply does not know what they're talking about." The presenter smiled at me but her eyes betrayed total confusion. I was going way off script.

I talked about the confusion my German client faced and how IBM built its massive blockchain project with Wal-Mart to track the food supply, but now Wal-Mart had more control than ever. How was that any better than the status quo?

I thought the cynicism might make me a pariah, but the MBAs stormed me afterward, now even more excited by my no-bullshit tone. I passed my card out by the dozens as they asked which startups to apply to for internships. These bright-eyed, bushy-tailed recruits came in two flavors – the Bitcoin stoners or the ex-bankers looking to jump to tech. To both I was living the dream. "Don't join any ding-dong projects," I said. They laughed at my terminology. Imagine the laughs if I told them about Spankchain.

The presenter handed me a small trophy as a thank you as I left. I turned it over on the subway home, laughing as I realized it had Omar's name on it. I had joined the ranks of the "thought leaders" to discover most had no real thoughts of their own. I found freedom in righteous fury. But even with the trophy for my "thought leadership," I knew I was still an idiot.

Fake it til you make it, they say. And if you don't make it, just hope no one notices you're a fake!

## III. Magic

All the marketing stuff is well and good, but at the end of the day no one pays attention unless you've got something special.

PegaSys had been grinding out code, already more than 50,000 lines of it. We were making progress but toiling in obscurity. When Vitalik started talking about the need to put more effort into Ethereum's software,

I jumped in to note PegaSys now had more engineers contributing to Ethereum than anyone, including the 2.0 upgrade.[21] I grabbed Dan by the hoodie sleeve when Vitalik tweeted his approval. No matter what happened now, I was legit: anointed by Ethereum Jesus himself.

21 The Ethereum 2.0 software upgrade would take us from fifteen transactions a second – not enough to operate a simple game like CryptoKitties – to a thousand times that and make Ethereum a better payments network than even Visa or Mastercard. Additional work would upgrade from the cryptography that was using more electricity than Belgium to something more environmentally friendly.

The other magic we needed was our equity. Now was the time to ask Joe for the numbers. Two of PegaSys' close competitors had raised over $50M each, even after the downturn, and with the right paperwork we'd create the same value out of thin air.

The price of Ether had stopped its free fall, bouncing hard off $378 and then coming up above $500 and beyond, and we could read the optimism in Joe's face when we met him. ConsenSys was at 1200 employees, a ship too big to turn and sailing full steam ahead. Plus, half the Mesh was rich. Not as rich as before, but still rich. ConsenSys took a respite from the days of testy town halls and pivoted back to dream mode.

We'd been trying to meet him for weeks, but with hundreds of employees now in twenty offices around the world, he had become nearly impossible to access. I spoke to him more when I lived in Dubai than when I sat two seats away from him in Bogart. He spent more time on planes than in that chair now, and when back there was an air of exhaustion. The bags under his eyes drooped just a little more. This time he looked more energized than usual: Consensus, the biggest conference in blockchain, was only a few days away and promised to bring the world's attention back to crypto. That would bring attention to the technological progress we made the last few months since the CryptoKitties hiccups, and prices would undoubtedly follow.

"Have you guys seen Braid yet?" he asked us, his bare arms crossed. Braid was a movie ConsenSys helped create with the first ever token sale for a movie, long before I joined. Joe had told the director, Mitzi, we could change filmmaking forever, and get rid of the predatory studios. Now, more than a year later it had been released. "The reviews are bad, but I liked it! Mitzi is a little crazy, but I appreciate that."

The genuine enthusiasm oozed from his pores. He had made a billion dollar bet on humanity, but the most exciting thing in his life was funding an indie horror movie. No wonder half the Mesh worshipped him still. These were the moments I doubted myself for doubting him.

We made small talk about my upcoming wedding. "Brown girls," I said, "are a little wedding crazy." He chuckled.

We turned back to the question of money. Joe agreed to doing a raise, but questioned why we wanted to be so traditional. Silicon Valley investors posed new problems. Ethereum offeredan infinitely better way to raise funds than depending on some capitalist shark. Hadn't we just shown that with Braid?

One gaping hole remained: the terms of the deal. If ConsenSys "incubated" your idea, Joe automatically owned a large percentage – but the exact terms always remained unclear. To any VC, that ambiguity posed an insurmountable hangup. In the old days Joe would have done this himself, but now he had a dozen minions at his summons. A sharp new lawyer he had hired would handle it. "Giovanni will help you get your term sheet," Joe reassured us.

Giovanni did not help us get our term sheet.

"Damn this Uber surge," he said, walking into the post-it smothered conference room. "I never take the subway," he explained smugly, wiping designer glasses. "Just gross." To a born New Yorker like Dan, he might as well have said he'd come from breakfast with the Klan.

He crossed his arms and gave us a litany of challenges. He joined ConsenSys from a white shoe law firm, where his job had been to negotiate the fine print of derivatives deals. That meant he was a black belt in the minutiae of how to financially screw you over. Why now, he kept asking.

That we did not want to reveal. Dan and I had seen Joe's choices since the prices began falling, and he was still giving the greenlight for anything. The latest announcement for a new project, ConsenSys Space, was bigger than anything that had come before. The Mesh was heading for a new frontier – the skies above. Asteroids carried untold wealth in minerals – platinum and other rare metals that would be worth trillions on Earth. Untold riches sat there, unexploited. Only a crazed billionaire could fund any pioneering attempts to retrieve them. Luckily…

Joe was now deep in negotiations with a company known for satellite tracking and mining asteroids. There were no regulators in space, and a token for the heavenly metals could rake in billions. No, his ambitions were not coming down to Earth any time soon. That was the nail in the coffin for Dan and I: we expected ConsenSys to hit bankruptcy one day, and, by then, we wanted to be long gone from depending on Joe.

But Joe had his own reasons to want to stop us. BlockApps, the spoke Joe's own son Kieran built, now was fully separated from ConsenSys.

Kieran started one of the first spokes at ConsenSys, before Pantheon, but the story turned Oedipal over conflicts on deals. That had to sting, and so ConsenSys would want to hold on tight. We were at Giovanni's mercy.

But Dan and I had a few tricks in our hoodie pockets. Omar was working on a deal for Meridio. We could learn from him and ask for the same terms. But until that closed, we were stuck in the ConsenSys nest. Our magic had run out.

I researched *Braid* that night and Joe was right: the reviews were abysmal. The plot caught my eye: two lawbreaking women who rob their wealthy friend, a schizophrenic heir living in a fantasy world they had dreamt up together as children. Ironic, I thought. But who was living in the illusion?

# CHUCK NORRIS MINES BITCOIN

*New York, May 2018. ETH:* $735.

The Hilton Midtown is a nondescript, perhaps even unattractive concrete slab nestled between Sixth and Seventh Aves in Manhattan. But inside, ten thousand crypto aficionados strained together to push a narrative: that crypto was changing from bubble to mainstream.

This was Consensus, the biggest conference of the year.

"Get your popcorn ready," Omar said, as we jostled for a seat in the main hall amongst the thousands of attendees. "Time to teach IBM the fear of God." The *God* in this case was Amazon Web Services, the most powerful and terrifying company in tech, and Joe was about to come on stage to announce they were joining hands with ConsenSys in a new partnership. After two painful months of doubters around every corner, Joe was coming to strike back against our rivals.

Omar fidgeted next to me, looking antsy. He had wanted to make an announcement as well, but his team worked around the clock only for the Plaza deal to fall through a few weeks prior. I knew behind the nonplussed exterior he was smarting. After the *Times* article everyone expected big things, but so far he was empty handed. It had to hurt to see others in the limelight. "Rome wasn't tokenized in a day," I had told him.

We all feared for the worst in Feburary when Bitcoin had crumbled to $8,000, but it roared back to $14,000, and even now it was worth five times more than last year's conference. Swarms of Midtown financiers descended on all sides and ConsenSys and our competitors elbowed each other like merchants in a bazaar for a moment of the bankers' attention.

Everyone blared their latest deal, and the prospect of breakthroughs heralded the potential for a new golden age.

The weirdos showed up in droves too, much to the delight of the attendees and the press.. The NYT took careful note: "Seth Kaye has hot pink hair and Pokémon stuffed animals on his shoulder," their article opened. There are no Bitcoins to hold, no Ether to pass from hand to hand, and so the spectacle of pink hair or the three bright orange and green Lamborghinis revving their engines outside (I saw them and fondly remembered the rides with Hani to KFC) was as real as crypto got. But beyond the costumes, cameras, and other circus acts crypto really was spreading deeper and deeper into the mainstream's consciousness. Even Kanye was tweeting about it.

Within minutes of Joe starting to speak I checked the news. The first article about the partnership was already out, front and center on CNBC. I leaned over to show Omar. The coronation was on schedule.

But Coindesk ran this conference, and as usual, they were not going to make it easy on Joe or Ethereum. After the announcement, which was making headlines in the financial press, he would have to "debate" Jimmy Song, a well-known Bitcoin maximalist. Amber Baldet, the former head of blockchain at JP Morgan, would attempt to moderate. She was a purple haired cyberpunk turned banker who believed in the decentralized promise.

Jimmy took the mic and the air in the room with it. I knew him only as the author of the boringly titled "Programming Bitcoin," but his obscene manner of speaking was nearly as jarring as seeing this tall Asian man in a ten gallon hat and big leather boots. He attacked immediately, describing Amber's new work as "buzzword bingo" and Joe's projects as "magic fairy dust." The audience jolted awake. Someone cheered loudly at his words. Jimmy went on for several minutes, ravishing his chance to trash Ethereum. "Just use a database!" he shouted. I strained my eyes to see Joe from my vantage point thirty rows back, his broad shoulders clearly stiff and still. Jimmy stopped only short of slapping him in the face. He added later in a parting shot after the debate that "the only reason dApps exist is to raise money from gullible people or from greedy FOMO [fear of missing out] people." Another swipe. "That's essentially what the Ethereum platform has done, and honestly a lot of what your companies have done."

Joe sat there, monk-like, taking the blows. At last he spoke. "I'll bet you any amount of Bitcoin that you're wrong," he said finally. He would bet Ethereum would have tens of thousands of users on its apps before long. Joe knew that the failure of so many tokens cast doubt blockchain. But he was not surprised; rather he expected it. The Internet, AI, or VR all went through bubbles. That was part of the hype cycle.[22] Things would come back. Faith would be rewarded.

Hoops and hollers leapt up from the audience. An *unlimited* bet? A man who burned $100M a year to fund ConsenSys would not shy away from putting more on the table. I felt a touch of pride. Even Jimmy, known to have his own crypto-millions, seemed taken aback. He knew, as everyone else did, that Joe could call a billion dollar bluff. But Jimmy took the bet.

Amber recovered from the daze of watching the two men standoff. She asked if they would shake for the deal. "We can sort it out on Twitter,"

22 I am not inferring his thoughts here: Joe himself said bubbles are "healthy" numerous times on TV and in articles. He usually added that they brought money and attention to accelerate the good ideas.

Joe said. I looked at Dan nearby, who shared my expression of amazement. We had always known Joe's dedication, but this was on a different planet. The higher we flew, the more Ethereum's doubters multiplied: the blockchain rivals, the Eth killers, the Bitcoin maximalists, Wall Street, the coin papers. One day they would bring Joe down. But for now, our gladiator had risen from the dust and fought back.

Back at our exhibition booth, I was fighting my own battles.

"You know, you don't want to use Ethereum! It's not safe. Do you want some mining pool in China handling your money?" A middle aged banker stood in front of our conference booth, shitting on us with no subtlety. The slick hair and arrogant demeanor jumped out to me: David Rutter, the CEO of R3, our rival that was everywhere at once. This asshole, who had raised hundreds of millions of dollars, would stoop so low to camp out in front of our booth and steal customers right before our very eyes. An Asian man listened to his diatribe with a confused face. I started to see shades of red off the visible light spectrum.

"Excuse me," I said, struggling to be heard over the noise. I raised my voice. "Could you insult us somewhere else?"

He looked me up and down, unimpressed. Even in my best startuppy getup, a blue blazer and tan jeans, I looked like roadkill to him. "Sure, pal." R3 took their clients to five star restaurants for dinner while I was passing out Snickers bars for attention. He turned away, putting his arm around the now more confused fellow and towing him away.

I wiped a bit of sweat from my face. Wave after wave of people were shoving their way through the exhibition crowds, fighting to grab swag or shake hands with a crypto-celebrity or see crypto bros do dumb stuff. I manned our booth, talking to everyone in earshot. We wanted honey and now we were in the hive.

My legs were tired from standing. At 7am I had printed hundreds of copies of flyers about PegaSys and ran here, arriving to a line that already snaked around the block. The pandemonium was heartening: PegaSys was crawling out of the grave just as things picked up. The conference hype could slingshot us towards autumn, when Pantheon's launch would be our chance to strike back. Rutter would hardly know what hit him. The thought put a little more spring in my step.

I walked through the floor, past a CNBC camera filming an interview and R3 and IBM's superyacht sized displays. The question of if David Rutter printed his own flyers wandered to my mind and I felt confident he did not. I eavesdropped on IBM's army of suits. "Did you see our Super Bowl ad?" one of them asked me. I shook my head. People in tech knew not to bring knives to gunfights. Instead they bought bazookas, and everybody killed each other.

I nodded as I passed a gaggle of ConsenSys employees doing the rounds. We had added 400 more people since Portugal, now topping 1000 employees. The floodgates reopened and I was interviewing people day and night, often those decades more experienced or infinitely more knowledgeable about cryptography and software. Crazy felt like an understatement. if announcements didn't do it, Hires would. Numbers were Joe's weapon of choice: *keep going.*

Back at the booth, another attendee walked up and asked for a t-shirt. Omar shrugged an apology. "Explain to me again how the Ethereum Virtual Machine works?" the inquirer asked me. After a few months in PegaSys I absorbed enough of Shadi's brain that I rattled off such explanations without thinking.[23] Smart contracts, Turing complete, byzantine algorithms. This was my lingo now.

---

23 For those interested, the Ethereum Virtual Machine is like a simulated computer (hence, "virtual machine") inside of the Ethereum protocol software, including the version PegaSys built. What the EVM did was process any type of code written in Ethereum's available programming languages – the most popular known as Solidity, which is very similar to JavaScript and therefore easily learned by tens of millions of software developers – and translate it into a series of simple instructions. That simplified translation was easily digestible to all participants in the Ethereum network, which made the EVM very elegant in that all participants could essentially run the same software program simultaneously. This is where the Ethereum founders came up with the phrase "world computer." The EVM is also Turing complete, a phrase in computer science that meant a programming language could perform any operation, meaning Ethereum, unlike R3 or IBM's software, could be used for far more than just finance and was capable of doing anything you could imagine.

A pair of tall, athletic men walked by as we went back to our perch at the booth. "The Winklevii," Omar said, grabbing my shoulder. I waved and the nearest one waved back.

"Oh shit," he mouthed. This was web 2.0 and web 3.0 colliding – the Winklevoss twins, most famous for suing Mark Zuckerberg and claiming he stole their idea for Facebook. The ensuing story became the movie *The Social Network*, which had let the world know that nerds did not always play nice, a lesson we were reminded of daily. The lives of young tech millionaires had been a hot story for Hollywood for a few years now. Now the Winklevoss twins were writing their own sequel.

The Winklevii had taken the $60 million they won from Zuckerberg and used Bitcoin to turn it into billions. Their crypto exchange, Gemini, ran slick ads all over the conference, painting themselves a notch above shitcoin salesmen. A guy wearing a suit with fabric made out of fake dollar bills walked by them, wearing B-shaped sunglasses and a shirt saying "Chuck Norris mines Bitcoin!" The Winklevii smiled and walked past. Crypto rolled right past its identity crisis: half joke, half revolution. They might laugh, but they knew these cartoons were making them richer by the minute.

I recalled our meeting the day prior with Coinbase. Gemini's massive rival was the investor darling of crypto, lauded by Silicon Valley for its focus and rewarded with an eight billion dollar valuation. They were the Jekyll to ConsenSys' Hyde.[24] Even over evening drinks our Coinbase counterparts seemed buttoned up, unable to let loose and enjoy the craziness around us. "I almost feel bad for them," I said to Omar after.

"Ah, the twins huh?" my old hedge fund manager said as I recounted the story later that day. He knew the Winklevii from Harvard. He cocked his head slightly. "By the way – why are you carrying so many flyers?"

---

24 Coinbase received accolades at that time for being the next Google or Facebook of crypto. However, exchanges are middlemen, charging absurd fees to give access to unsophisticated users – rubes – who did not know how to access Bitcoin and Ethereum directly. There was a pointed irony to the way crypto people spoke about the value of decentralization and then praised the new middlemen as evidence of revolution.

I shuffled the papers back into my messenger bag. My old boss noted his traders loved crypto and gestured to the row of men behind him, their eyes flitting from dozens of screens.

"Hopefully they are not trading crypto with our money," he said with a belly laugh, as if someone had suggested he invest in moon rocks. Which, in case you have forgotten, is something ConsenSys was trying to do.

One of the traders leaned over. "You're into crypto?" he chirped. A head of thick, well-combed hair sat above a white dress shirt opened at the top. "Can you tell us some of the hot ICOs?"

I hesitated. Our chief legal officer, who unfortunately ... you know. But he said specifically not to give investment advice. These guys did not want to hear that drivel. "Come on, we saw those Lambos on Sixth Ave," the trader said, goading me to spill.

Here we were, still standing on the precipice between punchline and financial revolution. "Okay," I said, easing up. "Have you heard of Filecoin?"

That Friday at Bogart the atmosphere was just as heated. Nearby in Queens we were hosting our own competing conference focused on Ethereum, known as Ethereal. PegaSys made our own announcements with the Enterprise Ethereum Alliance, and Ether jumped $70. We had delivered on our first promise. *Om nom nom nom,* one of the whales wrote on Slack as he bought up more Ether. Employees flew in from the four corners of the world – Korea, Australia, Chile, you name it – for the festivities. The air in Bogart was thick, mixing anticipation with the stifling heat after half the air conditioners broke. The body heat of the crowd in our undersized offices gave the office the muggy feeling of a dive bar in peak summer.

"Almost as hot as Singapore here," David said. He had flown in as well, flying twelve hours after his transfer to the Asia office right after I left Dubai. Omar showed us a portrait of himself he'd picked up at the Cellarius booth: a cyborg caricature with one robot eye on board a spaceship. Everyone posted their robot AI-selves all over Instagram. Tyler and his fish-tracking team held court there, hosting a chef in their booth to chop up a tuna they had tracked on its journey from "bait to plate" – all recorded on the blockchain. I stopped by with Omar and watched as he deftly sliced a thin piece from the giant hunk of fish before him, passing me a small paper plate with a dab of soy sauce.

How to make sure the fish we eat is safe

WIRED

FOLLOWING A TUNA FROM FIJI TO BROOKLYN—ON THE BLOCKCHAIN

David trying to bend his long Gumby legs underneath him as we sat on the floor. "Did Ether hit $10,000 yet?" he asked, referring to our old war cry. Around us, everyone smiled through the sweat with the confidence that crypto had gotten a new lease on life. Maybe not $10,000, but a sushi chef was just as good.

I barely heard David's next words over the hundred conversations going on in the same room, instead nodding a smile while scooping the digitally authenticated sashimi into my mouth. Somewhere between the cyborgs, bean bags, and endless swag, we had found a tiny island for ourselves amongst the madness.

# POPECHAIN

*"It's only when the tide goes out that you learn who's been swimming naked."* – Warren Buffett

*New York, July 2018. ETH:* $441.

ConsenSys was starting to defy gravity. After the conferences, prices came down again, but somehow our marketing prowess only grew. We revealed a new project called Civil, focused on using blockchain to fight fake news and censorship in media.[25] Forbes and the Associated Press soon signed up as partners, eager to see what the blockchain could do for the struggling industry. Senior execs joined from NPR bringing positive attention in double helpings. What better way to seize media attention than disrupting the media itself?

New York Times

**Goodbye, Denver Post. Hello, Blockchain.**

**Expenses for the fledgling outlet will be covered by a grant from Civil, whose sole investor, for now, is ConsenSys, a Brooklyn-based blockchain software ...**

Jun 17, 2018

---

25 For those wondering how, Civil used a token called a "TCR," a token curated registry. This strange acronym meant a list where users would give tokens to journalists who published accurate news, thus incentivizing good behavior, and storing the article text on Ethereum to ensure it could not be censored. Why? One ConsenSys engineer explained to me that if a million unpaid Internet nerds could build Wikipedia for free, imagine what they could do when rewarded by a token? The project *could* work. Why not? A TCR was also a great way to force feed a token into a project that did not need one.

The spotlight was now a floodlight, but I figured I could turn that attention to something positive for PegaSys with our launch in Prague only two months away. I wanted to follow the conference with an all-out assault, hitting at least ten cities in a month to pitch every financial institution we could lay our hands on.

I reached out to my old friends, the German bankers. Ritesh never landed the follow up deal, but it was worth asking. My German replied that he would have loved to, but he had actually just quit to join a blockchain startup. He never saw the value of the corporate stuff. I shook my head. Maybe I'd see him in Prague.

The summer eased into a lull. The long pause between Blockchain Week and our fall launch gave me a couple weeks to finally breathe. I stopped burning the midnight oil, instead finally taking time to help with the floral arrangements for our wedding and plotting out a minute by minute schedule with Excel. I shared my spreadsheet schedule with my family, orchestrating the events like a software release, worried for every detail. "*Beta,* a wife brings *barakah,*" my father said. Blessings. "Don't stress so much."

An engineer showed me a simulation of a new algorithm he had put together, the lines squiggling up and down like a shitcoin chart. That work had garnered an invite to speak at Stanford to the world's best cryptographers, bringing us into more exclusive enclaves. I asked Alec, our Ethereum research lead, what our upgrade timelines would be since we had doubled our forces.

"Now now," he said in his careful British way, "just because we have nine women does not mean we can have a baby in a month." Six months ago Ethereum's future had been clear as mud, but with a push from me and Dan, PegaSys was now one of the leading voices whipping the upgrade effort into shape, with Alec and a new hire named Tim becoming stars in the Ethereum world. Now, in a near miracle, they were nearly finished with the blueprint for Ethereum 2.0, but even then more code needed writing. Then, and only then, might we have a timeline for the "genesis block" – the first transactions birthing a new chain. But progress was now steady.

The only memorable misstep remained an intern we hired, one Raheem had reached out to recommend. On his first day kept showing me pictures of himself shaking hands with some government bigwigs in Malaysia. "The Prime Minister's advisor is my best friend, I swear," he said. "I know people that make things move," he wrote. Now he wanted to show me a presentation for his new startup idea. He extolled his personal network and connections, writing *THE FUTURE* on every page. Did the Clintons or Trumps know about blockchain? They would soon, apparently.

I motioned Dan over. He strained his neck to come close to my laptop screen. "Please let him present this."

"Don't let him?" I asked, thinking I'd misheard.

"Oh no, you must," he clarified. "Is that a picture of the Pope?" There was a drawing of a man in a white cassock, with a red cloak, large hat, and one hand raised above his head. There was no mistaking who that was supposed to be.

Dan was having a riot. "Should we add Rome to our travel plans?" he said, laughing.

I wondered aloud if we should fire the intern. I currently spent my subway rides on the L listening to an audiobook of *The Hard Things About Hard Things*, the memoir about startup leadership by Ben Horowitz, a famous investor in tech. The book blasted poor hiring as a death knell, and ninety percent of the book seemed to be about firing people. And when Horowitz was not firing people, he lashed out at them for sucking. *Hire slow, fire fast* was his Bible.

"Joe's probably not going to hold us to Horowitz standards," Dan replied, "and I guess we should be thankful he doesn't." Despite all the bravado, Dan was always a softie at heart. He had spent his first two years after college working on economic development in Tanzania and Kenya, something we bonded over early on as I had spent a summer doing similar work.

Joe often shouldered the blame for giving non-contributors too many second chances. To be a Silicon Valley god you needed clear psychopathic tendencies, and the data backed it up: by one estimate, 4%

of CEOs were psychopaths. Instead, he approved our crazy ideas by the dozen, from Civil to chess with eight types of pawns. I still thought it was an important trait. To invent anything world-changing, you had to see the world differently. Dorsey and Musk loved to toot their weirdness to the world, after all. No, Joe was not the prototypical startup CEO – not by a long shot. But did we even want him to be?

The summer crawled along until August. The days of wedding festivities had finally arrived. I took each weekend as a welcome distraction from the slog ahead for Pantheon's launch.

Saira and I had survived the gauntlet of family and invitations and logistics – the power in the hotel blew out hours earlier, right when two hundred aunties needed to straighten their hair – to arrive here.

Any worries from the last year released the moment we stepped onto the purple and white stage, even as hundreds of eyes watched every step. Before I could blink the *imam* was congratulating us on our vows. I thought back to the depths I'd felt in Dubai two years prior, crushed by the pressure and the loneliness. Saira smiled and I gripped her hand.

The crowds stormed the dessert table as my friends ran onto the dance floor, working to such a fever pitch that one went to the hospital with a torn Achilles. In an over the top year something lived up to the hype. Money, logistics, clothes, money, jewelry, money, all slipped out of my mind as the night stretched on. I was going to enjoy the moment for as long as it lasted.

# BAD TERMS

*"Gimme the Loot"* – The Notorious B.I.G.

*New York, September 2018. ETH:* $248.

Omar and I were sitting in an Italian restaurant near Washington Square Park, the red-checkered kind. After the summer spike, crypto was fading fast with the autumn leaves and the doubts about blockchain were now in full flight. Making money took more effort than ever: an employee from our rival Digital Asset told me IBM had finished over 400 blockchain projects and lost money on most. The Lambos at conferences, Super Bowl ads, and expensive salaries hung heavy over everyone's heads. *Forbes* humiliated R3 in an article, bashing the company as on a "rocky road" as it "goes for broke" while struggling to raise a new round of capital.

The Mesh cheered the toppling of the corporate Goliaths. I felt more troubled. If a rising tide lifts all boats, everything goes together when the toilet gets flushed. Ethereum's software fared worse, not better, than our rivals' despite the dozens of PegaSys engineers hammering away at improvements. TechCrunch predicted our demise, writing the "collapse of ETH is inevitable."

To survive in this environment Dan and I needed to double our efforts, and with the wedding done I could pound the pavement again. Pantheon's launch at the conference in Prague loomed a month away and we worked our contacts dry, calling every Wall Street bank or Big Tech or major corporate who would pick up to set up meetings for after Prague.

"Let's find every company that worked with JP Morgan on Ethereum and tell them we've got something better," I had said to Dan. Why stop there? We scoured the news for every company that our rivals claimed to work with. I pressed for every startup hack I had picked up in the last year and I still was not sure it was enough. Were we the awaited savior or the latecomer dud? The last few months hardened our skins enough to take the hit of dozens of rejections likely coming our way. Every major tech hub or financial center between San Francisco and Milan fell on our path to find the holy grail: a landmark customer.

I came to Omar now looking for advice.

"What's the point?" he said morbidly, catching me off guard. "They'll never close your equity deal. You won't own any of the success."

The restaurant was noisy and full of families. I leaned in closer to hear better. I had assumed he had finished his negotiations with Joe over equity. Was I wrong?

"Whatever they tell you," he finished, "get it in writing or it means nothing." He shook his head and the salt and pepper locks followed. Someone came by and dropped a dessert menu, unsure whether to pick up his half eaten meal. It had been months and neither side would budge. ConsenSys and Omar were in a standoff.

"What happened to radical transparency?" I asked.

"All talk," he said. "It's almost two years and you've got no equity. What's transparent about that?" The distress stood out on his face and I stopped pressing. Deep-pocketed competitors popped up everyday for him and us and stole what was left of our potential markets. VCs still came around, even in this market, but the window was nearly shut. Could ConsenSys be so myopic? I changed topics to complain that Vanessa had emailed me again about real estate, once more confusing us. He just shook his head.

The fear balled up in my stomach. There had been *promises*. You're an entrepreneur. It's not about control. Part of me still bought into the mythos. But without equity, those words were hot air. Our chances of ever getting the unicorn payday we dreamed of for PegaSys slipped to zero. All the work since I joined for no payoff. ConsenSys was a startup incubator that ate its young. Worse, crypto prices showed no sign of stopping their fall. An earthquake might be coming.

Omar had even managed to get rid of Giovanni the lawyer and negotiate directly with Joe, yet still he hit a wall. Maybe I'd had Joe all wrong.

Omar dropped his voice to a whisper and he leaned over. "We need to get the fuck out of this company."

I listened and nodded, deep in thought. Omar had always been aggressive. Perhaps he had asked for too much. His tenacity could have that effect. He'd probably screwed up, and now he was on Joe's bad side. After all, Joe had spent billions for no other reason but to help people. The launch was at hand and the rest would work itself out later. But I knew one thing now: Omar was no longer any help to me. If anything, he might be a hindrance. I had to trust Joe. I had no other choice.

# SATANISTS AND CAPITALISTS

> *"There's definitely, in all blockchains and cryptocurrencies, some notion of what I call a high priest. A high priest is basically someone who has high status inside a cryptocurrency community for whatever reason, and sometimes high priests say things. I don't know if you want to mix religious metaphors, but they can issue fatwas."* – Vitalik Buterin, creator of Ethereum, *Forbes*

*Prague, October 2018. ETH:* $203.

My Uber wound its way through the hills outside Prague as the sun rose. We were hours away from PegaSys' official launch of Pantheon at Devcon, the annual conference by the Ethereum Foundation. Nearly delirious from two nights without sleep, I thought back on remember my last time in Eastern Europe: a harrowing road trip gone wrong to Tbilisi. A group of soldiers looked at me with suspicion at the Turkish border, wondering what an American college student was doing in this remote corner of nowhere. One whispered to the other. *Jasoos*. I knew enough Turkish to know it meant "spy." After a long interrogation, I had missed the only bus out, and I stood by the side of the road looking for a ride. When one kind hearted soul picked me up in his van, only after a few minutes did it dawn on me my fellow passengers were all young, scantily clad women. They pointed at me and giggled. I was hitchhiking my way with a bus full of prostitutes.

I snapped out of the daze and started typing furiously on my phone. Coindesk would blast a headline about our launch in a few short hours, and the marketing team scrambled to fix our website after weeks of misfires. I had sucked up to Coindesk for months to earn enough cachet to get them to run this piece. We offered them an exclusive if they included a few quotes of our choosing and a link to download Pantheon. They happily obliged. In this market, even the journalists felt the screws turning and needed to drum up excitement.

"Sorry, I've been up all night," the web developer replied to me on Slack. "Working as fast as I can." It was 3 am in NYC and I told him there was only until 8 am to get it fixed. I had already dumped one marketing guy after he broke the page, and now the backup turned out to be worse. I needed to fire this one as soon as our launch was over. But first I needed my headline.

PegaSys had earned a little buzz from headlines in smaller crypto outlets before, but that limelight lasted about five minutes before Ripple announced Bill Clinton would speak at their shill conference. Two hours later the web dev finally finished and I could take a breather. The headline went up as promised: our team was about to give Ethereum "a shot in the arm." Pantheon had arrived. Sleep came soon after.

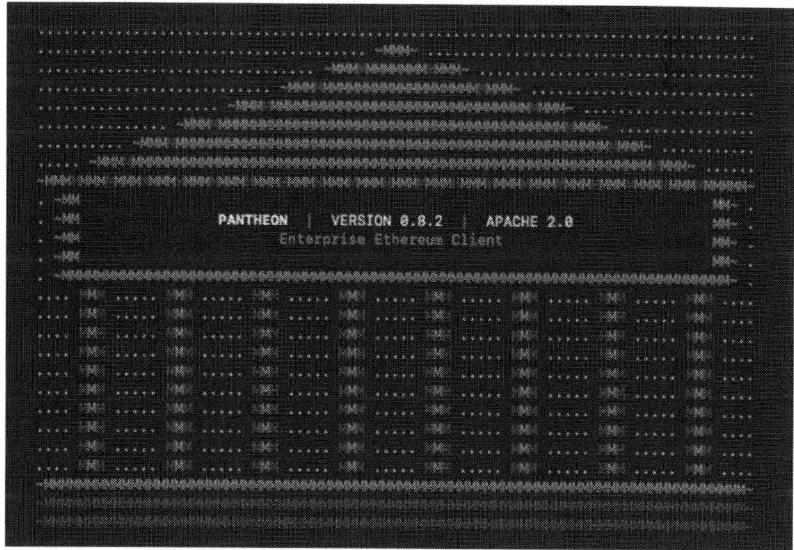

Crypto loved conferences as much as it loved Twitter. Tech conferences were always blowout events, because throwing a party was the only way to make software releases exciting. Crypto took that even further and tickets for Devcon sold out in seconds. Despite the price falling and then falling further, all of us at ConsenSys trekked to Prague with mountains of t-shirts and water bottles to give away because this was our best chance to get anyone's attention. We would either bring the excitement back to Ethereum, or this would be the last dance. Either way, the Mesh saw a chance to party.

Ethereum remained as slow as it had been for years but the community now could trumpet the research and effort to improve it. Ethereum still hosted hundreds of startups building new apps, including a large number now focused on "DeFi" – decentralized finance, a moniker for a collection of blockchain apps to lend and borrow money or create digital dollars. Excitement bubbled over these new ideas, many of which actually worked as well as any banking app. There was something encouraging about the focus on real progress even in the hard times. The narrative continued to shift, looking for the killer app that would stick. The downside of our launch's timing was obvious: we were far behind and the era of easy money was over. But the upside was now we had something to prove. The wheels of the startup world kept turning.

Crypto still had its flair for the outlandish, and ConsenSys knew how to steal the show. We had a new acquisition to announce: ConsenSys Space would merge with Interplanetary Resources, the asteroid mining company we had partnered with. As Joe noted in our press release, Ethereum formed the basis for "democratizing and decentralizing space endeavors to unite our species." ConsenSys would boldly go towards the final frontier, our aspirations further endorsed when even William Shatner chimed in to reveal himself an Ethereum acolyte. The acquisition was the signal that no matter what the price of Ether said, to Joe our trajectory always remained skyward.

Bob Summerwill Retweeted
William Shatner
@WilliamShatner
@BobSummerwill the Enterprise Ethereum Alliance? Are we absolutely sure @VitalikButerin isn't a Star Wars fan? I've heard rumors...some started by myself!
11/4/18, 8:27 PM
18 Retweets 51 Likes


"Now Joe really is *astronomically* wealthy," someone joked. Otherworldly profits awaited. Dan and I ignored the easy jokes and all the other noise. We wandered through the old, Soviet style conference hall, weaving among the brutalist concrete pillars to find a room for our slate of meetings. A little help from my friends got me rested and ready: melatonin and the Whale. The latter set up our most critical meeting of the trip with Microsoft, who had cooled off since ConsenSys' announcement with their sworn rival Amazon a few months before, but we wanted to get back in their good graces. These two companies were the backbone of the Internet, making money off every click in an app from ordering an Uber to ordering a pizza, a pair of trillion dollar behemoths that crushed unicorns at will. Convincing them to work with us over JP Morgan would be worth ten headlines, at least. This mouse might make the elephants dance just yet.

Their blockchain lead sauntered in, a giant at least 6'7" and well-built. But we brought our own weapon, our new head of product who was himself 6'6". The two shook hands as we all looked up. He lay out our plans and I focused on speaking about what they cared about most: their cloud. Microsoft saw blockchain software like ours as a way to get customers to pay Microsoft as much as thirty thousand dollars a month simply to run PegaSys' systems. We sold light bulbs while they owned the power plant. Our pitch hit the mark.

"As long as you're not going to march into Times Square waving signs about Microsoft buying your ICO, we think it's a great idea," the giant told us cheerfully. We had convinced them that we were the horse to bet on. The sleepless nights finally felt worth it. We were on our way.

The conference continued to put wind in our sails. After Microsoft next up was Brian Behlendorf, an Internet legend who had built some of the first piping for the modern web. He held the keys to the Hyperledger project, a blockchain group effectively run by IBM. There could be peace between us, he offered. Only if they acknowledge Pantheon as equals, we countered. Brian said he would see what he could do.

Our last meeting in Prague was with a rival: Parity, our Ethereum-based competitor. We assumed they hated us, especially after they had mocked us a month before Pantheon's launch to ask about our ICO. But instead the meeting took a turn: after hackers stole hundreds of millions from them, they no longer had money to compete with us. They offered to sell us their code for ten million dollars. Their CEO Gavin Wood hated Joe and regularly spoke ill of him, but now he had to bend the knee. I can only imagine the immense pleasure Joe took to see a rival so humbled. That alone was recognition that we still held the power in the ecosystem. We turned them down anyway.

We heard through the grapevine that the Foundation now wanted to hold a series of meetings with all of Ethereum's top engineers to discuss the future of the blockchain. We had to get in there, even if we had to sneak our way in. I walked around searching until Dan signaled he found them. We were in the rooms that mattered most.[26]

I sat in the lounge area afterward, exhausted from talking for hours and waiting for the next round of lemon tarts to come out at the refreshments table. My phone buzzed. Our winged horse t-shirts were caught up in customs, and I needed to wrangle with some European bureaucrat so we could give away swag during the all-weekend hackathon we were hosting. I called the shipping company and told them to deal with it.

I looked for a place to sit and relax but there was none: every talk was overcrowded, attendees sitting in hallways and aisles. Satisfied with the day's progress, I walked outside into the light drizzle with Matt, passing a poster of Deva the Unicorn, the official conference mascot. An army of marketing people stood by a line of empty blue buses. A woman with purple streaked silvery hair handed me a small, laminate flyer, black with bright blue text like a neon sign in the dark:

*see the next stage of human society unfold*

The note instructed us to come back to the buses at 9pm for a trip to a remote mansion hosting a party. She told us she had no other info. I turned to Matt, wondering what he knew. He always had his finger on the pulse of weird crypto things.

"I'm not sure, dude," he said. "Maybe they'll take us all into the mountains and kill us?" His usual sense of humor on display. "We had to reschedule our Satanist party because someone said everyone was going to this thing. Rumor is some big vainglorious blockchain project announcement costing millions. *Ye gods*, that stuff is the worst."

"Satanist party?" I asked. Never a dull day.

Matt explained it was the ten-year anniversary of Bitcoin, and a few of the ConsenSys crypto-rich wanted to host a devil-themed celebration. "Hell is going to be fucking lit," he exclaimed. He moved his hands like the shape of a flame, smirking at the pun on perdition.

"People want to spend so much when Eth is so low?"

---

26 We tried to help organize these meetings by taking notes. Unfortunately, Dan put these all in Google Docs, which were later leaked to Coindesk as proof of "secret closed door debates."

"This pricing is irrational," Matt said. "It'll come back up."

The wording evoked a memory of a saying by Keynes, the economist. "The market can stay irrational longer than you can stay solvent," I said in faux wisdom.

Matt gave me a mischievous look. "And we can stay stupid longer than the market can stay irrational."

The words meant more than he knew. I debated internally whether to go to either, given my experiences with unplanned excursions into remote parts of Eastern Europe. The party seemed badass, but the only time I thought of myself as a badass was when I did not put my phone in airplane mode after takeoff. But today I had something to celebrate.

That night necks craned around everywhere to see who else was coming. We rolled into the darkness of the Czech countryside. Crowds walked together towards the old mansion, and we could hear the loud music as we got closer. I saw a familiar face and grabbed his arm. "What's the deal here?"

"Oh, you don't know?" Hugo, our head of Paris replied in that French way signifying amusement and sarcasm. "It's Blockchains LLC!" I must have looked confused, as he kept going. "They're starting something, I don't know, in the desert, maybe in Arizona? A whole city run on blockchain. A massive experiment!"

I was confused. "So it's not a new blockchain?" I asked.

"*Non non non*," he said. "It's a whole new way of life!"

The lights went out as a giant screen lit up. A trailer began, cellos and violins playing over scenes in the desert. A little girl ran away into the dunes.

"We're building a different kind of sandbox," the girl explained. "Once you join us, we'll be the ones to change the world. Blockchain can, will, and should change the world." She ran into a small valley with what looked like an encampment behind her. "Everyone will get a fair shake, because no one will be shaken down. Your voice will be your vote." She started drawing in the sand. Soon we saw she had drawn a giant chain. The dramatic score signaled a conclusion. "There's only one problem. *I don't want to wait.*"

Aha. Someone had a lot of Bitcoin and wanted to use it. $300M, I would find out later. Where better to find potential new citizens than at Devcon? Banks and courts built on smart contracts. Burning Man except permanent. *Code will be law.* A massive bet on humanity: where had I heard that before? The prophecy of everyone becoming crypto rich might be failing, but the prophecy of a blockchain rapture still held promise. Some were willing to put their money where their mouth was, even yet.

I knew crypto was strange but this was only a slight outlier in software. All of Big Tech stared into its own navel endlessly, talking about the transhuman and bio-hacking and immortality. These blockchain investors chugged the Kool-Aid of Silicon Valley libertarianism, and added a splash of nerd revenge mixer about seizing power from the world of jocks in finance and suits in government. To us the only difference was that Big Tech was a bunch of hypocrites. I could see how someone might say the same about us. If we really cared about society, why couldn't we give our crypto gains to a food bank or something? To an outsider, the obsession with funding our own utopias or paths to the moon looked like lightspeed ego trips. I had moved past such judgements now. Egos were what made life interesting. People like this had one uncompromising belief: that technology made the world better, and history proved them right, over and over. What else had worked? Religions had come and gone, along with so many schools of philosophy and art and political systems. Only technology separated us from the barbaric past.

"How boring," Matt yawned. To him it was more investor-blockchain claptrap. "Tomorrow's party will be so much better. I would totally hang with a bunch of Satanists over lame capitalists any day."

I told him I could head back early with him, having had my fill. The music continued and the crowd cheered more because it felt right. Many of the engineers lived for these celebrations, booze soaked affairs where they could release the social inhibitions that only staring at a computer screen for twelve hours a day can drill into you. A man at the mic threw an arm in the air and grabbed the mic. "Now let's get this party started!"

*doi doi doi doi doi doi*

I was hitting stone after stone, nearly sick to my stomach as my head bounced up and down on the bright green electric scooter, but I could not slow down. Dan and I were racing past the Louvre, a mental break between the endless pitch meetings, and I'd elected a poorly timed shortcut from the banks of the Seine to a cobblestone street. The plastic scooter wheels shouted their objections and sounded like they might break. I looked back for the slightest second, seeing Dan come close, and I started to lose my balance. *Aaaaahhh*, I thought, afraid my next meeting with a finance CTO would being by explaining my bloody corduroys. I turned the scooter hard and jumped off, stumbling a few steps just as we pulled in front of the Jardins des Tuileres.

"You can't quit!" Dan shouted incredulously. I was in the lead when we stopped, but he was never, ever going to let me win like that. I conceded out of respect. That maniacal need to win of his was what had kept us going months before, when we had whistled right past the startup graveyard.

Three weeks had passed since Prague and Eth had fallen by another ten percent, adding ten percent more stress and a growing case of impostor syndrome for me. Dan admitted to the same. "I've felt like an impostor everyday for the last year," he said. "But growth is a man with a yo-yo walking uphill," Dan assured me. "Try not to focus on the yo-yo."

Even with the rough crypto seas, we earned enough attention to fill our days with glass conference rooms overlooking the Thames or the East River or Lake Ontario. For the entire month we passed out free t-shirts and candy and ground through meetings morning to evening. We held an all weekend hackathon, watching the room dimly lit by dozens of laptop screens as the engineers worked late into the night. I left Rob on the sofa, half asleep after midnight as he hacked Pantheon a new database connector. Joe came to hand out the prizes the next morning. "This is awesome," he said, shaking everyone's hands as we took photos. I was surprised at how much his approval meant to me.

IBM waved us through the gates, admitting to us they burned money on blockchain deals but every single dollar spent on their clunky centralized blockchain was leading to fifteen dollars of cloud revenue. Like Microsoft, they ran the power plant.

Our overtures for peace with JP Morgan found no welcomes, and instead we received a tongue lashing for even trying to compete with them. Dan's face turned red from arguing back. (One upside to being brown is blushing tends to be unnoticeable.) Screw them, we said as we left.

In San Francisco we fought uphill. We held court during a conference in the Moscone Center, near the stage where Steve Jobs revealed the iPhone. The SF tech scene was its own bubble, and I balked at the $1300 a night it cost to book the Marriott, staying in a budget hotel instead. I stared at the ceiling all night as I listened to a homeless man yelling in the parking lot. This was the tech dystopia we needed to replace.

"We're real software, not a white paper," Dan repeated to another bespectacled audience. But no matter how many stickers I handed to the tech giants like Oracle or SAP or Salesforce, we saw the doubts in their eyes. "Our innovation teams are out of budget," they said. "Maybe next year." We sulked back to the hotel, side stepping the human feces on the sidewalk.

In London, we started to turn the tables. The first two banks told us their blockchain budgets had run out. We arrived too late. "Nothing to do with the crypto prices, obviously," they claimed. We were yesterday's news. Someday you'll be big, they were all telling us, but not yet.

But the third meeting, another exchange, even bigger than the one I worked with, wanted to work together. They knew blockchain was early, but tokenizing small stocks still held promise. We posed for photos in front of the heavy, marble doors afterward, pointing at the gilded letters and proclaimed we would *decentralize this shit.* "I guess I slept well," Dan told me after. He arrived at his famous brother's house so tired from the red eye that he slept through Johnny Depp coming by for dinner.

Another European city, another conference to squeeze in. This time I was introduced to Joe's son, Kieran. He acknowledged me with a wary glance and nary a hello. His project, BlockApps, had already spent three years trying to build a better Ethereum, and now PegaSys was a direct competitor to him, one that was getting waves of funding from his own father. *I probably wouldn't like me if I was in his shoes,* I thought. I had read more about Joe and Kieran by that point, learning that Joe's ex-wife was an anthropologist who wrote about failing democracies and conflict. I wondered what each of them learned from her.

Now we were in Paris. By my count I had been working 34 days straight, but we finally felt like we were getting somewhere. I looked at my watch. Twenty past, meaning it was almost time. We stepped back on to our scooters and headed to the office as fast as we could.

In our meeting, Rob stood by the whiteboard, unfurling those long limbs that had been packed into economy seats for weeks. The French CTO looked like he might cry from joy, telling us he had been searching for months for a version of Ethereum that met his needs. He had been building an equity trading platform for a year and nearly gave up from the technical challenges, but now PegaSys fit exactly what he wanted. We had our first customer.

# PART III

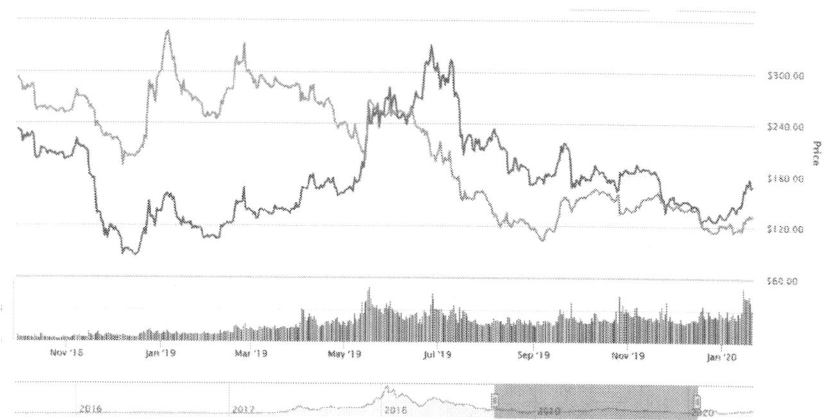


# COLLAPSE

# UNINDICTED CO-CONSPIRATOR

*"It's pretty much epic day after epic day."* – Joseph Lubin, *Breaker Magazine*, November 2018

*New York, November 2018. ETH:* $144.

I was in Bogart and annoyed. The assistant for the Chief Strategy Officer sat next to me, and since the latter had not shown up at the office for work in two years (*you don't have to be there physically to add value*, was the joke), she spent most of her day talking about her boyfriend troubles or asking other women about their boyfriend troubles and making everyone uncomfortable. Today she was calling car rental agencies, asking for SUVs with ski racks, as the CSO wanted to attend Davos in February but to also hit the slopes after his sessions with the world's central bankers on why they really needed crypto.

I had emails from governments and banks from Brazil to England to Italy asking for more detail. We hired two young associates for more of the blood and guts startup work: mid twenties and full of energy to help us grab more of the pie. But despite our successful roadshow, the mood in Bogart was sour. When the bubble peaked six months earlier, we knew we were in for a world of pain, but figured we would work hard and things would stabilize or even go up.

But Ether kept falling.

I tried to write an email but the assistant kept talking and I flipped to Twitter. The stock market had been puking for weeks and taking crypto with it. Even as things got better for PegaSys, they were looking worse for

ConsenSys. I felt a wave of trepidation. We ran on the startup treadmill as fast as we could, but someone kept turning up the speed. Another Coindesk article lashed IBM for struggling in its TradeLens blockchain with Maersk, the biggest shipping company in the world. Customers suspected TradeLens was too centralized, a trap in the guise of innovation. Ethereum fans cheered their failures, but neither centralized nor decentralized models worked well in corporate blockchains, IBM claimed. "You've got to pick your poison," their blockchain lead admitted. Startups outside Consensys were imploding by the day, and crypto was clearly not coping well.

Ether fell further.

Ari Paul and the other "Bitcoin investors" preached that crypto would be a safe haven in any crisis. Pomp, another Bitcoin talking head, issued a million dollar challenge that crypto would beat stocks over the next ten years. "Long Bitcoin, Short the Bankers!" he proclaimed. Only 'weak hands' sold from pain.

Still Ether fell.

People were still tweeting about Civil, our journalist blockchain project that had received so much hype. The token I struggled to explain months earlier turned out as inscrutable to everyone else. ConsenSys' CMO tried again to explain how Civil worked at Disrupt, a major tech conference, and the head of one crypto blog called the presentation nothing but a "word salad."[27] ConsenSys had become too good at spinning the media machine, and now it had spun out of control. Cynicism spread just as the token sale began.

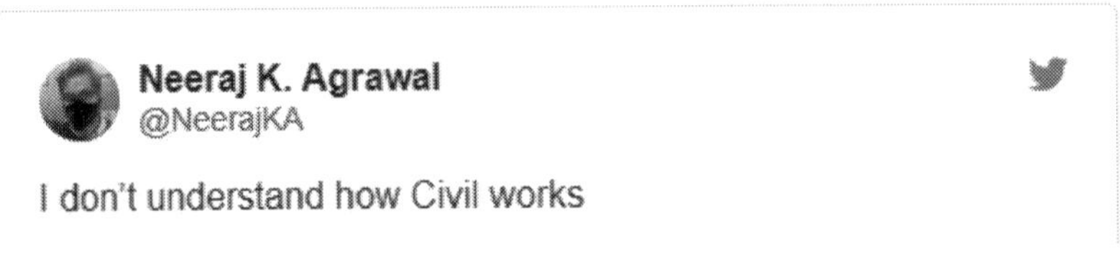


ConsenSys, chastened by the downturn, had set a goal of only $24M, miniscule compared to the billions we raised a year earlier. But now the

27 That might have been the best description of a TCR so far.

excitement around the token raise fizzled as the project went from media darling to punchline. The WSJ came for us first, noting the "skepticism" around Civil. I clenched a mental fist. I taught you what blockchain is, you ungrateful bastards.

Two weeks into the token sale, no one had invested. Desperation began to set in and ConsenSys ran non-stop ads on Facebook on Twitter. *Join us.* The bombardment only resulted in a pelting of digital tomatoes as the Internet townsfolk mocked us and our struggles.

Down and down Ether went.

A wizard with a long gray beard waved a long staff on Twitter. "Join us!" he exclaimed, next to his *magic internet news*, a play on the crypto phrase *magic internet money*. I couldn't help but laugh. This was now a full on PR crisis.

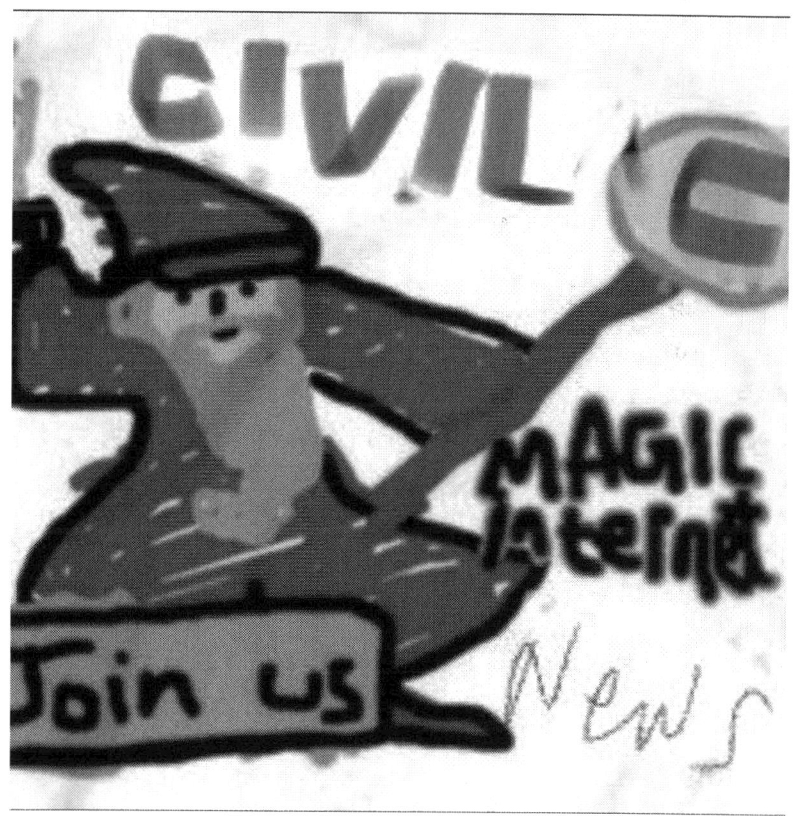

Nearly a hundred people from ConsenSys gathered at the last minute in Williamsburg to put all their mental firepower to try for one, final push. Civil's lead declared they were at the "eleventh hour" for the project. But the effort was for naught. When the token sale closed, we had raised only $500,000 in external investment. The NYT soon penned an obituary: "Alas, the Blockchain Won't Save Journalism After All." We were working for a good cause, their cause, but that meant nothing. "It was as if an Olympic weightlifter said that, at a minimum, he'd be able to clean and jerk 400 pounds, and then did not manage to move the bar more than an inch off the ground," they wrote. Ouch. We were not fixing fake news. We *were* fake news. Dan seemed depressed when we talked about it. "Never been afraid of failure," he confided. "I'm afraid of becoming an embarrassment."

More red. Everywhere.

Back in Bogart I grew frustrated as the assistant asked her fifth question about ski racks. Joe was at the cluster of five desks behind me, feet up as usual. I listened with one ear.

"So are we restarting negotiations?" he asked. He must be talking to the lawyers, I thought. There was a pause as the other side spoke.

"Well, if they have outside counsel, they can use them for negotiation in any other real estate deals." My ears turned a little red as I tried to keep my eyes locked on the screen in front of me. *Real estate. Meridio.* My eyes flicked around the room to see if anyone else was listening or watching. The drone of the EA loudly asking *is that SUV manual or automatic* drowned out the sound to everyone else in the room. The negotiations must be going poorly, I realized. With stocks collapsing, the fear of a tech winter made deals feel impossible. Our lawyers may have decided to cut Omar off.

Joe continued. "That sounds like something that could be construed as confrontational. Did he say anything you might consider an HR violation?" he asked. Was Joe looking for reasons to fire Omar? I was shocked. I maniacally typed nonsense to make it seem like I was not just sitting there listening.

*Kafka integrations into Ethereum will the quick brown fox jumped over the lazy dog the quick brown fox jumped over the*

"Well, make a note of it. Please keep this in your records in case we need it later." I heard a mouse click as he ended the Zoom call.

I sat perfectly still typing about brown foxes and ipsum lorems until another five minutes had passed. I felt a wave of guilt for doubting Omar. He had been right to question everything. I picked up my phone, slipped it in my pocket, and walked down the hall to the bathroom. I locked the door and sat down.

*O, you've got be careful man.*

The blue bubbles immediately popped up. *What do you mean?*

*Dude I'm in 22, and I think they're talking about you. Joe is looking for reasons to fire you. Or at least it sounded that way*

Bubbles popped up and disappeared. *Who was he talking to?*

*Not sure,* I wrote. *Probably the lawyers? It was on the phone.*

*Hmmmm,* he wrote back. *Yeah, I'm not surprised. They hate my guts.*

*It's pretty messed up,* I wrote.

I thought to ask what might be the "HR violation," but I decided to avoid the hornet's nest. And if the lawyers found out Omar heard about this, they might wonder who warned him, leading them back to ... no, I thought, I had given him enough warning. That was enough to be considered a good friend, right? I took a deep breath.

*Vanessa confused us again,* I texted. *How many times do I have to tell her I don't run the real estate spoke?*

*Lol,* he replied. *Some people. Still on for coffee?*

*Busy day,* I wrote back. *Raincheck?* The coffee shop was directly across the street from Joe's window. I wasn't trying to get dragged into this. The phrase "unindicted co-conspirator" came to mind, a smear tactic the Department of Justice had used against Muslim-American leaders after 9/11, naming anyone and everyone in court cases and knowing they would never have to prove anything in court. Guilty by association. That's what I would be if I was spotted at coffee with Omar. Unindicted co-conspirator.

I tried to process the voice I had just heard, but it did not reconcile with the Joe I knew. The Joe I had just complained a month ago was *too nice*. Did he really want a revolution? How could he if he wanted to retain control? I searched for excuses – were the lawyers manipulating him? We were already cutting staff left and right, including Harrison and his army of twentysomethings who would soon file suit against ConsenSys. But that team hired the wrong people. Omar was a golden child, or so I thought. This was more than expenses. This seemed personal. At that moment I realized that Ben Horowitz was wrong in his book about making the "hard choices" to be a good startup CEO. There was no Rocky Balboa-like training phase needed to steel yourself up to play hardball, no podcast or book required to teach you how to fire people without remorse. With enough power and money, anyone could become a psychopath.

# YE GODS

*"He who loses wealth loses much; he who loses a friend loses more; but he that loses his courage loses all."* – Miguel de Cervantes

*New York, November 2018. ETH:* $135.

Civil's implosion was the death knell for any hope of a PegaSys token. ConsenSys needed to lay low. My lovely pitch decks wilted unattended, unlikely to be seen by anybody.

Matt resigned soon too, much to my surprise. He stuck with us even when things were falling apart, and now he wanted to leave? *Ye gods,* I thought when he told me, remembering his signature catchphrase. "Now? Why?"

He apologized as he finally betrayed some emotion. He wanted to stay, but Google had offered him double his current salary to do crypto research. The Internet's royalty sensed opportunity in blockchain and would buy their way in. Sergey Brin, Google's founder, loved Ethereum, and the company could throw money at such a fledgling technology without thinking. Facebook announced plans to hire a team of hundreds. Meanwhile we were cutting staff: first, the architect, who had finished designing the squash courts we would never have. Leadership was finally learning to tighten the belt.

Big Tech's arrival showed crypto was more than yesterday's bubble. But it also meant only more competition for us. Soon they would vacuum up any good engineers they could and commandeer the market. They were taking back the zoo.

Alec, the British research manager we stole from another tech company, was presenting on the future of Ethereum and several hundred Meshians hung on to his every word.

The price of Ether had broken below $120 now. Most were too weary to register a reaction. The collapse had been slowing down, and there was still hope for a reversal. Omar told me he had planned his last resort: taking his real estate project to an Ethereum-killer still rich with token money.

The price headed downward and then upward in dizzying turns. With every $10 move up, the company Slack came alive buzzing with hope. Our future hung by one remaining thread, the research work to upgrade the blockchain to "Ethereum 2.0." Now we wanted to know how long that was going to take.

Alec had helped push the Ethereum Foundation from the informal horseplay of a year ago to an actual plan. Unfortunately, that plan hinged on writing tons of more code. R3 took the chance to kick us while down. "I don't think Ethereum is going to go anywhere, to be frank," their lead engineer announced. "They have announced they are going to rewrite everything from scratch."

Ethereum is not typical software, he explained. A blockchain is a strange thing – software involving thousands of computers at once. Keeping it free of fraud made it slow, and improvements required rigorous understanding of complex topics like game theory and byzantine fault tolerance.[28]

We had made dozens of hires, but they simply found more challenges: zero-knowledge proofs, roll ups, cross-chain atomicity. Behind every door were ten more that held more mysteries to be solved. Fixing Ethereum seemed like a house Agatha Christie designed, with every door leading back to the same room.

Dan finally cut to the chase – how long would it take for all these fixes to be made? How long until our castles in the air might have a foundation beneath them?

---

28 On a public network, every node must be equal. Because there was no quality check, the overall quality of the network thus became very low, and the blockchains became very slow. There was no clear way to fix this. By design, blockchain was meant to be peer-to-peer, but that meant having to deal with a large and unpredictable network.

He paused for a second and waved his hands. "Well," in a very English, very guarded tone, "we don't want to restrict ourselves with *timelines*..." At the core, blockchain faced massive bottlenecks: coordinating thousands of computers at once, a problem that grew exponentially in difficulty the larger the network was.

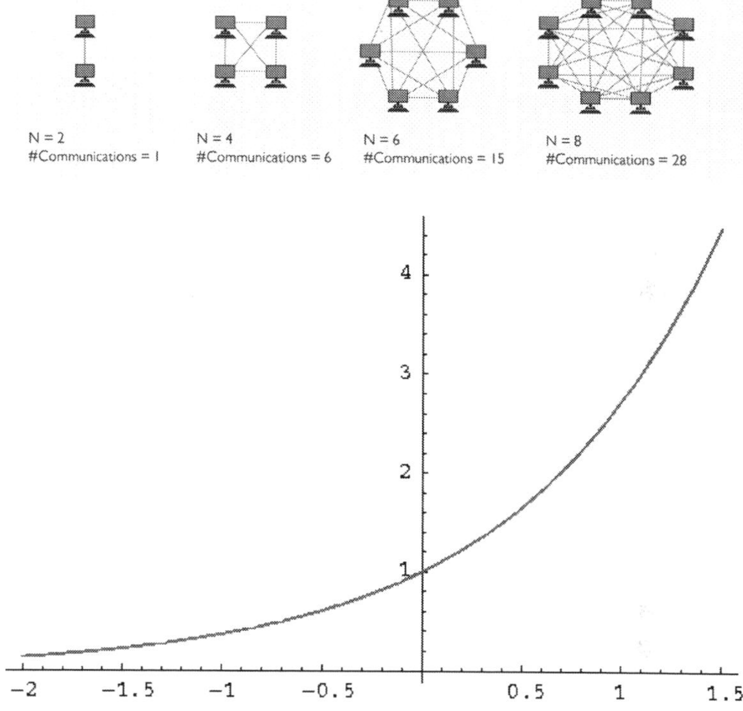


Only one potential solution might work, he said: a chain of chains. Ethereum would need over a thousand chains, an idea projects our rivals like Parity were already working on.[29]

29 As noted, a common solution is to make a 'chain of chains' so a thousand chains can talk to each other. The problem that arises there is how does one chain know to trust another? These smaller chains could be hacked, and that might pollute the database. Creating a thousand chains introduced a thousand more points of vulnerability. The Ethereum community eventually settled on a deposit system, where certain players acted as "validators," and if these validators were found to act dishonestly later on, they would lose their deposits.

"Getting this done right is more important than getting it done fast," he explained. "But I would probably guess three or four years, and that's if we get it to work at all."

I could see people doing the math in their heads. Three to four years of burning hundreds of millions of dollars at ConsenSys' size, over 1500 employees and sixty or seventy startups, with the Ether price where it was spelled disaster. Joe must know that too, I thought. He had come too far to risk losing it all. If the price fell further, the future of the revolution would take priority over everything else.

Oh dear, we thought. That does not sound good for the rest of us.

I recalled the saying my hedge fund boss had taught me years before. Dropped from a tall enough height, even a dead cat will bounce.

Shayan was a fellow Pakistani who hired me for my first foray into finance. (A little brown favoritism.) I had been tasked with covering oil stocks for the summer, right amidst the biggest collapse in the industry's history. Oil had fallen from $140 to $70 in less than six months, and the industry was reeling, from Texas to Abu Dhabi. Most times in history when oil had fallen sharply, there was a fast recovery, so investors were optimistic about a turnaround. Too much optimism, I told Shayan, based on my analysis.

"Did you break down all the assumptions in your model?" he asked me, not breaking eye contact in an eagle like stare. "You modeled out the inventories?"

Indeed, I confirmed. My models said the downturn would last six months longer than the market expected. Hope was the only thing holding these stocks up.

"Then short them to zero," he told me. The lesson stayed with me. When all you have left is hope, you're only fooling yourself.

At ConsenSys, we replayed the past in our minds. We looked back at the conferences and launch parties of yesteryear with regret. If we had saved a few more acorns, we might have lasted through the crypto winter. The price broke down again, and fell to $100 in the space of a week. A nondescript email arrived in our inboxes, inviting us to an important Town Hall. Doomsday was coming.

# GRANDMA'S REVENGE

*"Men, it has been well said, think in herds. It will be seen that they go mad in herds, while they only recover their senses slowly, and one by one."* – Charles Mackay, *Extraordinary Popular Delusions and the Madness of Crowds*

*New York. December 2018. ETH:* $112.

I closed my eyes as I read the article. The Mesh was in an uproar over how unfair the depiction of ConsenSys was.

**Cryptopia In Crisis: Joe Lubin's Ethereum Experiment Is A Mess. How Long Will He Prop It Up?**

Colleagues complained on Slack that Forbes published a "hit" piece on us which blamed us for Ethereum's challenges, dubbing the company "chaotic" and the portraying the list of spokes as a monstrous sprawl.

Would our own community defend us? Everyone in crypto knew full well we had done more than anyone else for Ethereum. If anything, Joe propped up the network when it teetered on the edge of collapse from CryptoKitties and the like, subsidizing the network with at least ten million dollars every year.[30] Did no one remember how he paid for

30 ConsenSys at the time had a service called Infura which any startup could use to access Ethereum, and for many years gave it away for free.

the first conferences, the hundreds of scholarships for engineers to study blockchain, the millions in free software we gave away? For all our missteps, Ethereum's flaws held us back from what we could have achieved.

I took a deep breath. I knew better than anyone our company was flawed, if you could even call it a company. But at least we stood by our principles. Our rivals like IBM and Digital Asset and R3 who were more focused on money were withering away, and most had already laid off huge chunks of their staff. Did these critics prefer we pursue profit over all else? I read on.

"Being the Daddy Warbucks of the Ethereum blockchain is fine when digital money is trading at stratospheric levels," Forbes continued, before going into depth on our "wobbly wheel" of spokes. The negotiations over equity were now tabloid fodder as well:

> When ConsenSys spokes have spun out and become separate businesses, for example, Lubin has retained ownership of 50% or more. Thus, like John Pierpont Morgan and Andrew Carnegie during America's Gilded Age and tech magnates Jeff Bezos and Mark Zuckerberg of the internet age, Lubin is setting himself up to become one of the controlling titans of the blockchain era.

The journalist kept pressing Joe. Was ConsenSys founded in part to make Ether more valuable? "Like, yeah, I'm going to build a company on an ecosystem that doesn't exist, so I can increase the value of my Internet magic-money holdings," he replied. He went on, the "people who were in the space early were there for philosophical reasons, for political or economic reasons not tied to their personal wealth." The writer would not let alone. What about the price?. Joe was as defiant as the generals at Thermopylae. He responded simply: "Who gives a fuck?"

These were the same journalists who had won clicks commending us months prior as the future of tech. Now they came not to praise Caesar but to bury him.

CoinDesk, the most popular "news" website in the space, reveled in our demise. CoinDesk reported with glee on the Civil failures and was now a declared enemy. Emails warned us not to trust anything to do with them or their leader Barry Silbert. His number two, Meltem, who came to crypto from oil trading, had left to become chief of investments at CoinShares, another crypto investment firm. With her massive social media following, she liked to flip between shitting on Ethereum to admitting how useful it was for investing in shitcoins like DeepBrainChain. "ConsenSys has done more for the Ethereum ecosystem in its first five years of development than any other firm," she admitted in a quote, at least giving us some credit. But once a maxi, always a maxi. "I don't think they even have the slightest idea what decentralization is," she added.

Gavin Wood, the co-founder of Ethereum who founded Parity, our rival who had tried to sell their code to us from desperation, relished the chance to castigate Joe openly again. He said Joe wanted to be the "Obi-wan Kenobi [of blockchain], but unfortunately he became the Darth Vader."

I realized the community's memory was clearly short. ConsenSys' fatal error was to overestimate blockchain's potential, even as all of our critics committed the same mistake. There was no room for human failures when Joe claimed we would remake the world of finance. No one was going to believe a multi-billionaire could be the victim of circumstance; his downfall was not the death of the dream but his own damn fault, the greedy hypocrite.

Every day the Ether price went down further. $120, $100, $80. The cable channels took delight in the ever growing sea of red – down 80% from peak, then 90%, then 95%. Every chart felt like another gut punch with no end in sight.

On whalepool people held up a good front. *I'm buying more!* many of them said. *Eth's on sale, you'll never see these prices again.* I sold the last of my shitcoins without even counting the proceeds.

One journalist texted me. Then another. Many had my number from the times when they feigned enthusiasm about our product launches just a few months prior. They were happy to write positive articles in the good times, but even more excited to chronicle our downfall. I felt a deep revulsion as the blue bubbles popped up probing for dirt. I asked a friend with a crypto-fund what he thought might happen.

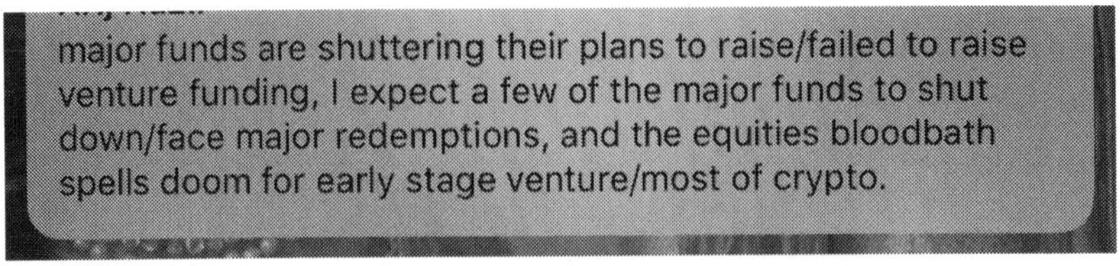

major funds are shuttering their plans to raise/failed to raise venture funding, I expect a few of the major funds to shut down/face major redemptions, and the equities bloodbath spells doom for early stage venture/most of crypto.

The worst part for me was that I had no idea what would happen next. Layoffs were coming, a town hall was scheduled in a couple days, but how many of us would make it through the week was anyone's guess. We were all sitting ducks. That did not matter to anyone outside of course. Who would give up the chance to give Joe his comeuppance? The sharks smelled blood and it was time to feed.

"Can you stop moving?" Saira complained. I had been tossing and turning in bed for hours, listening to my heartbeat in my ears like a song you can't forget.

I told Dan how much the uncertainty was gnawing at me. He looked at me almost surprised. "You're safe," he said. "Zero chance you get cut."

Even with those assurances, and Joe's word that PegaSys would be untouched, the anxiety shot through my chest. I replayed the words over and over in my mind, waiting for the pounding to stop, but my body seemed deaf to my pleas. I must be worried for my friends, I told myself. Or was I worried Dan and Joe were lying?

I wondered about the time. *Don't look at your phone,* I told myself. Every article on social media said that that blue light from your phone made you anxious and ruined your sleeping patterns. I fought the temptation. Of course, blue light was not the problem at all, except in the sense that blue light was a metaphor for the tech industry ruining people's lives, which was exactly what was happening to me. I squinted to check my watch instead. Five minutes past 3 AM.

"I can't sleep," I finally admitted to her and to myself. "I'm going to get some water." I stood up and walked to the living room in our tiny, well furnished Upper West Side apartment. We'd been married four months now, so we finally had acquired all the finishings – a gleaming, faux marble coffee table sitting on top of a turquoise, heavily patterned Persian rug her father had gifted us. He owned a few carpet and flooring stores in the tri-state area; Saira had grown up with the nickname *the carpet queen of New Jersey*, which she hated and to me was hilarious. Sometimes when I worried about the state of ConsenSys or reflected on how the tech bubble would inevitably collapse I imagined going to her father, hat in hand, to ask for a job as a carpet salesman. I was already helping him on the side, re-doing his website and trying to encourage him to modernize his business to sell more products online. I dug my toes into the carpet and noticed a stray gym sock; if Saira spotted it in the morning I would never hear the end of it. As I bent down to pick it up, I ran my hand over the lush, hand woven texture. *Yes sir, you see,* I rehearsed in my head, *the highest quality you can find, imported from Turkey. How big of a living room do you have?*

I stayed there for a moment, quadruped, eyes closed, imagining the smell of rooms and rooms full of carpets. Outside the high-rises on Manhattan's Upper West Side cast midnight shadows on our building. The scattered few apartments with lights on made for an urban Starry Night. I closed my eyes tighter and I could only hear my heart beating. *Would I rather be a salesman or admit defeat and go back to consulting bullshit?* Sales was honest work, I thought, or more honest than being an overpaid fluff. It was 3:36 AM as I considered my career dilemma.

My father promised blessings, I thought. When were those coming? I saw my late twenties in the rear view, the only real window to bootstrap that company or join the startup that can't pay you a full salary. I turned thirty in three months; in a couple years, there would be kids and the need for good insurance.

You really only get one swing, I realized.

*Is this it?*

I grabbed my iPad from the counter table and googled *columbus circle cardiologists.* A nice looking Iranian lady returned my gaze in the dark. She would take my insurance and I resolved to call her the next morning. I took an anxiety pill and forgot about carpets and screens for a few hours.

I woke up after 9am and by then the culling had already begun. Sharaf sent me a Slack first thing in the morning, before I even woke up, that he had been invited to an untitled meeting at 9 am. His last startup went belly up, and I had spoken to the analytics team leads and helped him get a role at ConsenSys last year. "Not sure what it's about, but I'm not feeling good about it," he wrote. Another message:

:(

My response never went through. By the time I opened it, his account was already deactivated.

Within an hour the entire Slack workspace blew up. People tagged the Mesh in farewell posts, replete with emojis of teary faces and broken hearts. Every fifteen minutes HR concluded a Zoom call to cut another team, and new goodbyes followed like clockwork. Amare, our self appointed "Chief Anarchy Officer," the constant thorn demanding we live up to our values, wrote a simple note. "bye friends" and "hopefully you stay meshy."

The head of our Chile office (*why did we ever have a Chile office?* I wondered) wrote an emotional missive encouraging everyone to stay strong through the hard times. *Latin people, we have tough skin over our souls*, he wrote. *We bounce back.*

Others defended their tenure. One team wrote a collective note, as bizarre as it was heart wrenching:

> *We were here by the values and principles: increased transparency, inclusion, social responsibility, decentralized organization and the opportunity to design the future ... we were always respectful and honest to one another, and we loved animals.*

News started to leak out of what was going on at ConsenSys. Within hours, TV hosts tweeted about our demise.

**Joe Weisenthal**
@TheStalwart

Imagine being an employee at Consensys. There's a good chance that you, personally, own a lot of Ethereum. So your wealth has been clobbered. And then your company's entire fate is tied to Ethereum and now laying off workers. That's a lot of embedded leverage.

11:31 AM · Dec 7, 2018 · TweetDeck

**19** Retweets **135** Likes

I felt like he was speaking to me directly, reminding me of my worthless pile of shitcoins. If I had just squeezed in a few more trades, I would be sitting on retirement money. What did I regret, really, I wondered: that I had been too greedy – or not greedy enough?

The wifi crashed from all the calls back and forth. I closed my laptop and went for a walk around our Brooklyn office.

*I ended up in the streets after the dot com bubble,* one colleague wrote, *but I made it back.* Hardly reassuring, I thought.

I knew we needed this. If anything, Dan and I would get more of Joe's focus. The last count I heard was over 1600 employees, growing and growing even as the price drifted down while the Mesh tried to will it back up. We had been a lobster in the pot, thinking it was a warm bath. But now the sharp drop forced us to face reality.

Our magic formula was genius for a time, as it seems in every bubble. Now humbled, we now had to make due with a smaller, leaner company, one that could survive the deep winter as crypto matured.

"This could be good," Dan said over Slack, mustering encouragement. "ConsenSys might learn something. I'm willing to try." Maybe Joe could find the balance between laissez-faire father figure and ruthless Silicon Valley CEO. Maybe we could even focus on our best work, raise outside funding, and wean ourselves off Joe's wealth. Maybe.

An engineer I barely knew stopped me as I passed on the sidewalk. His team was a goner – was there any way I could find him a role on PegaSys?

"You've got all the skills, you'll find something quick," I said, unable to promise anything.

"This was my dream job," he lamented. I realized suddenly why these layoffs hurt: most Meshians did not think of this as work. This was a mission, and the pain was not from a broken business model but from witnessing the very ideals they held dear fall apart. I said that I would forward his resume.

More goodbyes and tweets streamed by as I sat on the park bench, barely feeling the December cold. ConsenSys is a bunch of arrogant shitcoin scammers, one maxi tweeted to a nodding audience. The haters said we deserved the punishment, for all the taxi drivers and grandmas who had lost their life savings. Now the grandmas were selling and inflicting the same pain back on us. Karma was a bitch.

From what little I learned about layoffs in business school, this was the wrong way to do them. No one received a reason, other than "hard times." No warnings, either. Just one day we all woke up, and a third of us were gone. How was that fair?

In the meantime, the devastation continued. The entire social impact team – a group of sweet, naive recent grads – was cut next. (It seemed my writings had not been read by anyone in leadership after all.) Before leaving, the team lead demanded *fuck it, what happens to our equity* on the all-company thread. HR threw insincere apologetics to deflect and break up the stream of depressing messages. Each goodbye message was showered with emoji replies, crying faces, sad faces, swearing faces. This was a downsizing in the millennial age: Slack and memes made work feel fun, until the memes and gifs were of crying Elmos and broken bleeding hearts. Then it felt like a supervillain destroying the world.

*dude are you in today's WSJ?*

I hadn't spoken to this college friend in a few years, so his text message caught me off guard. I was at dinner with Saira and her friend, seated in the nightclub-style lighting of a Thai place near Union Square. I wanted to feel far from anything work-related.

*oh god*

"Sorry," I said, feeling rude as I tapped endlessly on my phone. "Got a weird text."

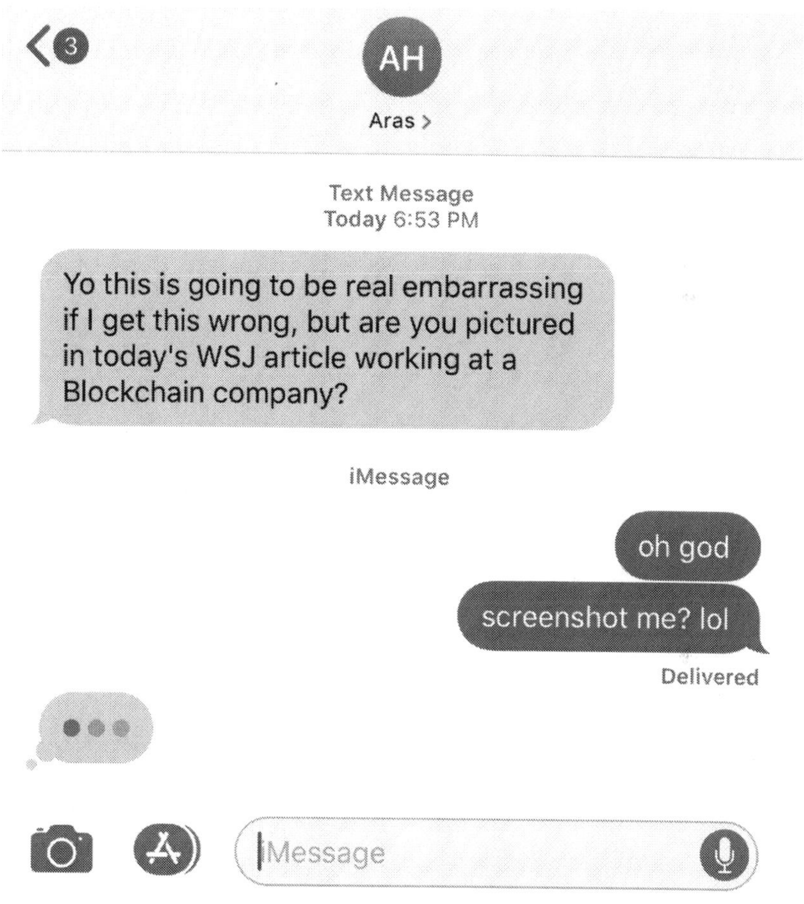


*I'll send you a picture of my copy*

A picture of a newspaper popped up, neatly folded over a subway seat. There, in the top left, I stared a hole into my computer screen. It was the same picture they had used a few months prior. There I was, seated at my desk, hoodie half up and a pair of giant headphones. I texted him back that yes, that is me. How ironic when they used the same picture in an article about how ConsenSys was the next big thing.

*Hope things are okay*, he said nicely. I'll be fine, I replied.

I searched around for the article: another commentary about the layoffs at ConsenSys. I pointed out to Saira that the woman next to me in the photo had been let go in the cutbacks. Her friend, a banker at JP Morgan, expressed disbelief. "This doesn't sound like a normal layoff," she said. "I don't know how I could do any work."

She was right, in a way. This wasn't the normal bump in the road; the entire narrative we wove was torn to pieces. Could Joe change? How much humiliation does a billionaire need to do that? The survivor's guilt returned. I would hunt for more hires knowing full well they might turn into cannon fodder for the next bubble.

"At least you're famous," Saira said, patting me on the shoulder as we rode back on the subway. Another sleepless night awaited.

Joe sent a note to the Mesh.

We built astronomical models and theorized about other planets, he wrote, but now we needed a rocket ship to get there. This would be the start of "ConsenSys 2.0," a new era of focus and sustainability. ConsenSys 1.0 was still an "astonishing" success, he explained in the seven page letter, and he would reveal more of the grand plan. I read through quickly, looking for any admission of fault or error. I found none.

As I scrolled through the pages on Google Docs, I saw the cursors of hundreds of my co-workers coming through along with me, hunting for any hint of the future. The screen flashed orange, then green – people were copy-pasting the entire thing. Of course Coindesk had the letter within minutes. Clearly other Meshians felt even more upset than I did.

Before the town hall, I turned the Bear Stearns pen case over in my hands and thought back to that afternoon in college I had watched the world economy melt down before my eyes.

There was something fascinating about being there on that particular day in 2008, like watching Gettysburg from a nearby hill. We had no idea how severe the effects would be for the world. For a bunch of 20 year olds, it just seemed exciting.

"What's the positive social value banking does for the world?" asked one of my friends during the Q&A in the Bear auditorium.

"Easier than the questions I thought I'd get," laughed the silver-haired director. "We provide financing to companies. Next question?"

"What's going to happen to banks given the current market turmoil?" asked a sharply dressed classmate. I recall his name being Bolton, though I might be wrong.

"Many will be challenged, and we'll need to make adjustments," the director responded as if he had rehearsed it the night before.

"What about Bear? Are there repercussions from the hedge fund collapses?" Bolton was feeling confident.

The director did not take this lightly. "I have been at this bank 26 years and have never doubted that we have the best people on the Street," he said, his voice rising. Suddenly he pounded the wooden podium like he had a gavel. "Mark my words, Bear *will* get through this crisis, and we *will* be stronger on the other side!"

I turned to my best friend Samim, an Afghan from Brooklyn who had managed to impress the bankers we'd spoken to that day. Was he trying to reassure us, I whispered, because it sounded like he was really trying to reassure himself.

The pen cases and notebooks I took that day have turned from souvenir into museum piece, a *memento mori* on my desk. Bank after bank had chased the mortgage market until they all went over the cliff like lemmings. The smartest people usually had the most hubris. And ConsenSys had a lot of smart people.

I told Dan this story as we walked to the town hall. Dan noted that Bear had been bought for $2 a share a few weeks after my visit, so at least most of those people got to keep their jobs.

The town hall showed a Mesh clearly torn about what happened. Many were happy to see accountability finally applied; the crypto-rich who barely showed up to work dragged down our reputation and needed the boot. More professionalism was due.

Others did not fall in line so quickly. A stream of questions poured in as Joe spoke on every possible topic.

Would there be additional layoffs? Joe only gave a vague reply.

Did his decision depend on the price? No, he told us, although no one believed that.

Who made the decisions about who was laid off? That even I wanted to know. How could these decisions be fair when ConsenSys refused to even admit anyone was "in charge"? Someone recalled Amare's warnings about a "shadow hierarchy." Who pulled the strings? We wanted to see their faces.

Joe would give no names. The process had been fair, he said.

I took umbrage at this last point. "It was pretty ridiculous," Sharaf told me of his final meeting. "Someone else said this was their first week." It seemed someone had simply gone down a list and picked the names they did not know.

After years of coddling, had Joe turned on his children? I did not blame him directly as much as the thick layer of yes-men that he congealed around him. The lawyers and Dolphin Men. The lack of structure produced not one Lady Macbeth but dozens, who simply echoed to Joe his beliefs about inevitable victory.

It struck me Joe was acting as if all of this had been part of the plan, a grand strategy, a tragic but inevitable result. How could we be so in denial, I wondered. Price had been prophecy in the good times.

A ConsenSys whale interrupted my thoughts to suggest everyone try micro-dosing LSD for their mental health. It did wonders for me, he said.

"Shouldn't leadership be held accountable?" another Meshian cried.

The pitchforks now came out, and heads needed to roll. *Fire Jared!* someone demanded. The confrontation turned hot as the desire for revenge grew. If Joe would not lay blame, he was going to bear the brunt of the Mesh's anger.

"If you used to be 'white Morpheus' are you now white Thanos?" someone posed anonymously, referring to the Marvel supervillain who killed half of humanity. A meme appeared of Joe's face superimposed onto Thanos' giant, purple, armored body, looking wistful as he considered his power.

I could simply snap my fingers and their jobs would all cease
to exist. I call that...ConsenSys 2.0.


Joe ignored these comments, offered a few positive words, and said goodbye.

HR emailed that these were difficult times and we would make it through. Unfortunately even our "I made it from the streets" colleague in DC had been worn down, replying-all:

> *I can honestly say I have never felt as isolated, under-used, and disempowered in all my professional career of more than 30 years than I do at ConsenSys*
>
> *All the best*

The nice Iranian doctor told me her husband was a banker. "You see, banking and startups, it's both very stressful work," she told me. "You get anxious."

I swung my legs, child-like, on the paper tissue of the exam table. "Yeah, definitely a lot of pressure," I said blandly. Just put the stethoscope on me already, I thought.

"Does your wife work?" she asked, trying not to seem too prying.

"Yeah," I told her, "she's a doctor too, actually."

"Oh!" she laughed. "Does she want a job? I need some young blood." Must be nice, that kind of job security, I thought. "But you know, it's like I tell my husband. We would be fine if anything happened. We're both able to provide."

I imagined a tall, graying brown man, eyes creased from being in banking for twenty years. I wondered if he'd ever left his friends out in the cold to save himself. Instead I asked if palpitations were normal with anxiety.

"Everyone has different symptoms. I don't want to give you pills because then you'll just be another finance guy on pills." *Banker husband with his hand in the cookie jar?* I wondered. "I'll give you a Halter monitor – it will listen to your heart for a week. If you feel anything weird, just press the button, and I'll know." I thanked her, went to pick up my monitor from the nurse, and walked home in the cold.

More cuts came in the coming weeks. Many of those not laid off, as spokes were "spun out" from the mothership, got a gentle shove off the diving board with $100,000 of funding to find their way. A lifeboat and some canned food to hold you over through the hurricane.

Omar's end was inevitable too. We both knew it. And when the time came, we had little to say. The energy had been sucked out of him, as a fire burns out its oxygen, and we simply shook hands and resolved to catch up later. In the business world, you can be a sailor riding the smooth corporate seas, or a startup pirate testing uncharted waters. But if it's the pirate's life for you, then don't be surprised when you have to walk the plank.

# GREEN SHOOTS

*A man asked JP Morgan, the banking titan of the 1920s and 30s, if he had any predictions for the stock market.*
*His response: "It will fluctuate."*

*New York, April 2019. ETH:* $165.

As 2019 dragged on the crypto bloodbath did not end so much as pause. Everyone had expected a final blow, but that was too predictable. Instead there was the slow, steady hiss of air being let out of a balloon.

Bitcoin bugs and crypto nuts spent the year arguing why the price would come back up. Another wave would come, they said: there had been five "Bitcoin recessions" already. The Bitcoin maniacs – Charlie Shrem, Anthony Pompliano, Tim Draper, Erik Voorhees, Ari Paul, and whole armies of charlatans trying to mimic them – continued pumping Bitcoin as the one true coin. Bakkt, the Bitcoin exchange heralded as the arrival of the big investors, became enmired in scandals and delays.[31] The price stayed down.

The 'thought leaders' slowly faded away, some becoming experts in new areas like machine learning or VR. The prognosticators stopped prognosticating. 'Experts' claimed everyone had been wrong all along: blockchain was clearly for payments, or for the back office, or something else that their hawkeyed hindsight had made obvious. Now you see me, now you don't.

---

31 The CEO of Bakkt was actually the wife of its chief investor's CEO. After Bakkt failed, she became a US Senator. See, it's not just crypto that's full of corrupt people!

The Whale insisted big money would still come soon. Fidelity and Blackrock are coming. The price would go up, and then down again. A golden metronome.

Other large companies focused on Ethereum like Status and Steemit soon cut up to 70% of their workforce. R3 even took the step of suing Ripple for billions of dollars on a deal gone sour, as the enterprise blockchains now tried to eat each other. Blythe Masters, the "quadrillion dollar" CEO of Digital Asset, stepped down with no explanation in the press release. None was needed. Life moved on.

The cardiologist said the tests had come back and I was fine. I took most of March off and went jet-skiing in the Maldives on a long delayed honeymoon. Blessings needed counting.

When I returned to Bogart the office was empty and eerily quiet. The Whale was in, looking sunburned. He had apparently been quite drunk the night before, Dan told me. This close to a billion, he had declared, two fingers close to each other and teary eyed. At a 95% loss, he probably had come down to fifty million or so. At least he had enough to keep a healthy tan.

I video called Ritesh a few days later to see if he'd had any luck with the banks. There was a blur of brown and black as he realized he had turned on the video accidentally to reveal himself sitting shirtless in his home office. "Oh shit," he exclaimed, switching off.

Doesn't look like much progress, Dan said to me as we piled into my rental car. Our team had convened in LA – the middle point for us and Australia – to find a new path forward now that we'd shelved the two hundred person hiring plans. The little Chevy purred as it climbed up to Griffith Observatory high above the Los Angeles skyline, where the purples and oranges of sunset were just climbing their way across from the Pacific to downtown.

We'd weathered the storm with a dozen or more customers in pilots, including a few major banks and governments. That might be a high success rate for blockchain, but not enough to raise venture funding in this environment. I leaned on the white concrete barrier and pulled out a napkin drawing I had made to show how all our paths to unicorn like growth were now cut off:

| | **Wall Street** | **Joe schmo** |
|---|---|---|
| **Public blockchain** | Too scary | Too slow |
| **Enterprise blockchain** | Too expensive | Too boring |

Dan shifted his weight as he looked from napkin to skyline. "Joe will never give up," he said, ever persistent. "That means we lay in wait until he's got ten billion dollars again."

I didn't disagree. There were armies of rich techie guys who had too much money and were too nerdy for gambling on football. Crypto would come back. We could build Joe's world anew.

But what about me?

I had already put two years into this. Loyalty to Dan kept me going. The teammates I'd hired who needed jobs. I looked over at the Aussies, happily snapping selfies with the Hollywood sign in the background. That was enough for some resolve. But was it enough?

After the fallout, things were starting to stir again. JP Morgan had announced "JPMCoin," a coin for banks that stole the financial world's attention for weeks, and it would be built on Ethereum. New apps were coming out, referred to as "DeFi," decentralized finance, that could create a digital dollar, lend or borrow money, or provide savings accounts, using only algorithms and smart contracts.[32] The story was shifting: from killing the banks to being the banks.

For Joe, that was perfect. DeFi sounded sexy, and we needed sexy to convince investors to come back. ConsenSys "2.0" had been trying for months to work backwards: to find the problems that Ethereum could

32 Most of the excitement then was around "stablecoins," essentially cryptocurrency backed by real currency, a salve for the nauseating fluctuations of crypto. The most popular stablecoin is the dollar-backed USDT, with over $17B in circulation – supposedly. From inception, USDT has been dogged by accusations it is not actually backed by US dollars, and its Virgin Islands auditors didn't help. MakerDAO, an "algorithmic stablecoin" run on Ethereum, instead relied on a deposit system that was more reliable.

solve and build a business worthy of investors. To me, trying to think of a problem to solve *after* starting the business was like trying to invent a new color. Even so, Joe and Jared had toured Silicon Valley looking for investors, yet none could make heads or tails of our hub and spoke model. Google had its moonshots, but we were no Google.

Satoshi gave guidance from the beyond. He, in his infinite wisdom, had created crypto to be a currency. That settled it: financial services would be the key focus, and a more reliable bet, than robot AI video games or satellites. DeFi would be the name of the game. More importantly, DeFi could create apps that promised stable returns – something crypto whales, and perhaps even Joe Schmo, would love. ConsenSys would take the zombie remains of Omar's code and spin it into a new platform. Would this be the story that could stick?

Ahmad, my old classmate and colleague, had come from Dubai for this year's Consensus, recurring now after a full year and a lifetime. Spurred by my encouragement and ConsenSys' gravitational waves, he had joined in 2018 and was now leading the Dubai office. "No Lamborghinis this year," I warned, trying to lower his expectations.

He updated me on Dubai. The government still believed, and our little office was making money. But all that paled next to the feeling when he walked into the massive new office we'd built and eighty empty seats stared back.

Across the crowded hotel lobby I spotted a familiar face. Not one that I knew in person, but still familiar: a Netflix documentary about Fyre, the doomed music festival in the Bahamas, had seized the popular imagination recently. An island concert advertised with bikini-clad models on jet skis had disastrously turned out to be little more than refugee tents in a hurricane, and viewers loved the *schadenfreude* of watching wealthy millennials suffer. Out of the organizing group of Ja Rule and fraudulent entrepreneurs, only one planner seemed sane, a long-haired banker turned yoga instructor who warned months in advance that they were headed for disaster.

And now here he was in front of me. Of course he went from Fyre to crypto, I thought. Natural transition. "Hey," I said, casually.

Small talk ensued. He was a crypto investor now, working to bring in more institutional investors. "Right on, man!" he said, fist bumping me when I told him about PegaSys. "Have you been to the DeFi lectures?" he asked me excitedly. "That stuff is the *future*."

Ahmad smiled as we walked away. "That was better than Lambos," he said with a smile. "Doesn't Fyre kind of remind you of a certain startup ...?" he trailed off.

Oh yes, I said. Even down to the superfluous y in the name.

An old colleague of mine was now leading a DeFi startup and had just raised tens of millions from Silicon Valley to build crypto-based lending tools. If anyone would help me see if DeFi was the escape hatch we thought, it was him. I texted him if he was in town.

Let's meet up for a drink, he replied. A fancy Midtown hotel was best. Company tab, I hoped. Were the good times back?

I sank into the dark leather chair set in dark wood in the dark hotel bar across from him. He was young and handsome and full of energy. He listened to my Fyre story politely, though his eyes kept jumping from side to side. "The waiter keeps coming by," he said finally. "I've been doing meetings here all day but haven't ordered."

The comment caught my ear. The amount VCs had invested suggested impressive business results. "You must be making real revenue," I wondered aloud.

"So far?" he asked. "Well, actually you helped us the most!" He went on to tell me his biggest customer was the Whale, an introduction I'd made last year, and that their total revenue was less than half his salary. They needed to find more whales to be profitable. That, or they might release a token.

The waiter came by again, asking for my order. It seemed like our second attempt at revolution might go the same way as our first.

# THE SCHOOLBUS

*"First rule of startups: if you own 100% of zero, you're still worth zero."* – Dan *New York, August 2019. ETH:* $224.

Dan and I shuffled up the misshapen steps in Bogart, unsure of what to expect. Giovanni, ConsenSys' lawyer, had asked us to a meeting for a discussion on equity. "Is there any point to this?" I asked Dan. "ConsenSys can't find investors anyway."

The market doldrums had lessened and Ether was slowly, steadily coming up. Momentum was on our side: more pilots and a couple paying customers.

That created a circular conflict: the better we did, the more we wanted to leave the Mesh and the more Joe wanted us to stay. ConsenSys "2.0" had changed little, other than nixing another spoke every week. I sent Dan our brochure, crossing out all of the dead projects.

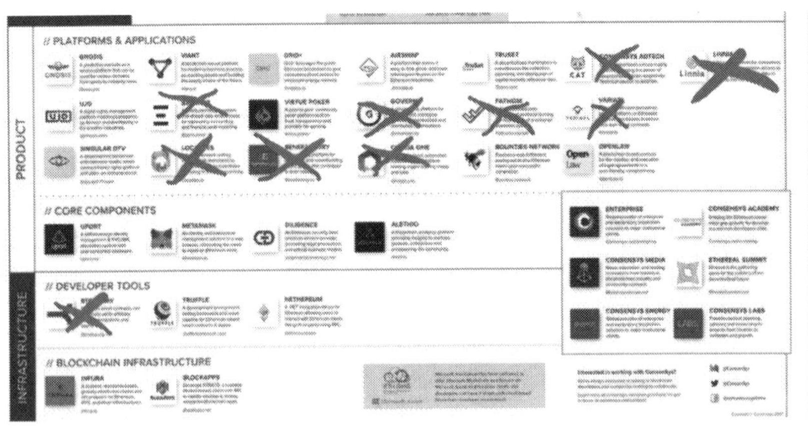

Halfway into 2019 I checked on a Slack thread I'd had with my other Pakistani friends in the Mesh. Omar, Sharaf, Azeem, Abdul, Zunaira, all gone: now I was in the chat by myself. Even the CIA could not drone strike Muslims in these numbers. Vanessa, the business development teammate who always mixed me up with the other browns, had figured out who I was now that there was no one else to confuse me for. I wished myself a happy Eid and felt sorry for having pitied myself.

Perhaps ConsenSys wanted to make amends, I thought. There were still promises to keep.

"Joe will be joining," Giovanni told us flatly as we sat down in our orange plastic chairs. That was unusual. A few others – our head of Legal, who unfortunately has to read every line of this book, looking for reasons to sue me – and Andreas, another friend of mine at the company, soon joined. We waited, and then Joe appeared, one hand rubbing the back of his bare head.

Joe started calmly. As we knew, ConsenSys wanted to raise funding from investors, and that meant streamlining. *Streamlining* is a swear word in corporate politics, which usually meant being shown the door. I worried for a moment. But he soon clarified his intentions: ConsenSys wanted full ownership of its best teams. These spokes would all be merged, like a super robot from a Japanese anime, to form the core of the new ConsenSys.

"So what does that mean for our equity?" Dan asked, cutting to the chase. Were our negotiations being canceled?

"For the good spokes with traction, like Infura, MetaMask, and you guys," Joe explained, "we will acquire the remainder of your equity."

I raised my eyebrows. Acquired?

With ... money ...?

This might be *deus ex machina* we'd been waiting for, I thought, or a pity deal for pennies on the dollar. Which one likely depended upon negotiating with the lawyers yet again.

Luckily, Joe informed us, we would be dealing with someone new. Joe had tasked Andreas to complete this deal.

Andreas looked at us through a pair of thick spectacles. "Joe wants me to get all the spokes on the bus, and I have been tasked with driving," he said with a smile while tugging on his ear. "It's time to pick you all up for school."

Dan and I sat down in a corner of the office near a pile of bean bags. He asked me to write down how much money we should ask for. I wrote down a number in the millions. A fraction of what we could have had a year prior, but large enough to me. I slid the paper back across to him.

He stared at it blankly. He took my pen, scratched out my number, and tripled it. Planets, man, *planets!*

He said, given my past in finance, I should chart the path to the number we'd go for. I went back to my apartment for the afternoon, staring at my laptop and wondering what to do. This might be beyond me, even with all the financial wizardry and tricks I'd learned over the last few years.

Our kitten jumped in my lap and began to meow loudly. He was a Bengal, striped and spotted like a tiger, meaning we obviously had to name him Sher Khan. I picked him up, barely the size of my palm, and set him on my desk, where he flipped over and splayed across my keyboard and filled my screen with nonsense.

*][pokkkkkkkkkkkkkkkkkkkkkkk*

Probably as good as my work, I thought.

I scrambled to conjure up something to fill the emptiness of my spreadsheet. Truth be told, the timing was on our side. Eth had fought its way to nearly $300, and ConsenSys' marketing had started using the phrase "crypto spring." We had just closed our first major customers; we could launch a token if we wanted. And above all else, if Joe wanted to sell investors on a vision of crypto-paradise, Ethereum 2.0 was the pearly gates for which PegaSys held the key. We held all the cards. But how much did we deserve?

I thought back to LA a few months prior. Crypto was coming back like Dan and I had figured. Take the right number and run.

No, I thought. Take more. I had a billionaire on the ropes, and the revolution didn't matter much now. Make it hurt. I remembered Ritesh's words. Guys like us, he said, we don't make the Bezos or Lubin money. Take your chance because it might be the only one.

I played with the spreadsheet. Up, down. The numbers coalesced now: even bigger than Dan's number. How much would that be for me? On paper, at least half a million.

Feels right, I thought.

Andreas looked at the spreadsheet with a mixture of surprise and consternation. He adjusted his glasses. We waited for a response. We expected laughter.

"I think this positions you really well," he said at last.

They barely negotiated. Andreas could not guarantee anything, but Joe would likely approve. We were shocked.

I missed the final details, taking another vacation in California. (My vacations piled up that year.) We hiked up the stairs hewn into the rocks of Yosemite, listening to the sightseers chatter in French about the lovely views. The waterfalls of the melting glacier draped over boulders hundreds, maybe thousands of feet tall, and we looked across the valley to the evening light coloring El Capitan with a perfect golden hue as it had everyday for the last ten thousand years. I thought about the buyout, which even as it constituted the pinnacle of startup success, felt oddly empty. The last three years I had rehearsed the dream of being acquired so many times in my mind it felt like a memory. Now I tried to piece together the mental flotsam and jetsam of the last few years that barely made sense, confused as if I'd just woken up from a half-remembered dream. I really hope Joe buys us out, I thought, because I don't think I can do this job much longer.

When I returned, Dan gave me the update: signed and approved. I congratulated him on the successful 'exit.' "First of many for you," I said as we high fived.

The number was enough to make Dan wealthy (wealthier?), and enough to make the last thirty or so months feel well spent. I told Dan to rub it in his brother's face, but he said his brother had just been nominated for an Oscar, and so he still had a long way to go.

"Just one condition," he finished. "We'll only get paid one eighth each quarter. So to get all of it, we have to stay at ConsenSys for two years."

I looked at him for a moment. Hmm, I thought. Two years. That is a long time.

Two years. I thought about that night. Is my heart beating fast again? ConsenSys had barely survived the last two years, and the price could – likely would – always crash and nix our deal. I was doubling down.

I tried to remember what the Iranian doctor had told me. Deep breaths. Sher Khan meowed late into the night, wondering how he'd ended up in a six hundred square foot Manhattan apartment. Curses spilled out of me as I pushed him out of our bed, and Saira asked me why I was blaming him for my own restlessness. I needed a change. It was time to consult my sherpa.

I waited for Omar on the corner by our office. The smell of halal chicken and rice from across the block tempted me to artery-clogging gluttony, but we would not be taking packets of white sauce back to the office like the old days. I squinted up at the graffiti spray painted near the roof. "PIGEONS KILL YUPPIES," the artist declared.

"Joe wants to buy our equity," I explained to Omar as we turned the corner. A horn blasted from a passing cement truck, pulling sharply in front of us into a mixing lot. A lone sushi chef stood in the back of the place we had chosen. Omar wanted reassurance we would avoid any run-ins with the Mesh.

"Don't take it," he said. "When they fail at fundraising, they'll just screw you over later. They don't have any good people left." I wondered if he was referring to himself.

Our talent pipeline was certainly weakened. Someone, Amare probably, had left a comment on a talent website that ConsenSys "had fired all the black people." Ouch.

*Oh no*, I whispered looking up from our table. Omar turned just in time to see Joe walk in, the two locking eyes in a moment of silence before both put on fake smiles. He faced me again, his eyes stony and cold.

A hot beat passed before both of us nodded. We passed the menus to a puzzled looking waiter and waved to Joe as we left.

The ride underground to Washington Square Park was short and quiet. ConsenSys planned to focus heavily on DeFi, I said, using the old spokes' smart contracts to build a new platform.

Omar suddenly came alive. "They're using my team's work," he declared to half the park. "Aren't they?"

I lied and said I wasn't sure.

"Man, I should've told Joe I'm suing him right then and there." He would not have been the first, or even the last – only a couple days prior Giovanni was on the phone discussing terms with someone's opposing counsel. He had hung up and said his next call would be another disgruntled employee, who had gone to the lengths of hiring Mark Zuckerberg's attorney.

My next words hung in my throat. I had been about to say the DeFi project was a mess and that team kept asking for my help. I thought the change of scene might do wonders.

But that would not go over well now. Omar would see me working with his old team undoubtedly as a betrayal. We sat down on a bench and I told him he might have success with a lawsuit, given what I'd heard from Giovanni.

I wouldn't be getting any more advice today, at least not from Omar. For now, I was on my own.

# THE DING DONG HALL OF FAME

*"A man who stands for nothing will fall for anything."* – Malcolm X

*New York, November 2019. ETH:* $173.

Omar was wrong. The first check from Joe came in the mail, and it cashed. My PegaSys teammates were effusive with their thanks, telling me about a new house they had an eye on.

Startupland calls these often multi-year periods of waiting for checks the time to "rest and vest." But I showed up for work and went home each day feeling uneasy with ennui. Thirty was too young to come in each day to stare at the clock. The napkin I'd drawn for Dan haunted me, and I heard the mockery from the tiny Bill Gates on my shoulder: *Less than a million? That's the best you can do?*

The crypto markets churned and boredom begat curiosity. I began to experiment with DeFi, logging on to dy/dx, a trading tool where I could buy complicated derivatives of Ethereum and other crypto.[33] The friendly, brightly colored interface of buttons and popups invited me to play pinball with my bank account. I could see the man on the street enjoying this. It felt more personal than trading stocks.

The trading instincts, long dormant, suddenly turned hot and loud. I managed to buy a synthetic form of Ether that was five times as volatile. Still smarting over my losses during the boom, I pounded the keys

33 An impressive pun which I hope you appreciate.

looking for my second chance. I made two thousand dollars the first week, but three days later I had lost it all.

Someone had crossed stock trading with a video game, and I wanted more. No bank would ever give people that experience. Rat, meet cheese. The wheels started turning in my head. People would actually want to use this.

I reached out to Corbin, the DeFi project lead. I wanted in.

The Frenchmen were looking at me with great distaste, as only Frenchmen can.

I was barely a month into my DeFi tenure and already making enemies. DeFi apps had picked up steam in the last few weeks, marching towards one billion dollars in activity. The charts showed fitful jumps upward that were horrifyingly encouraging, evoking Ethereum in early 2017, just before I joined the Mesh. The countdown to liftoff was starting.

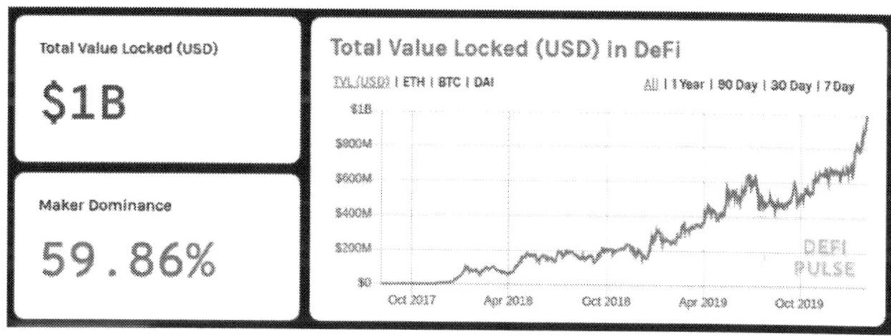


*Source:* DeFiPulse.com

But a deep fissure emerged: whether to build the apps for banks or to kill the banks. One team of engineers, based in Ireland, still lived by the *disrupt or die* motto while another, based in France, had a major financial services customer already signed and delivered. Now we met in Dublin face to face to settle the debate.

The Irish, knowing I was on their side, welcomed me to their office by the Dublin docks with their typical warmth and an offer of Guinness. (I declined). Smooth-cheeked and pouty faced, the Frenchmen sat across from us in the colorless conference room and ran over the long list of pointless requirements their bankers wanted.

I wanted to rub the lead Frenchie's face in the charts of orange and green. Crypto payments, loans, collectibles: these were the future, I said. Hadn't we learned anything from the last bubble? Silly made money and serious got fired. I had spent years pitching banks and knew they were only tourists in startupland, never staying long enough to truly innovate.

But there was only one potential customer Corbin and I could scrounge up that was willing to take payments via crypto, a company based in California unable to accept credit cards because the US government still considered their industry illegal. They hoped crypto might be a good substitute.

Cannabis was to be the bedrock for the next Internet.

The Frenchmen weren't buying it. They had billion dollar investors. We had weed. This was not the rocket ship scenario that I had envisioned, but if Dan taught me one thing, it was to forget the odds.

I huddled with the Irishmen near the snack table where we resolved to go ahead on our own, screw the consequences (and the French). I was all-in: you take off or you blow up on the launchpad.

On my return from Ireland I stopped by Bogart to find it emptier than usual. By the end of the day only Joe and I were left. I asked him about his plans for Thanksgiving.

"No plans," he said. "I usually spend it with my son, but he's with his mom. Probably just going to work." I gave him a smile and said to enjoy some rest, but a feeling of sadness bubbled up. This man, for all his billions and his legions of admirers, would spend the holidays very much alone. Crypto was his only mistress now, avaricious as she was, and their dalliance would likely never end until he had given everything.

The next two months of mornings were filled with fighting with Frenchmen and building code for DeFi. Victory and defeat came hand in hand. In six weeks, we had our first app: with just the click of a button, I could instantly deploy an ERC-20 smart contract. I created a billion

FaisTokens and sent them to my friends. Zero to one was still the best feeling in startup.

The cannabis company called soon after to cancel on us. Crypto, their last lifeline, had come too late: they were declaring bankruptcy.

We pitched a few banks, but that still went nowhere. The crypto markets were slipping downwards quickly, a spring with no summer. Ritesh might know which had potential, I suggested to Corbin as we pecked at our laptops on the undersized table of an Upper West Side cafe.

"ConsenSys cut him last month," Corbin told me, surprise turning to amusement at my shocked expression. "He's been tweeting some pretty angry stuff." My jaw hung for a moment.

Alas, poor Ritesh. I knew him well. Maybe some DeFi startup would pick him up. He and hundreds of other Meshians had been scattered to the winds, many landing at Amazon Blockchain or Coinbase or Facebook's Libra coin, ready to tell a new blockchain story, the tirades against Big Tech long forgotten.[34] Dozens of mice lost in the maze, looking for the cheese that might not be there.

My own pickings were desperate and few. But I told Corbin that Leanne, another colleague, had approached me in Bogart last week. "The DeFi stuff got me thinking," she said. "Can you keep this to yourself?"

The next day I sat with her looking at the smiling visage of an NBA player on the big screen in Bogart. Metta World Peace was known as a champion, All-Star, and the biggest weirdo in all of sports. I told him this was perfect timing: Spencer Dinwiddie, a forward for the Brooklyn Nets, wanted to use DeFi to make it possible to "invest" in players by turning their contracts into tokens.

34 In fact, the Libra project would soon became a whipping boy for Congress to highlight tech companies' excessive ambitions. Jerome Powell, the Federal Reserve Chairman, called Libra a source of "serious concerns regarding privacy, money laundering, consumer protection, [and] financial stability." Even Joe went on TV to say he was a "big fan" of Libra, as stablecoins would be the impetus for blockchain to finally get widespread adoption.

An impossibly wide grin came in reply. "I know all about that," he said, his jittery fingers waving on screen. "Love that. Did I tell you about my app?"

Metta was not alone in his enthusiasm for tech. Andre Igoudala, Kevin Durant, and even Lebron James were making VC investments. I guessed there was another reason NBA players had become obsessed with startups: with their formidable funds they wanted to join America's new cabal of the rich and powerful – tech entrepreneurs.

"I have always been super into crypto," he continued with another excited head bob. "I feel like now is a great time to work with y'all."

I subtly took a photo of the screen while spitballing ideas. His eyes lit up when I mentioned a coin to make bets on pickup games. "You could even have a leaderboard," I said. This conference room, its past littered with so many of my marker drawings of complex software architecture, now might be the site of a victory based on my simplest idea yet. It was no replacement for a bank, but Metta had a lot of money and cachet to take us to the big time.

But I told Corbin in the cafe that as the call went on our lanky customer's patience with the technicalities wore thin. "I got the impression," I began to confess, "that he just wanted a coin to name after himself."

Corbin hemmed and hawed while looking into his coffee. "Not great," he replied. Was the future of crypto selling goofy coins to people with too much money? At least we'd be the best at it.

Omar called me again days later with more startup ideas. Was I ready to quit yet? "You see this DeFi stuff Consensys is prattling on about," he said. It was like he was reading my mind. "Bunch of clowns. Ding dong shit."

"Absolutely," I replied. I imagined what he would say if I told him the truth, that I was selling that stuff using his old code. But there was, I decided, no need to give him the opportunity to call me a traitor or a fool. I already knew that I was.

# ROLLER COASTER

*New York, February 2020. ETH:* $186.

Everyone loves roller coasters, but stay on one too long, and you'll throw up on your own face.

The desire to jump ship grew until it became unbearable. Someone told me high quality LinkedIn photos attracted recruiters, and I picked the photo where I looked the least brown and photoshopped my skin even lighter. I would change it back once I scored some interviews, I told myself, but the interviews soon started and I changed nothing.

A fellow Meshian asked if I could help in a meeting with NIST, the National Institute of Science and Technology, the US agency which set the industry standard for cryptography and whose approval we needed to make banks happy if they were ever going to use Ethereum. The metal detectors and endless hallways of fluorescent lighting at their headquarters outside DC warned us what the faceless gatekeepers of government might think of our revolution.

"We might fall behind China soon," my colleague Mike said in the meeting, hoping to add expediency. How long could it take to potentially add Ethereum to their approved lists? I added that Ethereum 2.0 was being written as we spoke, and if the US government didn't pay attention they would miss the next crypto wave, too – one that would be based on technology 1000x more scalable.

"Unless we see massive industry adoption," their cryptography lead replied, "we probably wouldn't approve any new algorithms in the next ten years, at least."

Good God, I thought. Ten years? Were they just rubbing it in? The straw fell heavy on the camel's back.

The price of Ether fell steadily again from $200 to $150, and when the price collapsed again to $120, nearly a year to the day after the first drop, we knew what to expect. We all filed into year-end strategy meetings to debate why we had missed our revenue targets. But at the end of the day Alec's equation could not be broken: nine women could not make a baby in one month and 100 engineers could not finish a five year blockchain upgrade in one. ConsenSys had built a Ferrari with no engine.

The inevitable town hall came and went without the accusations of perfidy from yesteryear. The sycophants tried to lighten the mood, asking Joe silly questions. "It's 2030, and Ether is $10,000. Joe – where do you go for vacation?"

Joe smiled, always happy to daydream about the future. "Well, by then, ConsenSys Space will likely have an extraterrestrial base, so I assume that will be a good escape from these earthly coils," he declared. He considered for a moment the likelihood of touristic viability on the moon. "I like scuba, too? Perhaps there will be some good undersea space diving to be had."

ConsenSys Space's continued existence revealed what the town hall did not: that Joe wasn't willing to cut to the bone, at least not in the way investors wanted. Not yet.

But Omar's warnings contained some truth. We'd clearly tried to pitch Silicon Valley, but they found "ConsenSys 2.0" wanting. One plus one still did not equal three. More cuts would be needed, and they would come soon. I wondered if this time I might be on that list.

I reached out to Metta. We had been speaking on and off for a month, but nothing had closed yet.

He had been sending me emails regularly, but his questions showed he still was unsure on what to do. "I've spent a mil building my app already," he said, "and I'm not sure I understand the crypto stuff. Can't we just make a coin?"

My ideas didn't make sense to him yet, and I didn't know if they really made any sense to me. In one meeting, I tried to explain NFTs, but lost his interest as soon as I tried to explain the definition of *non-fungible*. I had rarely had a second thought about spending Joe's money, but Joe was different: he would die before giving up on crypto. But for Metta, there was either helping on his frivolous ideas or just using his fame for marketing and money. Self-respect was missing from the equation.

I knew I was crazy to give up on such an obvious chance for fun and profit. But I had grown tired of spending my life trying to realize the fantasies of the wealthy. Leaving Wonderland was all I could think about.

A second town hall invite arrived. We understood what this probably meant: after months of searching, ConsenSys' search for investors had still yielded nothing. The mother lions had hunted all they could for food and found none.

Joe said a few words, describing in his usual *sotto voce* how the events of the last two years had been inspiring, and how much he had enjoyed – loved – working with each one of us. He paused for a long moment, looking down. When he came back to looking at the camera, it was clear he was near tears. The cowboy bravado (*who gives a fuck?*) was missing. We had to keep going in our mission, he said, and to do so there would have to be hard cuts to reach ConsenSys 3.0. He looked around the room at the somber expressions. Someone put a hand on his arm.

"3.0?" David messaged me. "In ten years we'll be at ConsenSys 6.0 and it'll just be Joe by himself." Not everyone felt moved.

Joe's voice broke a few times while he delivered the rest of the bad news. There would be more spin-outs, more layoffs, more difficult goodbyes, but we had learned and we would grow. "I'm proud to work for this guy," Dan whispered to me, as we listened to the elegiac descriptions of our near future.

HR came on afterward to deliver hard numbers. The company had shed some 500 people in the last year or so, leaving us with a shade under 1000 or so on the payroll. The right number was much smaller. There was no official target, however, because they were afraid someone would leak it to the media. That was all they would say.

When a spaceship takes off, it is the size of a large building. It loses most of its bulk in the Earth's atmosphere, burning fuel and detaching the boosters halfway through the atmosphere. Even then, the remaining shuttle is not capable of landing on anything extraterrestrial – the atmosphere is too thin. The only way to get to the surface is to deploy a small lander, the size of a car, usually with just two seats. Only a select few get to make it to the moon.

I told Saira about the call that had just happened. A hot pizza sat between us, warming us up like a fireplace in the chill of February rains. I was still wet, having come in after going outside to listen to Joe.

"It's good you have that job offer then," she said. I agreed. At long last I had an offer for the role I wanted. "So you're going to take it?"

I told her I was on the fence. I thought about my friends that still worked here. DeFi still had some promise. The potential for a virtual currency remained huge – billions of people in developing countries from India to Nigeria to Argentina were stuck with depreciating currencies or runaway inflation and no sound alternatives. Ethereum could fill that gap.[35] But until Eth 2.0 came through – at least a few years at the current pace – I would have to work on more betting tokens and weed networks. There were eighteen more months for me to "rest and vest," but I could not ditch the feeling I was waiting for a revolution that might never come.

I told Dan I had a job offer in hand. Maybe an optimist can convince me, I thought. It was the night after the Oscars and we had been surprised over his brother's shock loss. We met for lunch at our usual taco place where no one else spoke in English and we could speak frankly.

"We're meeting with Microsoft again next week," he said, "and then JP Morgan again. They've finally come around. Don't give up now." The window was opening, he felt, regardless of the price.

I couldn't admit to him that deep down, somewhere, I knew this had been the time of my life. But my heartstrings led me to this job, and I

35 Digital payments in many of these places is "stuck" because banks and payment processors earn their living by charging transaction fees to handle these transactions – an average of about 2.5% on every transaction. Unfortunately, that made very small payments – anything less than a few dollars – uneconomical, which in turn hurt everyone from food trucks to Internet artists to most of the developing countries of the world.

needed my head to lead me out. "I want to see some tears, Dan," I joked with him. "Then I'll feel like you really need me."

The blue eyes looked amused but the pursed lips signaled determination. "Fine, come over for dinner tomorrow," he said with a wave of his hand. "I'll make some guacamole with lots of onions, and you'll get your tears."

"Good," I replied, "someone in your family will finally win an Oscar." Dan just shook his head.

I messaged David, Bilal, Shadi, and a few others to check their thoughts on staying for ConsenSys 3.0. They did not have a choice, they informed me. They were all being cut.

I resigned that evening.

What was Joe's real mistake? Was it believing too much in how much one technology could change the world? Or was it just trusting us too much – making his "billion dollar bet on humanity" – that with enough money and creativity a group of passionate entrepreneurs really could change the world? Did we fail because we aimed too high or because we did not beat our waxen wings hard enough?

Everyone at ConsenSys had been moved by Joe's tears on the call. Some, like Dan, wanted to stay and fight for such a vision. I had my reservations. I wanted to fault him but I knew the blame lay equally with us. So many people in ConsenSys had coveted money over impact, or power over revolution, and the anarchy that had held us back so many times was our collective failure. Joe had aimed to change the world, even conquer the stars. Now we heard ConsenSys would auction the space invaders arcade games from the ConsenSys Space office to make a few bucks.

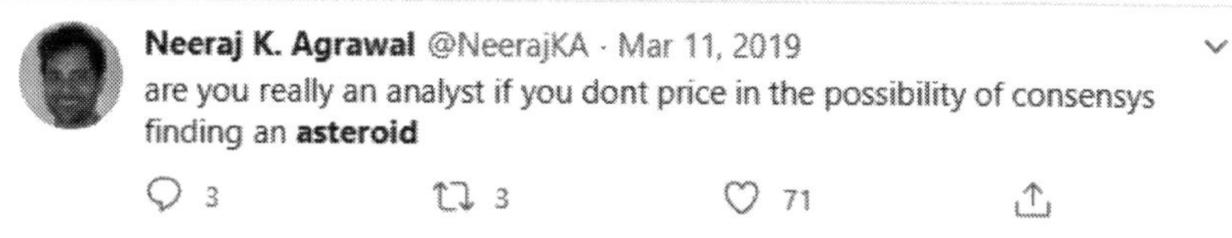

Neeraj K. Agrawal @NeerajKA · Mar 11, 2019
are you really an analyst if you dont price in the possibility of consensys finding an **asteroid**
3
3
71


There are those who will interpret Joe and our collective failings as clear signs for the failures in tech, or capitalism, or both, an intoxicating cocktail that convinces men and women they are more powerful than they really are. But by and large, everyone I met in ConsenSys, Joe most of all, started with good intentions. We only wanted to create a better future, but sometimes we forgot to ask: better for who? We obsessed over building perfect machines and forgot we were imperfect people. Blockchain, and the enigma we created around it of an infallible technology, simply formed a mirror for our altogether too human failings.

Emotions had taken over for so many – greed, FOMO, pride, hope. Our mission had started around the seriousness of money: something too serious to be left in the hands of inept governments. But in the end we became reckless: easy come, easy go. We laughed at Dubai's splendour, and its wastefulness, but when we experienced the same excess we did little better.

I still didn't know whether to feel angry at Joe for experimenting with our livelihoods so recklessly. I doubted that Zuckerberg had ever thought his app for sharing college party photos would transform into a Russian propaganda site or that Jack Dorsey foresaw his texting service could be so used by a President to spew racial hatred. Tech is an industry for optimists, and we had all been too optimistic every time we opened Pandora's box, and yet we did it again and again. We tried to infuse the software we built with the best of our values, but technology always outlived us: there was no way to control what our colleagues, let alone our descendants, might do with it. In the end, tech defined the future's norms more than our norms defined the tech. That was what made it so exciting to us, after all.

It dawned on me that Joe had not cried the first time he had to fire hundreds. He had cried the second time, when he was *forced* to, when he finally had lost control of what he had built. I wondered what it felt like to be so rich that you feel invincible, only to find out that you are as subject to destiny as everyone else.

My two weeks notice ticked by uneventfully. Dan emailed me. He knew my last day was coming up, and he was going to make one last stand to convince me to stick around. Persistent to the last. I knew he stayed partly from the golden handcuffs to vest his equity, but I admired his determination nonetheless. "All the foundations you laid are paying off," he told me. "We're doing another negotiation this week. At least come to the meeting."

I walked into the fourth floor meeting room in Bogart for the last time. The team was on lunch break, filing in line to pile up Roberta's pizza on paper plates. I stood in the back of the line behind who else – Dolphin Man. "Good to see you!" he said, full of energy.

As I took a bite of my pizza he addressed the room. "I know it's supposed to be a working lunch, but I thought I would take the stress off by showing you guys some photos from my trip to the Bahamas!" He plugged in his laptop and pulled up a photo of a boat floating in turquoise waters. "Paradise, isn't it?" he asked. The Microsoft guys nodded politely, uncertain what to think.

"Oh dear," he exclaimed suddenly, "can't show you that!" He jammed his keyboard trying to skip over the close ups he had taken of his wife in her bikini. Ten seconds of awkwardness ensued. "Boy, she's going to kill me now!" he said, trying to lighten the mood.

Dan looked like he wanted to jump out the window. He messaged me silently. *This is not convincing you at all, is it?* he asked.

*No,* I replied. *But I'm going to miss it.*

Mohamed, my Sudanese friend from Dubai who had introduced me to Raheem so long before, was in Manhattan for the evening. He had moved to Texas once Dubai's glamour grew thin. He asked if I wanted to meet up for hookah like the old days.

The cafe by Hell's Kitchen was lit dimly in orange as we watched people pass by on the sidewalks outside. He told me I sounded resentful. "At the end of the day, Joe is human," he told me. "How could he have predicted all of this?"

I paused. "Yes," I said. "A human who fired most of my friends." I turned my face as he exhaled a puff of smoke towards me. My eyes stung momentarily.

He laughed. "Well, he's under a lot of pressure. Now he needs to find a way to keep this thing viable, right? Doesn't seem easy."

I did not want to hear it – not on that particular day. "He got rich and powerful like everyone else," I said. Over time I would mellow out. Mohamed was right that the only future that had seemed obvious three years ago was an ending with billions of dollars for everyone.

Mohamed seemed pensive as he blew out a cloud of smoke. "Can you believe this all came about because I needed a place to stay for a few weeks? How crazy is that?" I wanted to say he missed a few steps, but he kept going. "Do you feel like you have a takeaway from all this?"

I was getting tired. The wooden high chairs were uncomfortable, and I wondered if 10pm was too early to excuse myself to go and crawl into bed. "I learned a lot," I offered, half hearted. "Learned some stuff about life, that's for sure."

But through all three years, one question had always remained with me. I had tried to stay above the fray, away from the ridiculousness that seemed to define crypto at every turn. I had doubted myself every step of the way. At times I failed, but I had put every ounce of effort I had to try and be professional and adult and *valuable*. I had hoped success – startup riches, or big, *change-the-world* impact – might finally give me the validation that I was above the anarchy and greed and absurdity.

But, when it came to it, I had been a part of that world. And in the end, I never found the validation I sought. Was I fooling myself now? Had I just been a ding dong like everyone else? What if the ding dongs were going to figure it out? I did not ask Mohamed what he thought. I figured the answer was that I would never really know.

Stay meshy, my friends.

*February 22, 2020*
*New York, NY*

# EPILOGUE: ETHEREUM, THE DIGITAL COUNTRY

*New York, April 2021. ETH:* $2190.

For the rest of my life, I will wonder how I missed so many chances to make millions.

Even on my last day, I held a golden ticket: I was working on a project for NFTs, the digital baseball cards CryptoKitties used, which only a year later took the world by storm, immortalized in a Saturday Night Live skit. Ether and Bitcoin surged again to double, triple their 2017 highs. Dan raised tens of millions from investors for another crypto startup. Omar raised a billion. How could I have been such a blockhead?

There is nothing you can do with Bitcoin or Ethereum you cannot do with a normal database. But that does not change that there are tens of thousands of crypto-believers working endlessly to change that. We wanted to rebuild the world based on crypto, a world automated by smart contracts, but pesky realities – lawyers, hackers, governments – always came in the way. So instead, crypto has built a parallel world: a digital economy, funded by millionaires, who patronize its artists and entrepreneurs. And that economy is humming: billions sloshing around DeFi, NFTs, DAOs, and the rest of the alphabet soup.

What a waste, the critics chirp.

But the most powerful empires in human memory created their wealth out of nothing. Spain found gold. What is gold worth? Zilch. England created colossal wealth from spices that grow in the dirt, as I discovered tasting pepper straight from the vine on a trip to Zanzibar the week I quit ConsenSys. They colonized the tropics for spices that they barely use in their food, I thought to myself, spitting out the fiery little berry. Of course, the spices themselves weren't valuable; it was their scarcity in the cold places that drove Columbus across the ocean and a thousand ships behind him. The true motive was money. For that illusory wealth, the colonizers committed unspeakable atrocities; from it, they funded art, philosophy, and science.

Bitcoin and Ethereum follow these empires. Their discovery was a way to create scarcity in a world of plenty. That scarcity has such a rarity, an appeal so strong that it seems almost holy. An electronic Kaabah, a digital See.

The crypto barbarians will always be there, waiting on the other side of the gates, ready to invade the real world. They will delve the darkness of human imagination and plumb the depths of human greed. Out of that who can say what treasures the crypto-explorers may find? The story of these empires may have only begun.

Made in United States
Orlando, FL
15 September 2022

22442295R00146